American Vistas
1607-1877

American Vistas
1607-1877
Second Edition

Edited by **LEONARD DINNERSTEIN**
UNIVERSITY OF ARIZONA

AND **KENNETH T. JACKSON**
COLUMBIA UNIVERSITY

New York OXFORD UNIVERSITY PRESS
London 1975 Toronto

To
Andrew Dinnerstein
and
Kevan Parish Jackson

PREFACE TO THE SECOND EDITION

We are grateful that the enthusiastic response to *American Vistas* has made a second edition necessary. In making revisions, we have been guided by the philosophy which motivated our initial effort, namely, that history is an exciting and vibrant discipline and that good historians should convey a sense of the complexity and richness of the past without sacrificing scholarly accuracy. Once again, we have sought to concentrate on subjects which are not given extended coverage in typical textbooks, and this has again led to an emphasis on social rather than political history. We have not overlooked significant political events, however, as our new selections indicate.

Concerns of historians differ according to the times, and we have attempted to reflect changing interests in *American Vistas*. Five of the essays in this volume, three of which are new, deal with the role of women and the family; five others explore facets of black history. We have also included material on witchcraft, the Indians in colonial America, the role of immigrants in the development of the nation, and the growth of an urban police force. The essays on "England's Vietnam: The American Revolution" and "The Impeachment of Andrew Johnson" have a kind of relevance not often found in collections of historical articles.

Most instructors prefer to shape their courses to their own style. We have, therefore, deliberately kept our volume brief so that it might be used in conjunction with a text or with other readings. Without attempting to cover every significant topic in American history, we have endeavored to include essays which illuminate important developments in the past.

We hope that this second edition meets with the approval of its readers. Suggestions for improvement from both professors and students would be welcomed by either editor.

Leonard Dinnerstein
University of Arizona

Kenneth T. Jackson
Columbia University

November 1974

PREFACE TO THE FIRST EDITION

Perhaps more than any other generation in American history, college students of the 1970's have grown up in an age of almost constant domestic and international crisis. Aware of and extremely concerned about the maladies and the future of the world, they sometimes regard history as less relevant and less useful than other problem-related social sciences or activist fields of study. At a time when war, pollution, unemployment, crime, narcotics, and the generation gap confound American youth, what can history tell them? When tolerance and understanding are in short supply between the young and the old, the black and the white, the militant and the conservative, the study of the past may appear distressingly insignificant.

Actually, the notion that our dilemmas or our attempted solutions are unique is superficial, if not absurd. Our search for panaceas in the present must be informed by a knowledge of past times and places. The insights garnered from the way in which others handled their problems add an extra and necessary dimension to contemporary analysis.

The thirteen essays included in this volume deal with the panorama of human experience through an examination of the ingredients of everyday living in America: sex, race, taxes, and the appropriate role of women in society. Unfortunately, popular history has been a term with unsavory connotations because most works in this category are more popular than they are history. The essays within were selected on the basis of interest and readability, but they also represent the work of some of the most distinguished scholars in the United States. With this combination, it is hoped *American Vistas* will offer to the student an exciting, rich, and intelligent sampling of this nation's past.

Because we assume that this anthology will be used chiefly in conjunction with a survey textbook, we have focused upon questions and events generally lightly treated in the basic classroom volume. This has meant more attention to Puritan attitudes toward sex than Puritan attitudes toward God; the three-cornered relationship between blacks, whites, and Indians rather than the usual two-sided analysis; and the character of Thomas Jefferson the man rather than Thomas Jefferson the philosopher and politician. At the same time, however, we recognize that the major topics dealt with in the basic text must also be illuminated here. Consequently we have included essays on slavery, the American Revolution, national expansion, the coming of the Civil War, and Reconstruction.

In such a short volume the problem of proportion has been especially difficult. Obviously all of the main issues in American history could not be included but we have tried to maintain a rough chronological and geographical balance. The essays do encompass a wide range of subjects, and each one is preceded by a brief introduction that places the selection in context and points out some of the more important questions which the article might raise. The complete citation is also included so that students seeking documentation may refer to the original source.

For aid in the selection of articles we wish to thank Professor William E. Leuchtenburg of Columbia University, and Professor William H. Hackett of Henry Ford Community College. Joseph A. Fineman and Christina Sharp assisted with the proofreading. Finally, we must acknowledge the substantial participation of Barbara Bruce Jackson at every stage of the compilation. She represented the intelligent nonprofessional historian in our deliberations and worked as an equal partner to help make our anthology both scholarly and literate.

Leonard Dinnerstein
University of Arizona

Kenneth T. Jackson
Columbia University

December 1970

CONTENTS

I   AMERICAN BEGINNINGS
1607–1800

The Puritans and Sex

EDMUND S. MORGAN

• In 1630, after an arduous Atlantic crossing aboard the Arabella, John Winthrop and a small band of followers established the Massachusetts Bay Colony. In their "Holy Commonwealth" the Puritans emphasized hard work, severe discipline, and rigid self-examination and self-denial. Ministers had great political influence in the theocratic government, and profanation of the Sabbath day, blasphemy, fornication, drunkenness, and participation in games of chance or theatrical performances were among their many penal offenses. Even today the term "puritanical" suggests narrowmindedness and excessive strictness in matters of morals and religion. Yet, as Daniel Boorstin and others have observed, the Puritans were not simply an ascetic group of fanatics who prohibited all earthly pleasures. Actually the severity of their code of behavior has frequently been exaggerated. The Puritans were subject to normal human desires and weaknesses, and they recognized that "the use of the marriage bed" is "founded in Man's nature." Moreover, numerous cases of fornication and adultery in the law courts of New England belie the notion that all Puritans lived up to their rigid moral ideology. In the following essay, Professor Edmund S. Morgan cites numerous examples of men and women, youths and maids, whose natural urges recognized no legal limits. In viewing their enforcement of laws and their judgments of human frailty, we may find that the Puritans do not always conform to their conventional stereotype as over-precise moralists.

From *New England Quarterly*, XV (1942), 591–607. Reprinted by permission of the author and the publisher.

3

Henry Adams once observed that Americans have "ostentatiously ignored" sex. He could think of only two American writers who touched upon the subject with any degree of boldness—Walt Whitman and Bret Harte. Since the time when Adams made this penetrating observation, American writers have been making up for lost time in a way that would make Bret Harte, if not Whitman, blush. And yet there is still more truth than falsehood in Adams's statement. Americans, by comparison with Europeans or Asiatics, are squeamish when confronted with the facts of life. My purpose is not to account for this squeamishness, but simply to point out that the Puritans, those bogeymen of the modern intellectual, are not responsible for it.

At the outset, consider the Puritans' attitude toward marriage and the role of sex in marriage. The popular assumption might be that the Puritans frowned on marriage and tried to hush up the physical aspect of it as much as possible, but listen to what they themselves had to say. Samuel Willard, minister of the Old South Church in the latter part of the seventeenth century and author of the most complete textbook of Puritan divinity, more than once expressed his horror at "that Popish conceit of the Excellency of Virginity." Another minister, John Cotton, wrote that

> Women are Creatures without which there is no comfortable Living for man: it is true of them what is wont to be said of Governments, *That bad ones are better than none*: They are a sort of Blasphemers then who dispise and decry them, and call them *a necessary Evil*, for they are *a necessary Good*.

These sentiments did not arise from an interpretation of marriage as a spiritual partnership, in which sexual intercourse was a minor or incidental matter. Cotton gave his opinion of "Platonic love" when he recalled the case of

> one who immediately upon marriage, without ever approaching the *Nuptial Bed*, indented with the *Bride*, that by mutual consent they might both live such a life, and according did sequestring themselves according to the custom of those times, from the rest of mankind, and afterwards from one another too, in their retired Cells, giving themselves up to a Contemplative life; and this is recorded as an instance of no little or ordinary Vertue; but I must be pardoned in it, if I can account it no other

than an effort of blind zeal, for they are the dictates of a blind mind they follow therein, and not of that Holy Spirit, which saith *It is not good that man should be alone.*

Here is as healthy an attitude as one could hope to find anywhere. Cotton certainly cannot be accused of ignoring human nature. Nor was he an isolated example among the Puritans. Another minister stated plainly that "the Use of the Marriage Bed" is "founded in mans Nature," and that consequently any withdrawal from sexual intercourse upon the part of husband or wife "Denies all reliefe in Wedlock vnto Human necessity: and sends it for supply vnto Beastiality when God gives not the gift of Continency." In other words, sexual intercourse was a human necessity and marriage the only proper supply for it. These were the views of the New England clergy, the acknowledged leaders of the community, the most Puritanical of the Puritans. As proof that their congregations concurred with them, one may cite the case in which the members of the First Church of Boston expelled James Mattock because, among other offenses, "he denied Coniugall fellowship vnto his wife for the space of 2 years together vpon pretense of taking Revenge upon himself for his abusing of her before marryage." So strongly did the Puritans insist upon the sexual character of marriage that one New Englander considered himself slandered when it was reported, "that he Brock his deceased wife's hart with Greife, that he would be absent from her 3 weeks together when he was at home, and wold never come nere her, and such Like."

There was just one limitation which the Puritans placed upon sexual relations in marriage: sex must not interfere with religion. Man's chief end was to glorify God, and all earthly delights must promote that end, not hinder it. Love for a wife was carried too far when it led a man to neglect his God:

> . . . sometimes a man hath a good affection to Religion, but the love of his wife carries him away, a man may bee so transported to his wife, that hee dare not bee forward in Religion, lest hee displease his wife, and so the wife, lest shee displease her husband, and this is an inordinate love, when it exceeds measure.

Sexual pleasures, in this respect, were treated like other kinds of pleasure. On a day of fast, when all comforts were supposed to be foregone in behalf of religious contemplation, not only were tasty food and drink to be abandoned but sexual intercourse, too. On other occasions, when food, drink, and recreation were allowable, sexual intercourse was allowable too, though of course only between persons who were married to each other. The Puritans were not ascetics; they never wished to prevent the enjoyment of earthly delights. They merely demanded that the pleasures of the flesh be subordinated to the greater glory of God: husband and wife must not become "so transported with affection, that they look at no higher end than marriage it self." "Let such as have wives," said the ministers, "look at them not for their own ends, but to be fitted for Gods service, and bring them nearer to God."

Toward sexual intercourse outside marriage the Puritans were as frankly hostile as they were favorable to it in marriage. They passed laws to punish adultery with death, and fornication with whipping. Yet they had no misconceptions as to the capacity of human beings to obey such laws. Although the laws were commands of God, it was only natural—since the fall of Adam—for human beings to break them. Breaches must be punished lest the community suffer the wrath of God, but no offense, sexual or otherwise, could be occasion for surprise or for hushed tones of voice. How calmly the inhabitants of seventeenth-century New England could contemplate rape or attempted rape is evident in the following testimony offered before the Middlesex County Court of Massachusetts:

> The examination of Edward Wire taken the 7th of october and alsoe Zachery Johnson. who sayeth that Edward Wires mayd being sent into the towne about busenes meeting with a man that dogd hir from about Joseph Kettles house to goody marshes. She came into William Johnsones and desired Zachery Johnson to goe home with her for that the man dogd hir. accordingly he went with her and being then as far as Samuell Phips his house the man over tooke them. which man caled himselfe by the name of peter grant would have led the mayd but she oposed itt three times: and coming to Edward Wires house the said grant would have kist hir but she refused itt: wire being at prayer grant dragd the mayd between the said wiers and Nathanill frothinghams house. hee then flung the mayd downe in the streete and got atop hir; Johnson seeing it hee caled vppon the fellow to be sivill and not abuse the mayd then Edward wire came forth and ran to the said grant and took hold of him asking him what he did

to his mayd, the said grant asked whether she was his wife for he did nothing to his wife: the said grant swearing he would be the death of the said wire. when he came of the mayd; he swore he would bring ten men to pul down his house and soe ran away and they followed him as far as good[y] phipses house where they mett with John Terry and George Chin with clubs in there hands and soe they went away together. Zachy Johnson going to Constable Heamans, and wire going home. there came John Terry to his house to ask for beer and grant was in the streete but afterward departed into the towne, both Johnson and Wire both aferme that when grant was vppon the mayd she cryed out severall times.

Deborah hadlocke being examined sayth that she mett with the man that cals himselfe peeter grant about good prichards that he dogd hir and followed hir to hir masters and there threw hir downe and lay vppon hir but had not the use of hir body but swore several othes that he would ly with hir and gett hir with child before she got home.

Grant being present denys all saying he was drunk and did not know what he did.

The Puritans became inured to sexual offenses, because there were so many. The impression which one gets from reading the records of seventeenth-century New England courts is that illicit sexual intercourse was fairly common. The testimony given in cases of fornication and adultery—by far the most numerous class of criminal cases in the records—suggests that many of the early New Englanders possessed a high degree of virility and very few inhibitions. Besides the case of Peter Grant, take the testimony of Elizabeth Knight about the manner of Richard Nevars's advances toward her:

> The last publique day of Thanksgiving (in the year 1674) in the evening as I was milking Richard Nevars came to me, and offered me abuse in putting his hand, under my coates, but I turning aside with much adoe, saved my self, and when I was settled to milking he agen took me by the shoulder and pulled me backward almost, but I clapped one hand on the Ground and held fast the Cows teatt with the other hand, and cryed out, and then came to mee Jonathan Abbot one of my Masters Servants, whome the said Never asked wherefore he came, the said Abbot said to look after you, what you doe unto the Maid, but the said Never bid Abbot goe about his businesse but I bade the lad to stay.

One reason for the abundance of sexual offenses was the number of men in the colonies who were unable to gratify their sexual desires in marriage. Many of the first settlers had wives in England. They had come to the new world to make a fortune, expecting either to bring their families after them or to return to England with some of the riches of America. Although these men left their wives behind, they brought their sexual appetites with them; and in spite of laws which required them to return to their families, they continued to stay, and more continued to arrive, as indictments against them throughout the seventeenth century clearly indicate.

Servants formed another group of men, and of women too, who could not ordinarily find supply for human necessity within the bounds of marriage. Most servants lived in the homes of their masters and could not marry without their consent, a consent which was not likely to be given unless the prospective husband or wife also belonged to the master's household. This situation will be better understood if it is recalled that most servants at this time were engaged by contract for a stated period. They were, in the language of the time, "covenant servants," who had agreed to stay with their masters for a number of years in return for a specified recompense, such as transportation to New England or education in some trade (the latter, of course, were known more specifically as apprentices). Even hired servants who worked for wages were usually single, for as soon as a man had enough money to buy or build a house of his own and to get married, he would set up in farming or trade for himself. It must be emphasized, however, that anyone who was not in business for himself was necessarily a servant. The economic organization of seventeenth-century New England had no place for the independent proletarian workman with a family of his own. All production was carried on in the household by the master of the family and his servants, so that most men were either servants or masters of servants; and the former, of course, were more numerous than the latter. Probably most of the inhabitants of Puritan New England could remember a time when they had been servants.

Theoretically no servant had a right to a private life. His time, day or night, belonged to his master, and both religion and law required that he obey his master scrupulously. But neither religion nor law could restrain the sexual impulses of youth, and if those impulses could not be expressed in marriage, they had to be given vent outside marriage. Servants had little difficulty in finding the occasions. Though they might be kept at work all day, it was easy enough to slip away at night. Once out of the house, there were several ways of meeting with a maid. The simplest way was to go to her bedchamber, if she was so fortunate as to have a private one of her own. Thus Jock, Mr. Solomon Phipps's Negro man, confessed in court

> that on the sixteenth day of May 1682, in the morning, betweene 12 and one of the clock, he did force open the back doores of the House of Laurence Hammond in Charlestowne, and came in to the House, and went up into the garret to Marie the Negro.
>
> He doth likewise acknowledge that one night the last week he forced into the House the same way, and went up to the Negro Woman Marie and that the like he hath done at severall other times before.

Joshua Fletcher took a more romantic way of visiting his lady:

> Joshua Fletcher . . . doth confesse and acknowledge that three severall nights, after bedtime, he went into Mr Fiskes Dwelling house at Chelmsford, at an open window by a ladder that he brought with him. the said windo opening into a chamber, whose was the lodging place of Gresill Juell servant to mr. Fiske. and there he kept company with the said mayd. she sometimes having her cloathes on, and one time he found her in her bed.

Sometimes a maidservant might entertain callers in the parlor while the family were sleeping upstairs. John Knight described what was perhaps a common experience for masters. The crying of his child awakened him in the middle of the night, and he called to his maid, one Sarah Crouch, who was supposed to be sleeping with the child. Receiving no answer, he arose and

> went downe the stayres, and at the stair foot, the latch of doore was pulled in. I called severall times and at the last said if shee would not open the dore, I would breake it open, and when she opened the doore shee was all undressed and Sarah Largin with her undressed, also the said Sarah went out of doores and Dropped some of her clothes as shee went out. I enquired of Sarah Crouch what men they were, which was with them. Shee made mee no answer for some space of time, but at last shee told me Peeter Brigs was with them, I asked her whether Thomas Jones was not there, but shee would give mee no answer.

In the temperate climate of New England it was not always necessary to seek out a maid at her home. Rachel Smith was seduced in an open field "about nine of the clock at night, being darke, neither moone nor starrs shineing." She was walking through the field when she met a man who

> asked her where shee lived, and what her name was and shee told him. and then shee asked his name, and he told her Saijing that he was old Good-man Shepards man. Also shee saith he gave her strong liquors, and told her that it was not the first time he had been with maydes after his master was in bed.

Sometimes, of course, it was not necessary for a servant to go outside his master's house in order to satisfy his sexual urges. Many cases of fornication are on record between servants living in the same house. Even where servants had no private bedroom, even where the whole family slept in a single room, it was not impossible to make love. In fact many love affairs must have had their consummation upon a bed in which other people were sleeping. Take for example the case of Sarah Lepingwell. When Sarah was brought into court for having an illegitimate child, she related that one night when her master's brother, Thomas Hawes, was visiting the family, she went to bed early. Later, after Hawes had gone to bed, he called to her to get him a pipe of tobacco. After refusing for some time,

> at the last I arose and did lite his pipe and cam and lay doune one my one bead and smoaked about half the pip and siting vp in my bead to giue him his pip my bead being a trundell bead at the sid of his bead he reached beyond the pip and Cauth me by the wrist and pulled me on the side of his bead but I biding him let me goe he bid me hold my peas the folks wold here me and if it be replyed come why did you not call out I Ansar I was posesed with fear of my mastar least my mastar shold think I did it only to bring a scandall on his brothar and thinking thay wold all beare witnes agaynst me but the thing is true that he did then begete me with child at that tim and the Child is Thomas Hauses and noe mans but his.

In his defense Hawes offered the testimony of another man who was sleeping "on the same side of the bed," but the jury nevertheless accepted Sarah's story.

The fact that Sarah was intimidated by her master's brother suggests that maidservants may have been subject to sexual abuse by their masters. The records show that sometimes masters did take advantage of their position to force unwanted attentions upon their female servants. The case of Elizabeth Dickerman is a good example. She complained to the Middlesex County Court,

> against her master John Harris senior for profiring abus to her by way of forsing her to be naught with him: . . . he has tould her that if she tould her dame: what cariag he did show to her shee had as good be hanged and shee replyed then shee would run away and he sayd run the way is befor you: . . . she says if she should liwe ther shee shall be in fear of her lif.

The court accepted Elizabeth's complaint and ordered her master to be whipped twenty stripes.

So numerous did cases of fornication and adultery become in seventeenth-century New England that the problem of caring for the children of extra-marital unions was a serious one. The Puritans solved it, but in such a way as to increase rather than decrease the temptation to sin. In 1668 the General Court of Massachusetts ordered:

> that where any man is legally convicted to be the Father of a Bastard childe, he shall be at the care and charge to maintain and bring up the same, by such assistance of the Mother as nature requireth, and as the Court from time to time (according to circumstances) shall see meet to Order: and in case the Father of a Bastard, by confession or other manifest proof, upon trial of the case, do not appear to the Courts satisfaction, then the Man charged by the Woman to be the Father, shee holding constant in it, (especially being put upon the real discovery of the truth of it in the time of her Travail) shall be the reputed Father, and accordingly be liable to the charge of maintenance as aforesaid (though not to other punishment) notwithstanding his denial, unless the circumstances of the case and pleas be such, on the behalf of the man charged, as that the Court that have the cognizance thereon shall see reason to acquit him, and otherwise dispose of the Childe and education thereof.

As a result of this law a girl could give way to temptation without the fear of having to care for an illegitimate child by herself. Furthermore, she could, by a little simple lying, spare her lover the expense of supporting the child. When Elizabeth Wells bore a child, less than a year after this statute was passed, she laid it to James Tufts, her master's son. Goodman Tufts affirmed that Andrew Robinson, servant to Goodman Dexter, was the real father, and he brought the following testimony as evidence:

> Wee Elizabeth Jefts aged 15 ears and Mary tufts aged 14 ears doe testyfie that their being one at our hous sumtime the last winter who sayed that thear was a new law made concerning bastards that If aney man wear aqused with a bastard and the woman which had aqused him did stand vnto it in her labor that he should bee the reputed father of it and should mayntaine it Elizabeth Wells hearing of the sayd law she sayed vnto vs that If shee should bee with Child shee would bee sure to lay it vn to won who was rich enough abell to mayntayne it wheather it wear his or no and shee farder sayed Elizabeth Jefts would not you doe so likewise If it weare your case and I sayed no by no means for right must tacke place: and the sayd Elizabeth wells sayed If it wear my Caus I think I should doe so.

A tragic unsigned letter that somehow found its way into the files of the Middlesex County Court gives more direct evidence of the practice which Elizabeth Wells professed:

> der loue i remember my loue to you hoping your welfar and i hop to imbras the but now i rit to you to let you nowe that i am a child by you and i wil ether kil it or lay it to an other and you shal have no blame at al for I haue had many children and none have none of them. . . . [i.e., none of their fathers is supporting any of them.]

In face of the wholesale violation of the sexual codes to which all these cases give testimony, the Puritans could not maintain the severe penalties which their laws provided. Although cases of adultery occurred every year, the death penalty is not known to have been applied more than three times. The usual punishment was a whipping or a fine, or both, and perhaps a branding, combined with a symbolical execution in the form of standing on the gallows for an hour with a rope about the neck. Fornication met with a lighter whipping or a lighter fine, while rape was treated in the same way as adultery. Though the Puritans established a code of laws which demanded perfection—

which demanded, in other words, strict obedience to the will of God, they nevertheless knew that frail human beings could never live up to the code. When fornication, adultery, rape, or even buggery and sodomy appeared, they were not surprised, nor were they so severe with the offenders as their codes of law would lead one to believe. Sodomy, to be sure, they usually punished with death; but rape, adultery, and fornication they regarded as pardonable human weaknesses, all the more likely to appear in a religious community, where the normal course of sin was stopped by wholesome laws. Governor Bradford, in recounting the details of an epidemic of sexual misdemeanors in Plymouth, wrote resignedly:

> it may be in this case as it is with waters when their streames are stopped or damned up, when they gett passage they flow with more violence, and make more noys and disturbance, then when they are suffered to rune quietly in their owne chanels. So wickednes being here more stopped by strict laws, and the same more nerly looked unto, so as it cannot rune in a comone road of liberty as it would, and is inclined, it searches every wher, and at last breaks out wher it getts vente.

The estimate of human capacities here expressed led the Puritans not only to deal leniently with sexual offenses but also to take every precaution to prevent such offenses, rather than wait for the necessity of punishment. One precaution was to see that children got married as soon as possible. The wrong way to promote virtue, the Puritans thought, was to "ensnare" children in vows of virginity, as the Catholics did. As a result of such vows, children, "not being able to contain," would be guilty of "unnatural pollutions, and other filthy practices in secret: and too oft of horrid Murthers of the fruit of their bodies," said Thomas Cobbett. The way to avoid fornication and perversion was for parents to provide suitable husbands and wives for their children:

> Lot was to blame that looked not out seasonably for some fit matches for his two daughters, which had formerly minded marriage (witness the contract between them and two men in *Sodom*, called therfore for his Sons in Law, which had married his daughters, Gen. 19. 14.) for they seeing no man like to come into them in a conjugall way . . . then they plotted that incestuous course, whereby their Father was so highly dishonoured. . . .

As marriage was the way to prevent fornication, successful marriage was the way to prevent adultery. The Puritans did not wait for adultery to appear; instead, they took every means possible to make husbands and wives live together and respect each other. If a husband deserted his wife and remained within the jurisdiction of a Puritan government, he was promptly sent back to her. Where the wife had been left in England, the offense did not always come to light until the wayward husband had committed fornication or bigamy, and of course there must have been many offenses which never came to light. But where both husband and wife lived in New England, neither had much chance of leaving the other without being returned by order of the county court at its next sitting. When John Smith of Medfield left his wife and went to live with Patience Rawlins, he was sent home poorer by ten pounds and richer by thirty stripes. Similarly Mary Drury, who deserted her husband on the pretense that he was impotent, failed to convince the court that he actually was so, and had to return to him as well as to pay a fine of five pounds. The wife of Phillip Pointing received lighter treatment: when the court thought that she had overstayed her leave in Boston, they simply ordered her "to depart the Towne and goe to Tanton to her husband." The courts, moreover, were not satisfied with mere cohabitation; they insisted that it be peaceful cohabitation. Husbands and wives were forbidden by law to strike one another, and the law was enforced on numerous occasions. But the courts did not stop there. Henry Flood was required to give bond for good behavior because he had abused his wife simply by "ill words calling her whore and cursing of her." The wife of Christopher Collins was presented for railing at her husband and calling him "Gurley gutted divill." Apparently in this case the court thought that Mistress Collins was right, for although the fact was proved by two witnesses, she was discharged. On another occasion the court favored the husband: Jacob Pudeator, fined for striking and kicking his wife, had the sentence moderated when the court was informed that she was a woman "of great provocation."

Wherever there was strong suspicion that an illicit relation might arise between two persons, the authorities removed the temptation by forbidding the two to come together. As early as November, 1630, the Court of Assistants of Massachusetts prohibited a Mr. Clark from "cohabitacion and frequent keepeing company with Mrs. Freeman, vnder paine of such punishment as the Court shall thinke meete to inflict." Mr. Clark and Mr. Freeman were both bound "in XX£ apeece that Mr. Clearke shall make his personall appearance att the nexte Court to be holden in March nexte, and in the meane tyme to carry himselfe in good behaviour towards all people and espetially towards Mrs. Freeman, concerning whome there is stronge suspicion of incontinency." Forty-five years later the Suffolk County Court took the same kind of measure to protect the husbands of Dorchester from the temptations offered by the daughter of Robert Spurr: Spurr was presented by the grand jury

> for entertaining persons at his house at unseasonable times both by day and night to the greife of theire wives and Relations &c The Court having heard what was alleaged and testified against him do Sentence him to bee admonish't and to pay Fees of Court and charge him upon his perill not to entertain any married men to keepe company with his daughter especially James Minott and Joseph Belcher.

In like manner Walter Hickson was forbidden to keep company with Mary Bedwell, "And if at any time hereafter hee bee taken in company of the saide Mary Bedwell without other company to bee forthwith apprehended by the Constable and to be whip't with ten stripes." Elizabeth Wheeler and Joanna Peirce were admonished "for theire disorderly carriage in the house of Thomas Watts being married women and founde sitting in other mens Laps with theire Armes about theire Necks." How little confidence the Puritans had in human nature is even more clearly displayed by another case, in which Edmond Maddock and his wife were brought to court "to answere to all such matters as shalbe objected against them concerning Haarkwoody and Ezekiell Euerells being at their house at unseasonable tyme of the night and her being up with them after her husband was gone to bed." Haarkwoody and Everell had been found "by the Constable Henry Bridghame about tenn of the Clock at night sitting by the fyre at the house of Edmond Maddocks with his wyfe a suspicious weoman her husband being on sleepe [*sic*] on the bedd." A similar distrust of human ability to resist temptation is evident in the following order of the Connecticut Particular Court:

James Hallett is to returne from the Correction house to his
master Barclyt, who is to keepe him to hard labor, and course
dyet during the pleasure of the Court provided that Barclet is
first to remove his daughter from his family, before the sayd
James enter therein.

These precautions, as we have already seen, did not eliminate fornication, adultery, or other sexual offenses, but they doubtless reduced
the number from what it would otherwise have been.

In sum, the Puritan attitude toward sex, though directed by a belief
in absolute, God-given moral values, never neglected human nature.
The rules of conduct which the Puritans regarded as divinely ordained
had been formulated for men, not for angels and not for beasts. God
had created mankind in two sexes; He had ordained marriage as desirable for all, and sexual intercourse as essential to marriage. On the
other hand, He had forbidden sexual intercourse outside of marriage.
These were the moral principles which the Puritans sought to enforce
in New England. But in their enforcement they took cognizance of
human nature. They knew well enough that human beings since the
fall of Adam were incapable of obeying perfectly the laws of God. Consequently, in the endeavor to enforce those laws they treated offenders
with patience and understanding, and concentrated their efforts on
prevention more than on punishment. The result was not a society in
which most of us would care to live, for the methods of prevention
often caused serious interference with personal liberty. It must nevertheless be admitted that in matters of sex the Puritans showed none
of the blind zeal or narrow-minded bigotry which is too often supposed
to have been characteristic of them. The more one learns about these
people, the less do they appear to have resembled the sad and sour por-
traits which their modern critics have drawn of them.

Anne Hutchinson Versus Massachusetts

WELLINGTON NEWCOMB

• The Puritans of the Massachusetts Bay Colony left the old world for the new in order to escape persecution for their unorthodox theological beliefs. In their new "Bible Commonwealth," however, they did not propose to establish a system of religious freedom. As Francis Higginson wrote in the earliest days of settlement, "we have here the true Religion . . . thus we doubt not but God will be with us." What the Puritans wanted was the freedom to practice their own form of religious persecution; they did not intend to make room for dissidents.

Anne Hutchinson and her followers were dissidents who challenged the church authorities by conducting unauthorized evening meetings and by introducing the question of the covenant of grace. When Mrs. Hutchinson refused to modify her views, she was brought to trial. The verdict was excommunication and banishment from the colony. Careful readers of the following essay, however, will discover that Anne Hutchinson's difficulties had as much to do with her sex as with her theology. Women were not considered fit to teach males and thus could not be accepted as religious leaders.

In all the important western religions—Catholic, Protestant, Jewish—women have had an ambivalent role. On the one hand, they have constituted the backbone of the church and have been expected to teach the faith and to set high moral standards for their husbands and children. On the other hand, they have not been accepted as ministers, rabbis, and priests, and their theological contributions to church affairs have been primarily in the area of baking cakes, arranging flowers, and raising money.

From *American Heritage*. © 1974 American Heritage Publishing Company, Inc. Reprinted by permission of the publisher (June 1974).

It would have been no pleasant thing for any defendant to hear John Winthrop, governor of the Massachusetts colony, declaim the serious charges brought against Anne Hutchinson at her trial in 1637. In the Puritan society of early Massachusetts they were among the gravest that could be imagined. As recorded by the court reporter, they seem to evoke the gravity with which John Winthrop must have delivered them: "Mrs. Hutchinson, you are called here as one of those that have troubled the peace of the commonwealth and the churches here. You are known to be a woman that hath had a great share in the promoting and divulging of those opinions that are causes of this trouble. . . . You have spoken divers things, as we have been informed, very prejudicial to the honour of the churches and ministers thereof. And you have maintained a meeting and an assembly in your house that hath been condemned by the general assembly as a thing not tolerable nor comely in the sight of God nor fitting for your sex."

Anne Hutchinson, forty-five years old, stood listening to these charges on a November day when the New England fall had turned to its bleakest season. She faced her adversaries in the somber meeting-house in Newtown, later to be called Cambridge. It was a square, rude building with small windows admitting little light. The grays, browns, and blacks of Mrs. Hutchinson's surroundings were relieved only by the pallor of earnest English faces all focussed on her. But despite the severity of the setting, the meetinghouse was crowded to capacity with people eager to see how this woman, who had stirred the greatest storm yet in the young colony, would acquit herself. For people who eschewed the theatre as sinful the Newtown meetinghouse had become the stage for an exciting performance.

From what we know of Anne Hutchinson, she probably did not flinch for a moment upon hearing the charges against her. She was a woman of keen intelligence and strong personality, possessed of stubborn convictions not the least of which was that she had found direct favor with God. Even Winthrop, writing in his journal, begrudgingly described her as "a woman of a ready wit and bold spirit," and he had good reason to know. But nowhere in his writings did it ever occur to him to describe what she looked like. Puritans were like that.

The daughter of a clergyman, Anne Hutchinson had been born Anne Marbury in Lincolnshire, England. By the time of her trial she had borne her husband, William Hutchinson, thirteen children; she was now expecting her fourteenth. Husband, wife, and children had arrived in Boston in September, 1634, on the ship *Griffin*, and Anne had been the motivating force that had started them on the long and arduous voyage to the New World. She had felt the need to follow their former minister, the Reverend John Cotton, to Massachusetts. His departure had caused a spiritual crisis in her life, for there had been no other minister in England whom she felt she could trust to preach the Word without adulteration. Once her beloved Mr. Cotton had left their native land, there had been no doubt in her mind that she must join him in the New World.

Her journey had taken her now to stand before the Great and General Court of Massachusetts to be accused of traducing the ministry, as sure an act of sedition as could be imagined in a community where the church was, in effect, the government. It appears, though not conclusively, that the ministers who were to be witnesses against her were also her judges, and they must have constituted a fearsome and awesome presence.

John Winthrop continued to recite his statement. "We have thought good to send for you to understand how things are, that if you be in an erroneous way, we may reduce you that so you may become a profitable member here among us. Otherwise, if you be obstinate . . . then the court may take such course that you may trouble us no further." The defendant paid close attention to him, as did, presumably, everyone in the room.

Among the listeners was the Reverend Mr. Cotton. He was a man of fifty-two whose light curly hair fell to his shoulders, framing a benign countenance. He was an eloquent preacher and had the reputation of being one of the greatest of Puritan scholars; it had been a momentous event to welcome him to the Bay Colony in 1633. The Reverend John Wilson was already pastor of the Boston church when he arrived; Cotton had been called to be its "teacher." It was an equally important position and gave broad scope to his preaching. In his journal Winthrop described Cotton's almost immediate success: "It pleased the Lord to give special testimony of his presence in the church of Boston, after Mr. Cotton was called to office there. More were converted and added to that church, than to all the other churches in the bay. . . . Divers profane and notorious evil persons came and confessed their sins, and were comfortably received into the bosom of the church." But as much as Anne Hutchinson, too, admired Cotton's preaching, the one uncertainty that may have disturbed her as her trial opened was the question of what role her idol might play in it.

Cotton had long admired Mrs. Hutchinson. He thought she too did great good works for the Christian faith. When, after her arrival in Boston, she had experienced some trouble in being admitted to church membership, Cotton quickly smoothed matters over. By no means unaware of her intense esteem of him, Cotton had been truly glad to see her near at hand once again. Yet the troubles leading to her trial were related to that esteem.

As well as having a sharp mind and tongue, Mrs. Hutchinson was a woman of practical bent. She had borne many children herself, and she knew how to help other women through their confinements. An accomplished herbalist, she seems to have known as much about medicine as anyone in those times. And, together with her other virtues, this talented woman knew how to speak the language of religious comfort to the sick. This all played its part in her growing influence in the nascent town of Boston.

But whatever its causes, her influence grew to surprising proportions. Winthrop credited her with gathering at least sixty women at the weekly meetings she began to hold in her house. And, as she admitted at her trial (with no little danger to herself, for women were not considered fit to teach men), some males had attended meetings in her house. All in all, according to Winthrop, "she had more resort to her for counsel about matter of conscience, and clearing up men's spiritual estates, than any minister . . . in the country."

At first these gatherings were nothing more than discussions about the sermons of the week, a "godly" activity much encouraged in a Puritan society. But with Anne Hutchinson discussion became commentary, and commentary became criticism. In short, she began to attack the clergy, only the Reverend John Cotton and her own brother-in-law, the Reverend John Wheelwright, being excepted.

Mistress Hutchinson was an individualist living in an authoritarian age. Given her make-up, it was perhaps inevitable that she would attack the orthodoxy on those very matters of faith which constituted the foundation of the state. The concrete issue of Anne Hutchinson's trial was whether she had accused the clergy of preaching "a covenant of works" instead of "a covenant of grace." It was by raising this charge at her meetings that Mrs. Hutchinson had "troubled the peace of the commonwealth and the churches here." To accuse the ministry of preaching a covenant of works was, in the temper of the time and place, to destroy it if the accusation stuck.

The Puritans adhered to the Calvinist doctrine that sinful man was saved by God's grace alone. No man could do a thing, no matter how worthy or wonderful, to effect his own salvation. To stress the point that God saved whomsoever He desired with no help from man or church was, in essence, to preach a covenant of grace. A "covenant of works" was the contemptuous Puritan term for the antithesis of Calvinist teaching—the doctrine that a man by his own good works could achieve the salvation of God. To the Puritans (Anne Hutchinson included) this was blasphemy, for it detracted from that all-sovereign and perfect will of God by which He had in the beginning predetermined the entire future of the universe. To put it bluntly, the Calvinist doctrine of predestination held that you were already either saved or damned and that, in either case, there was nothing you could do about it.

Not only was this doctrine somewhat less than comforting to anyone who had doubts about his state of grace; it also left something to be desired from a social point of view. What incentive was there to live a moral and useful life if one had already been picked, willy-nilly, for heaven or hell? The town drunk might in the end turn out to be among the saved, and the governor among the damned. The Puritan divines, who were also the colony's rulers, therefore devised a system that, although it left the statement of the doctrine intact, reduced its formidable practical impact. They decided that they could look to the outward signs of a man's life—among which would be his good works— as the evidence, or lack of evidence, of his salvation by God's grace. Thus in Massachusetts the clergy, among their other duties, became the earthly arbiters to decide what people had in fact been saved by God's grace. When a person applied for church membership, he was examined at great length to determine whether his behavior suggested a state of grace. If the clergy and the laity of the church agreed that the applicant had been saved, he was thereupon admitted to membership. It was this feature of Puritan practice in Massachusetts that Anne Hutchinson denounced as in effect preaching a covenant of works.

But she went even further. Not only did she accuse the ministers of preaching a covenant of works, but she also asserted that they were incapable of preaching a covenant of grace. It is little wonder that these leaders, being thus called both deluded and incompetent, responded as they did. Mrs. Hutchinson's accusations also robbed church members of their hardearned assurances of salvation. In a commonwealth founded on the rock of a ministry supposed to know its business, this was highly subversive.

In contrast to the ordained clergy, Anne Hutchinson told her adherents, she herself preached a pure covenant of grace. She claimed she received direct revelations from the Holy Ghost, which, as the horrified Winthrop later reported it, gave her infallible knowledge of the salvation of her followers. "If she had but one half hour's talk with a man, she would tell whether he were elect or not." In a day when hell gaped beneath the feet of every mortal, every man and woman longed to hear of his salvation from the highest authority available. Here then was Anne Hutchinson's tremendous message: if the ministry could not honestly give the people knowledge of their salvation, she could.

Being a clergyman's daughter, a keen Bible scholar, and a "student" of Mr. Cotton as well as a brilliant woman, Anne Hutchinson was able to offer a mass of theological argument to support her heavenly credentials. The extensiveness of her doctrine may be judged from the fact that the synod that had been convened at Newtown in the summer of 1637 to deal with her heresies condemned no fewer than "eighty opinions, some blasphemous, others erroneous, and all unsafe." It also condemned her meetings as disorderly "where sixty or more did meet every week, and one woman (. . . by resolving questions of doctrine, and expounding scripture) took upon her the whole exercise."

As her chief points of doctrine Mrs. Hutchinson denied that sanctification (that is, a good life) was any proof of salvation, and she asserted instead that only the indwelling of the Holy Ghost constituted such proof. With the very first mention of her name in his journal these were the items listed by Winthrop as her "two dangerous errors." It is not hard to see why. If good works, or a good life, were not the outward evidence of a person's salvation, what objective basis was left in the Puritan scheme of things?

Men, as well as women, became Mrs. Hutchinson's adherents.

Among them were some of the colony's notables, including William Aspinwall, John Coggeshall, and William Coddington, who was at one time treasurer of the commonwealth. But the most eminent of her adherents had been the young Sir Henry Vane, son of a privy councillor to King Charles and easily the foremost aristocrat of the colony. Although he was later to play a most important role in the Puritan Revolution in England, it was his connection with royalty that led to his being elected governor within seven months after his arrival in October, 1635. Such prominent people as these, together with others like the Reverend John Wheelwright, constituted Anne Hutchinson's faction—a faction that, Winthrop felt, threatened the power of the established order.

This was the background of the struggle that had now crowded the meetinghouse at Newton with anxious spectators. As John Winthrop finished making his long statement their eyes were now fastened upon the person of the accused. One may well imagine that as Winthrop himself stared at her the aristocratic features of his face—the thin lips and pointed nose and beard—appeared colder than usual. He had labored selflessly to build this Puritan commonwealth on the firm foundation of the Word. To him this pestilential woman, this emissary from the underworld, was doing her utmost to ensnare the people in an evil trap and thereby overthrow that foundation.

But Mrs. Hutchinson was unimpressed. With that histrionic sense common to many religious leaders, which she abundantly possessed, she probably waited so that the room would become perfectly quiet. Then she calmly replied: "I am called here to answer before you, but I hear no things laid to my charge."

It was a simple but brilliant opening. It jolted Winthrop by its effrontery, and he spluttered back, "I have told you some already and more I can tell you."

"Name one, sir," was Mrs. Hutchinson's quick challenge.

"Why! for your doings, this: you did harbour and countenance those that are parties in this faction that you have heard of. . . ."

"What law have I broken?"

"Why, the fifth commandment. . . ."

"Wherein?"

"Why, in entertaining them."

"What breach of law is that, sir?"

"Why, dishonoring of parents!" (By this, Winthrop meant to say that she had dishonored the fathers of the state and the elders of the church.)

"But put the case, sir," she replied, "that I do fear the Lord and my parents. May not I entertain them that fear the Lord [just] because my parents will not give me leave?"

Winthrop had no answer except to burst out, "We do not mean to discourse with those of your sex." The defendant had piqued his masculine vanity, and the depth of it may be judged by another of his outbursts, which followed shortly. "We do not call you to teach the court but to lay open yourself." To make her "lay open herself"—to confess her sins—was the main purpose of the trial.

After more fruitless argument with the accused, Winthrop made another statement. "Your course is not to be suffered. . . . It is to seduce many honest persons that are called to those meetings. . . . We see no rule of God for this. We see not that any should have authority to set up any other exercise besides what authority hath already set up. And so what hurt comes of this, you will be guilty of and we for suffering you."

"Sir, I do not believe that to be so."

"Well, we see how it is. We must therefore put it away from you or restrain you from maintaining this course."

"If you have a rule for it from God's word, you may."

"We are your judges and not you ours," Winthrop exploded, "and we must compel you to it."

Governor Winthrop was, for a Puritan, a man of magnanimous spirit. He also possessed great ability. Yet so far he had made little headway with Anne Hutchinson. It was probably with great relief that he allowed his cantankerous deputy governor to assume direction of the trial. The mean and petty-minded Thomas Dudley was soon to display a much greater capacity for the unpleasant business at hand.

Dudley, with telling succintness, restated the charges against Mrs. Hutchinson: ". . . About three years ago, we were all in peace. Mrs. Hutchinson from that time she came hath made a disturbance. . . . But now it appears by this woman's meeting that Mrs. Hutchinson hath so forestalled the minds of many by their resort to her meeting that now she hath a potent party in the country. . . . And if she in particular hath disparaged all our ministers in the land that they have preached a covenant of works, and only Mr. Cotton a covenant of grace, why! this is not to be suffered."

This was the first mention made in the trial of the two covenants. It is surprising that Winthrop had said nothing about them. But Anne Hutchinson remained confident and challenged Dudley as boldly as she had Winthrop. "I pray, sir, prove it that I said they preached nothing but a covenant of works. . . . Did I ever say they preached a covenant of works then?"

"If they do not preach a covenant of grace—clearly, then they preach a covenant of works."

"No sir. One may preach a covenant of grace more clearly than another. So I said."

Thomas Dudley had fared no better than John Winthrop in making the defendant "lay open herself." But at least he had framed the most important issue of the trial, and the accused had been forced to reveal the nature of her defense somewhat earlier than she probably wanted to.

Now the deputy governor put a question that seemed to contain the nub of the whole case. "I do but ask you this: when the ministers do preach a covenant of works, do they preach a way of salvation?" But it was really an ambiguous question, and Anne did the only thing she could do: she refused to answer. "I did not come hither to answer questions of that sort," she proclaimed.

There was nothing else for him to do but to present his evidence, and he did so. Apparently—or so Mrs. Hutchinson made it seem—it came as a surprise to her when he called as witnesses six ministers who had, the year before, remonstrated with her about her meetings. She claimed that their discussion with her was to be held in confidence. But Winthrop quickly ruled that there had been no basis for any confidence. What the six ministers had to state was more than sufficient evidence for the charges against her. The gist of their testimony was that she had told them that only the Reverend John Cotton preached a covenant of grace; that they preached a covenant of works; that they were not able ministers of the New Testament; and that they *could not* preach a covenant of grace because they were not sealed of the Holy Spirit to do so. She might just as well have called them Pharisees. The trial had taken an ugly turn against the woman who had had the indiscretion to give such vent to her convictions about the ministers.

Anne Hutchinson did her best to deny what she could of this testimony. But for her to prevail required more than denying the testimony of—as Winthrop put it—"six undeniable ministers." Although the day had started badly, Winthrop was pleased with its outcome. With evident satisfaction he said, "Mrs. Hutchinson, the court you see hath laboured to bring you to acknowledge the error of your way that so you might be reduced. The time now grows late. We shall therefore give you a little more time to consider of it and therefore desire that you attend the court again in the morning."

Back from Newtown, across the tidal basin and mud flats of the Charles River, back upon the small and hilly cape of land that held the town of Boston—dotted only here and there with a few feeble lights in the autumn darkness—back in the temporary sanctuary of her home, there was much indeed that Anne Hutchinson could "consider of." By the flame of a candle she must have pored over whatever papers she had that concerned her trial. As she did so it could not have failed to remind her of all the events of her three years in Boston.

She could have wished that young Sir Harry Vane were still there, but he had returned to England. If he had still been governor, her good "Brother Wheelwright" would not have been tried and sentenced to banishment for a fiery sermon he had preached in January. And after his trial those men who had signed a petition asking mercy for him found that Winthrop would deal with them, too. Aspinwall, Coddington, Coggeshall, and Captain John Underhill were all being called to account.

But there was one ominous even by which Anne Hutchinson doubtless was baffled. It concerned the Reverend John Cotton, who in her eyes was incapable of wrongdoing. At first Cotton had refused to join in the condemnation of all eighty errors attributed to her by the synod. And those he balked at condemning included some of the most objectionable. But Cotton finally adopted the synod's statement of condemned errors completely. Probably he did so because he felt that Anne was sure to be found guilty, and he could no longer afford to be regarded as her mentor. Too intelligent a man not to know what he was doing, he well understood the blow he had thus dealt his admirer.

But whatever her thoughts about past events Mrs. Hutchinson found time that night to deal with her immediate problem. Although the ministers' testimony against her had been damaging in the extreme, it had not been given under oath, and she now plotted a way around it. The next morning, back in court, she boldly stated, "The ministers come in their own cause. Now the Lord hath said that an oath is the end of all controversy. Though there be a sufficient number of witnesses, yet they are not according to the Word. Therefore, I desire they may speak upon oath."

Winthrop tried to ignore her demand. But this woman was no one to be brushed aside. She went on to say, "I have since I went home perused some notes out of what Mr. Wilson did then write and I find things not to be as hath been alledged.' She was referring to notes that Wilson had written after the occasion of the ministers' remonstrance. Although neither she nor the Reverend John Wilson had the notes in court, the effect of it all was to throw doubt on the ministers' testimony. In these circumstances her demand for the oath loomed large.

One Simon Bradstreet pointed out that if by chance the ministers had misunderstood Anne's doctrines, "You would make them to sin if you urge them to swear." But this was precisely the pressure she wanted the ministers subjected to, pressure to make them hedge their testimony and destroy its effect. She insisted upon the oath. "If they accuse me, I desire it may be upon oath." Then she struck from the other flank: "There are some that will take their oaths to the contrary." She was gaining ground; she had pushed the ministers into a tight spot.

There was a growing commotion in her favor in the court after Winthrop called out, "Let those that are not satisfied in the court speak." The transcript reads "Many say: —We are not satisfied." Ever a realist, Winthrop decided to give way. "I would speak this to Mrs. Hutchinson. If the ministers shall take an oath, will you sit down satisfied?"

Having virtually forced this concession from the unwilling Winthrop, Anne made a mistake. Her reply was "I can't be—nothwithstanding oaths—satisfied against my own conscience." This seemed to be the answer of a person whose self-assurance had become an arrogant contempt of those not in agreement with her, and it weakened the effect of her demand for an oath.

After some further argument it was decided to first call the witnesses appearing on behalf of Mrs. Hutchinson. No oath was administered to them. The first, John Coggeshall, did his ineffective best. As he was already under the threat of banishment for having disturbed the peace, his state of mind may easily be imagined. But having been present at her meeting with the ministers, he stated that the accused had not said all that they had charged against her. Whereupon one of the ministers, Hugh Peter—later a chaplain in Cromwell's army—exclaimed, "How dare you look into the court to say such a word."

"Mr. Peter takes upon him to forbid me," Coggeshall said. "I shall be silent." And he was.

The next witness was Thomas Leverett. A ruling elder of the Boston church, he had also been present at the meeting of Mrs. Hutchinson and the ministers. He stated that she had merely said the other ministers did not preach a covenant of grace so clearly as did Mr. Cotton. If that could have been substantiated, Anne Hutchinson might have overcome the prejudgment of the court against her. But even Leverett's testimony, standing alone, was hardly sufficient to refute that of six "godly elders."

Now came the most important witness of all, John Cotton. A prudent man, Cotton opened his testimony by laying out his line of retreat in case he should find himself in trouble: "I did not think I should be called to bear witness in this cause, and therefore did not labour to call to remembrance what was done." He went on to say he was sorry that the comparison between his brethren and him had ever been made. But on the important issue he did stand by the accused. "And I must say that I did not find her saying they were under a covenant of works, nor that she said they did preach a covenant of works."

That the ministers were concerned by this testimony was demonstrated when Peter began to cross-examine Cotton. Some of the theological points they argued along the way are obscure, but Cotton seems to have held his own. One wonders what was going on in the mind of the defendant all this while. Certainly she failed to realize that things were going her way. Had it been otherwise, she would not have intervened at this point to make her second and final mistake.

Dudley had just restated the charge that Anne had disparaged the ministers as unable to rightly preach the New Testament; Cotton had replied that he did not remember it. Had Anne Hutchinson been able to content herself with renewing her demand for the minister's oath, she might well have walked out of the court a free woman. But she chose this moment to declaim a confession of faith. The Lord had given her to see, she said, that those who did not rightly preach the covenant of grace had the spirit of Antichrist, and "upon this he did discover the ministry unto me and ever since, I bless the Lord, he hath let me see which was the clear ministry and which the wrong. . . . Now if you do condemn me for speaking what in my conscience I know to be truth, I must commit myself unto the Lord."

Dudley, who had sized up the defendant more shrewdly than anyone else, immediately pressed his advantage. He began to taunt her, driving this now overwrought woman into traps that she had previously avoided with great skill. When she claimed she could distinguish between right and wrong ministers by an immediate revelation, he encouraged her to go on by asking. "How! an immediate revelation?"

With that, Mistress Hutchinson launched into a tirade bordering on hysteria. She called on Scripture to support her claims and compared herself to Daniel in the lions' den. It was an apt comparison but hardly one to charm the court. She closed by screaming, "You have power over my body but the Lord Jesus hath power over my body and soul. And assure yourselves thus much: you do as much as in you lies to put the Lord Jesus Christ from you. And if you go on in this course you begin, you will bring a curse upon you and your posterity! And the mouth of the Lord hath spoken it!"

In the shocked silence that followed this outburst, Dudley turned to the court and asked sarcastically: "What is the Scripture she brings?" Then Israel Stoughton, who earlier had favored administering the oath to the ministers, declared: "Behold, I turn away from you." The tide of opinion was now running against Anne Hutchinson.

John Winthrop now triumphantly addressed the court: "We have been hearkening about the trial of this thing and now the mercy of God by a providence hath answered our desires and made her to lay open her self and the ground of all these disturbances to be by revelations. . . . And that is the means by which she hath very much abused the country that they shall look for revelations and are not bound to the ministry of the Word, but God will teach them by immediate revelations. And this has been the ground of all these tumults and troubles, and I would that all those were all cut off from us that trouble us." And after further unflattering remarks Winthrop summed

up: "I am persuaded that the revelation she brings forth is delusion."
The transcript then reads "All the court but some two or three ministers cry out, 'We all believe it—we all believe it.' "

However unnecessary it may now have been, there was one remaining scruple to be satisfied. Winthrop asked the ministers to take the
oath. The transcript reads "Here now was a great whispering among
the ministers. Some drew back, others were animated on." Three of
them then took the oath and testified to more or less the same effect
as before. The heresy of Anne Hutchinson, which had been presumed
throughout, was now officially established.

William Coddington, beseeching the court not "so to force things
along," courageously maintained her defense until the end. "No man
may be a judge and an accuser too," he cried out. But his efforts were
useless. All but three members of the court voted to banish her.

John Winthrop solemnly pronounced the sentence of the court:
"Mrs. Hutchinson . . . you are banished from out of our jurisdiction
as being a woman not fit for our society, and are to be imprisoned till
the court shall send you away."

It was not possible to banish Anne Hutchinson immediately. First
she had to be excommunicated, and this raised an inconvenient com-
plication. The power of excommunication, by established New England pratice, was held by the whole congregation. But since Anne
Hutchinson still had a considerable following in the Boston church,
it was a good question whether the congregation actually would do the
job. The ministers, fully recognizing the challenge they faced, made
their preparations with great care.

Anne was confined in a house in Roxbury (out of the reach of her
Boston following), where, as Winthrop put it, "divers of the elders
and others resorted to her." This went on for more than three months,
and the visitations seem to have succeeded in breaking down her resistance. On March 15, 1638, a defeated and debilitated Anne Hutchinson was called before the congregation of the church in Boston. As
teacher of the Boston church the Reverend John Cotton presided.

Various of her "errors" were read to her, and she was asked whether
she would renounce them or not. Although she still showed faint signs
of her old fire, she seemed to have given up. It must have been a crushing experience for her to hear John Cotton say, ". . . let me warn
you . . . the dishonour you have brought unto God by these unsound

tenets of yours is far greater than all the honour you have brought to him, and the evil of your opinions doth outweigh all the good of your doings. Consider how many poor souls you have misled."

Winthrop, who was present and who took a minor part in these proceedings, wrote in his journal, "Mr. Cotton pronounced the sentence of admonition with great solemnity, and with much zeal and detestation of her errors and pride of spirit." When the great John Cotton turned against her, Anne Hutchinson's last hope was extinguished.

On March 22, 1638, Anne Hutchinson stated to the congregation of the church of Boston, "As my sin hath been open, so I think it needful to acknowledge how I came to fall into these errors. Instead of looking upon myself I looked at men. . . . I spake rashly and unadvisedly. I do not allow [that is, sanction] the slighting of ministers, nor of the Scriptures, nor any thing that is set up by God."

This confession did make an impression on John Cotton, and perhaps he briefly hoped that Anne might be spared excommunication after all. When it was asked if her confession could be repeated for those who had not heard it, he said, "The sum of what she said is this: . . . She doth utterly disallow herself and condemn herself for [her] carriage. And she confesseth the root of all was the height and pride of her spirit. [As] for her slighting the ministers, she is heartily sorry for it . . . and desires all that she hath offended to pray to God for her to give her a heart to be more truly humbled." Any good this might have done, however, was quickly wiped out by Anne herself. With a flash of her old stubbornness she spoke up and said: "My judgment is not altered, though my expression alters."

This gave the ministers exactly what they needed. One after the other, while the great Cotton remained silent, they all stated their opinions. What they had to say is best summed up by the words of the Reverend Thomas Shepard: "Yea, this day she hath showed herself to be a notorious imposter. It is a trick of as notorious subtlety as ever was held in the church to say . . . that she all this while hath not altered her judgment, but only her expressions." And the Reverend John Wilson pointedly added that it would be a sin against God not to rid themselves of a woman who could tell such a lie.

John Cotton saw what was expected of him, and he remained silent no longer. Whatever Anne Hutchinson may have been to him, he now joined the majority of the ministers. "I see this pride of heart is not healed but is working still," he said. "God hath let her fall into a manifest lie, yea, to make a lie. And . . . I think we are bound upon this ground to remove her from us and not to retain her any longer, seeing that she doth prevaricate in her words, as that her judgment is one thing and her expression another."

As the sin of telling a lie was considered a matter of practice rather than doctrine, Cotton turned the proceedings over to Pastor Wilson, who wasted no further time. Before any member of the church could express dissent, the pastor quickly pronounced the sentence of excommunication, calling her a heathen, a publican, and a leper.

The transcript of Anne Hutchinson's second trial comes to an end with the pastor's command to her to depart. Writing of this moment at a later time, Winthrop related the following: "In her going forth, one standing at the door said, 'The Lord sanctify this unto you,' to whom she made answer, 'The Lord judgeth not as man judgeth. Better to be cast out of the church than to deny Christ.'"

Two or three days after her excommunication Governor Winthrop sent Anne a warrant ordering her departure from the jurisdiction before the end of the month. Anne Hutchinson sailed to what is now Quincy and thence walked overland through the wilderness to Roger Williams' Providence Plantations. With her family and a number of her followers she settled on the island of Aquidneck in what is now Portsmouth, Rhode Island. The faithful Coddington became governor of her colony.

But the strain of her prosecution and the hardship of her journey in her pregnant condition had been too much for her. She fell sick, and when the time of her delivery came, she had a stillbirth. Rumors quickly spread that the stillborn child was "a monster."

The "monstrous birth" of Anne Hutchinson's child became the instrument for a sharp attack upon her. Even Cotton preached two sermons on the subject. The story was bruited about Massachusetts for the rest of the century, so that impressionable minds could not fail to draw the desired moral: God had punished Anne for her heresy. Long after the child had been buried, it lived as a ghost to haunt all would-be nonconformists.

Mrs. Hutchinson never fully recovered from the shocks of her experience. Although surrounded by her family, followers, and friends in the colony and presumably enjoying some happiness, she left Rhode Island after her husband's death in 1642 and went to the New Netherlands. Her tragedy was soon to run its full course. Finally settling near the present limits of New York City (her name is perpetuated by the Hutchinson River Parkway), she and five of her children were massacred there by Indians in 1643. Writing of her death, the Reverend Thomas Welde asserted that the Indians had gone to more barbaric lengths than usual: "And therefore God's hand is the more apparently seene herein, to pick out this wofull woman, to make her and those belonging to her, an unheard of heavie example of their cruelty above all others."

John Winthrop later described Anne as an "American Jezebel." He could not have failed to think that like Ahab's wicked wife, who had led another chosen people in the way of false worship, Mrs. Hutchinson had also met a violent end as part of God's judgment. In any event, the trial and banishment of Anne Hutchinson were only the beginning of the Puritan theocracy's repression of religious and social deviation. Her punishment was relatively mild, but it foreshadowed the fate of the unhappy "witches" who were to die by hanging in the hysteria that swept over the colony at the end of the seventeenth century; and it was to be another hundred years before true freedom of conscience would be tolerated in Massachusetts.

Witchcraft in the American Colonies, 1647-62

• Religious persecution of supposed "witches" began in the fourteenth century. The church was particularly anxious to convert everyone to the Catholic faith and regarded dissenters and heretics as pagans who were controlled by the power of evil. Trials, convictions, and executions became common throughout Europe and reached a peak during the sixteenth and seventeenth centuries. Under the auspices of the Spanish Inquisition as many as one hundred persons were executed, usually by burning at the stake, in a single day. Such auto-da-fés, as these mass burnings were called, came to take on the qualities of a carnival, where one could buy souvenirs, rosaries, holy images, and food. Suspicion even fell on professors doing scientific experimentation. An accusation of witchcraft became a means of destroying an opponent and confiscating his estate or business.

As a witch hunt, the American one was small compared with others of the time in Europe. The most famous outbreak centered around Salem, Massachusetts, in 1692. But as Frederick C. Drake indicates in his essay on "Witchcraft in the American Colonies, 1647-62," several areas had witnessed an explosion of mass hysteria and civil chaos a generation earlier.

It is easy to condemn seventeenth century Americans, and especially the clergy and the gentry, for their appalling moral cowardice. Their fears and passions led to a disregard of individual liberty. One might ask, however, whether our own century has witnessed a higher regard for human life or has been more resistant to tyranny and demagoguery.

From *American Quarterly*, Vol. 20, no. 4, pp. 694-725 (Winter 1968). Copyright 1968, Trustees of the University of Pennsylvania. Reprinted by permission of the journal, the author, and the University of Pennsylvania, publisher.

The witchcraft events that shattered Salem society in 1692 led directly to nineteen human executions by hanging, one by pressing with heavy weights, and the imprisonment of scores of people. Since that date they have also inspired a multitude of narrative accounts and stimulated at least three different controversies among historians.

The first of these controversies dealt with the role of Cotton and Increase Mather in the trials of 1692. Attacks upon the Mathers have varied from insinuations of responsibility for guiding the hysteria, in order to drive people back to church, to open condemnation for being slow to speak out against spectral evidence, a charge of ignoring the rules in judging the presence of witchcraft. During the last quarter of the 19th century a second argument developed over the legality of the courts which dealt with the indictments of 1692 and the adequacy of the compensation awarded to the dependents of those who suffered in the trials. Two of the foremost witchcraft historians of the 1880s, George H. Moore and Albert Goodell Jr., were the chief protagonists in this debate. Yet a third dispute, which arose in the first decade of the 20th century, between George Lyman Kittredge of Harvard and George Lincoln Burr of Cornell, concentrated more intently upon establishing the significance of witchcraft in America. The echoes of this debate, which evaluated the Salem outburst of 1962 within the overall context of European witchcraft, can still be heard today.

Professor Kittredge pointed out that belief in witchcraft was a constant quality in mankind; it was "the common heritage of humanity." Professor Burr dissented sharply from this view, claiming that witchcraft rose and fell in less than five centuries during "the greatest burst of Christian civilization." For Burr witchcraft meant the practice of worshiping the Devil thrown down from Heaven, and using powers gained from him to work evil. As the witch hunters justified their activities by reference to chapters from the Old Testament, it followed that witchcraft was a phenomenon within the Christian religion embracing both New and Old Testament doctrine. Necromancing, spiritualism and types of voodoo lay beyond the scope of this definition, and Burr accordingly rejected Kittredge's more universal view of witchcraft. Obviously, these respective definitions of the phenomenon led toward totally different conclusions. When both historians examined the New England record on witchcraft they differed considerably. Kittredge drew up a list of 21 theses on the subject, the twentieth of which stated: "the record of New England in the matter of witchcraft is highly creditable, when considered as a whole and from the comparative point of view." Burr, however, was unable to acquit his own ancestors upon the grounds that their belief in witchcraft was universal, or was more logical than disbelief. He affirmed that:

> it was superstitious and bigoted and cruel, even by the standards of their own time . . . their final panic [Salem] was the last on such a scale in any Christian land. Their transatlantic home I cannot think an excuse. . . . One thing is sure: we must not blow hot and cold with the same breath. If our fathers were the helpless victims of circumstance, then they were not its masters.

The multiple effect of these three controversies has been to elevate Salem to a position of being the only significant point of reference in colonial witchcraft literature. The prelude to the hysteria of 1692 is usually acknowledged to be the Goodwin case of 1688, when Goodwife Glover was executed in Boston after accusations that she had bewitched four young Goodwin children suffering from convulsions. Cases of witchcraft prior to 1692 have generally served merely as introductory material for the main discussion on Salem. John M. Taylor, an historian who provided evidence of early cases in Connecticut, nevertheless clung to this approach. References to earlier cases are often incorrect on numbers and important details. For example, W. N. Gemmill wrote of "over twenty trials for witchcraft" before 1692, when "many people were convicted and several hung [sic]." This estimate alone reduced the numbers indicted to 25% of the actual total and vaguely underestimated the numbers convicted and executed. Rossell Hope Robbins in the excellent *Encyclopedia of Witchcraft and Demonology* concentrated so intently upon Salem that he termed it "the best known name in the entire history of witchcraft." He asserted that the colonial witchcraft delusion was "sporadic and mild and, compared with the holocausts in sixteenth and seventeenth century Europe," it was largely "insignificant." Robbins affirmed, moreover, that the "relative freedom" from witchcraft for the 40 preceding years made the Salem trials overshadow everything else to such an extent that "it may be said the history of American witchcraft is Salem."

In some cases a tendency has developed to dismiss the crisis of 1692 as "a mere bubble in Massachusetts history." Thus Ola E. Winslow in her biography of Samuel Sewall, Salem judge in 1692, has commented that the "sporadic" witchcraft cases before the Salem troubles, were "surprisingly few in comparison with the disasters that might so naturally have been attributed to evil spirits in human flesh." A further example can be found in an essay by Stuart Henry upon Puritan character displayed in the Salem crisis. Henry generalized about the entire Puritan response to witchcraft from the one example at Salem. Closely following Kittredge's arguments to exonerate Puritanism, he flatly asserted that "the first vibration of the acute, high-strung Puritan mind to the demons of the spirit world was in Boston, 1688." Consequently, the Salem story polarizes as "one of the few chapters of American history which seems to have a definite beginning, middle and end." In searching for the source of the Salem story Henry observed that some English cases in 1683, "were instances of witchcraft, not in America, but in England, the memory of which might have been in the minds of the American colonists."

Salem has thus become the focal point of historical analysis of colonial witchcraft. The outburst of 1692 has been effectively separated from its American ancestry, and its origins located somewhere in the 1680s. Earlier cases have been ignored and miscounted. For there were over 95 incidents involving colonial people with witchcraft before 1692. Nearly 60 of these incidents occurred between the adoption of the Cambridge platform of 1648 and the acceptance of the Half-Way Covenant of 1662. These incidents led to at least 83 trials between 1647 and 1691 in which 22 people were executed, and many others suffered banishment, whipping and financial loss. Yet, of the 22 executions 20 had taken place between 1647 and 1662, and the first eight occurred in less than four years. The following table lists the witchcraft trials which directly involved the colonies from 1647 to 1662.

The two questions upon which this table can cast no light are, firstly, why did so many cases occur and, secondly, what characteristics did they possess? Both questions may be approached through an analysis of the three factors most likely to contribute to the occurrence of witchcraft activity in a society, namely the theological (or ideological) background of the people suspecting witchcraft, the presence of external stimuli and evidence of internal pressures in society likely to produce an active awareness of witches.

In his monumental survey of the theological framework of Puritan New England, Perry Miller wondered why no more cases of witchcraft

A Table of Witchcraft Cases and Incidents in the American Colonies: 1645-62

Name of Witch	Date	Accusers	Victims	Town	Colony	Verdict of the Jury	Final Verdict, Date and Sentence
Mary and Hugh Parsons?	1645	Not known	Rev. Moxon's children	Springfield	Mass.		Not accused in 1645, but several were disturbed.
Alse Young	1647	Not known	Not known	Windsor	Conn.	Guilty	Executed, May 25, 1647.
Margaret Jones	1648	A Neighbor	Neighbor's children	Charlestown	Mass.	Guilty	Executed at Boston, June 15, 1648
Thomas Jones	1648	A Neighbor	Neighbor's children	Charlestown	Mass.	Not known	Arrested, fate unknown, possibly released.
Mary Johnson	1648	Her Employer	Animals in the fields	Weathersfield	Conn.	Guilty	Guilty, Dec. 7, 1648, and executed at Hartford.
Mary Oliver	1649	Not known	Not known	Boston	Mass.	Not known	Confessed to witchcraft, fate not known but probably executed.
Mrs. H. Lake	1651	Not known	Not known	Dorchester	Mass.	Guilty	Executed at Boston
Hostile Indians			Uncas, Mohegan Indian				Inquiry by the Commissioners of the United Colonies.
John Carrington	Feb. 20 1651	Not known	Not known	Wethersfield	Conn.	Guilty March 6, 1651	Executed after March 6, 1651.
Joan Carrington	Feb. 20 1651	Not known	Not known	Wethersfield	Conn.	March 6, 1651	Executed after March 6, 1651.
Goodwife Bassett	May 1651	Many people	Not known	Stratford	Conn.		Guilty after a review by the Governor and Magistrates, and executed.
Mary Parsons	1651	Neighbors	Her own children and the Rev. Moxon's children	Springfield	Mass.	Guilty	Imprisoned at Boston, May 1, Acquitted of witchcraft by the General Court on May 7, 1651, but guilty of the murder of her child. Between May 7 and 27 confessed to witchcraft, and executed May 29, 1651, at Boston.

Name	Date	Accusers	Witnesses	Place	Colony	Verdict	Remarks
Hugh Parsons	1651	Neighbors and Mary Parsons	Rev. Moxon's children	Springfield	Mass.	Guilty	The jury verdict was set aside by the Magistrates, and the case went to the General Court in Boston, Acquitted May 31, 1651.
John Bradstreet	1651	Not known	Not known	Rowley	Mass.	Guilty	A fine of 20 shillings or a whipping.
Mrs. Kendal	1651	Godman Genings' nurse	Godman Genings' child	Cambridge	Mass.	Guilty	Executed.
Elizabeth Godman (First case)	1651	The Mrs. Goodyeare, Atwater, Bishop Thorp and Rev. Hooke	As Accusers	New Haven	New Haven		The Court of Magistrates issued a warning to Mrs. Godman that she was suspected as a witch, and she was informed that if she appeared in court again her evidence and case would be reconsidered.
Goodwife Knapp	1653	Roger Ludlow Mrs. Lockwood and seven others	Not known but several	Fairfield	Conn.		Executed at Fairfield.
Mrs. T. Staples	1653	Roger Ludlow	Not known but several	Fairfield	Conn.	Not Guilty	Released, and her accuser Roger Ludlow surrendered a total of £25 for defamation.
John Godfrey	1653	Job and Moses Tyler	Mary Tyler	Andover	Mass.		Deposition and evidence not presented until 1659.
Mary Lee	1654	Sailors on the Charity	Sailors and the vessel	En route to the Chesapeake	Md.		Mary Lee was hanged at sea; no verdict found on John Bosworth, master of the Charity.
Mrs. R. Manship	Oct. 16, 1654	Peter Godson	Peter Godson		Md.	Not Guilty	Released, and Peter Godson was judged to have defamed and slandered Mrs. Manship.

A Table of Witchcraft Cases and Incidents—(Continued)

Name of Witch	Date	Accusers	Victims	Town	Colony	Verdict of the Jury	Final Verdict, Date and Sentence
Lydia Gilbert	Sept. or Oct. 1654	Not known	Henry Stiles	Windsor	Mass.	Guilty	Executed.
Nicholas Bayly	July-Oct. 1655	Not known but several	Not known	New Haven	New Haven	Suspicious of witchcraft	Released, but banished from the colony.
Mrs. N. Bayly	July-Oct. 1655	Not known but several	Not known	New Haven	New Haven	Suspicious of witchcraft	Released, but banished from the colony, for "Impudent and notorious lying."
Elizabeth Godman (Second case)	1655	See the first Godman case, and Allen Ball	Stephen Goodyeare's step-daughters. and several animals		New Haven	Suspicious of witchcraft	Bound over to another court meeting on October 4, 1655.
Elizabeth Godman (Third case)	Oct. 4, 1655	As above	As above		New Haven	Suspicious of witchcraft	Released upon payment of £50 security for future good conduct.
Ann Hibbins	1656	Not known	Not known	Salem	Mass.	Guilty	A Court of Magistrates set aside the verdict but the General Court found her guilty on May 14, 1656 and she was hanged June 19, 1656.
Jane Welford	1656	Several Not known	Not known	Dover	New Hamp.	Acquitted	Freed upon condition of future good behaviour.
Eunice Cole	1656	Goodman Robe, Thomas Coleman, Abraham Drake	A cow and a sheep	Hampton	New Hamp.	Discharged	Released.

Name	Date	Accuser/Defendant	Role	Place	Colony	Verdict	Outcome
William Harding	1656	Mr. David Lindsaye	Not known	Northumberland County	Va.	Guilty	Ten stripes upon his bare back, and forever banished from the county, as well as paying all costs of the trial.
William Meaker	1657	Thomas Mullener	Not known		New Haven	Not Guilty	The Court found against Mullener and ordered him to pay £50 estate security or removal from the colony.
Jane Hogg —Knap	1657	Not known	Not known		Mass.	Not known	Unknown.
Goodwife	1657	Not known	Not known		Mass.	Not known	Unknown.
Batchelor	1657	Not known	Not known		Mass.	Not known	Unknown.
Ann Pope	1657	Not known	Not known		Mass.	Not known	Unknown.
Elizabeth Garlick	1657-1658	A fellow servant	Servant's child	Easthampton, Long Island	Conn.	Acquitted	Released, but had to pay the costs of transport to and from the trial.
Elizabeth Richardson	1658	The Ship's company of the *Sarah Artch*	Ship's Master and company	At Sea	Md.		Executed. Edward Prescott, the Ship's Owner, was released and freed from a charge of allowing the hanging to take place on his vessel.
Katherine Grade	1659	Captain Bennett	Not known	At Sea and Jamestown	Va.		Executed. Captain Bennett summoned before a General Court at Jamestown, but the verdict is not known.
Mrs. N. Robinson	1659	Ann Godby	Not known		Va.	Acquitted	Mrs. Godby's husband had to pay 300 pounds of tobacco, the cost of the suit, and the witnesses' charges at the rate of 20 pounds of tobacco per day, for the slander.

A Table of Witchcraft Cases and Incidents—(Continued)

Name of Witch	Date	Accusers	Victims	Town	Colony	Verdict of the Jury	Final Verdict, Date and Sentence
John Godfrey (Second case)	1659	Job, Moses, Mary, and Mary Tyler	Mary Tyler	Andover	Mass.		Depositions were made before the Governor, Simon Bradstreet, and six years later, in 1665, Godfrey was tried in Boston for witchcraft.
Mrs. W. Holmes	1660	Dinah Sylvester	Not known	Scituate	Old Plymouth Colony	Not Guilty	Dinah Sylvester had to make public acknowledgment for a false accusation.
Mary Wright	1660	Not known	Not known		Long Island	Suspected of witchcraft	Arraigned before the General Court of Mass., and acquitted of witchcraft, though convicted of being a Quaker, and banished.
Winifred Holman	1660	Not known	Rebecca Stearns	Cambridge	Mass.	Not known	Two affidavits signed by 7 and 18 persons respectively were produced to clear her, though the verdict is not known.
Nicholas Jennings	1661 Sept. 5	Not known	Several people	Sea Brook	Conn.	Disagreed	Freed after a jury disagreement "the major part thinking them guilty, and the rest strongly suspect it that they are guilty."
Margaret Jennings	Sept. 5, 1661	Not known	Several people	Sea Brook	Conn.	Disagreed	See verdict on Nicholas Jennings.
Nathaniel Greensmith	1662	Rebecca Greensmith, and the daughter of John Kelley	Anne Cole	Hartford	Conn.	Guilty.	Executed.
Rebecca Greensmith	1662	Anne Cole, William Ayres	Anne Cole	Hartford	Conn.	Guilty	Executed.

Andrew Sanford	1662	Not known	Anne Cole or the daughter of John Kelley	Hartford	Conn.	Not known	Not known.
Mary Sanford	1662	Not known	Not known	Hartford	Conn.	Guilty	Executed, sometime after June 13.
William Ayres	1662	Daughter of John Kelley	Anne Cole	Hartford	Conn.	Guilty	The water test was applied and confirmed witchcraft; he escaped prison and fled the colony.
Goodwife Ayres	1662	Daughter of John Kelley	Anne Cole	Hartford	Conn.	Guilty	The water test was applied and confirmed witchcraft; she fled the colony with her husband.
Mary Barnes	1662	Not known	Not known	Farmington	Conn.	Guilty	Executed.
Judith Varleth	1662	Daughter of John Kelley	Not known	Hartford	Conn.	Guilty	Found guilty, Jan. 6, but released after the personal intervention of Peter Stuyvesant, Governor of New Amsterdam and brother-in-law of the accused.
Elizabeth Seager (First case)	1662	Anne Cole	Anne Cole	Hartford	Conn.	Guilty	
Elizabeth Seager (Second case)	1662	Anne Cole	Anne Cole	Hartford	Conn.		Discharged, but under suspicion.
James Walkley	1662	Daughter of John Kelley	Not known	Hartford	Conn.	Not known	Probably guilty, because he fled to Rhode Island.
Katherine Palmen	1662	Not known	Not known	Hartford	Conn.	Not known	Not known.
Mrs. Peter Grant	1662	Not known	Not known	Hartford	Conn.	Not known	Not known.

had occurred before 1692, "for it was axiomatic that the Devil would try hard to corrupt regions famous for religion." He accepted without reservation, however, that cases of witchcraft before 1692 were "sporadic" but speculated that:

> Perhaps the reason there were so few witches in New England . . . is . . . the people were good enough Calvinists to resist temptation. They might not always be able to refuse an extra tankard of rum, but this sin—although it was the most plausible and the most enticing—they withstood.

Many of those indicted for witchcraft were judged to have failed in withstanding the sin. This was relatively easy to do for a covenant could be applied with equal diligence to a relationship with the Devil or with God, and the American Puritans were openly confronted with the Indians as positive instruments of Satan's power and determination to conquer New England for himself, permitted to torment all because of God's terrible judgments against his wayward people. Once it had been decided that the assumption of redemption through God's grace no longer applied to an individual, the twin assumption of original sin worked against him with devastating effect. The next step backward was seduction by the Devil, then open covenanting with him. For example, the indictments against Mary Johnson indicated that she was an allegedly lazy servant girl who prayed to the Devil for aid, and "by her own confession she is guilty of familliarity with the Deuill." The evidence against her cited the fact that she had been able to command the services of a goblin to perform her household duties. When she was chastised for not carrying out the ashes "a Devil afterwards would clear the Hearth of Ashes for her," and when she was sent into the fields to chase out marauding hogs "a Devil would scowre the Hogs away, and make her laugh to see how he scared them." In her confession she admitted uncleanness "both with men and with Devils." At Wethersfield, Connecticut, the indictment against the Carringtons claimed they had "Intertained ffamiliarity with Sathan, the Great Enemy of God and Mankinde," and in the Mary Parsons case the indictment accused her of not having fear of God before her eyes, nor in her heart, seduction by the Devil, familiarity and covenanting with the Devil while having used several devilish practices by witchcraft "to the hurt of the persons of Martha and Rebeckah Moxon," and yielding to the Devil's instigations and "malitious motion." Similarly, in the cases where people were released they were warned, generally, that they were "suspitious of witchcraft." These warnings were given to Mrs. Godman, the Baylys and the Jennings.

Evidence of witchcraft was accumulated in three ways: by confession, by searchings for witchmarks and by the collection of testimonies and accusations of witchcraft. The first two alone meant automatic proof of guilt followed by execution. Margaret Jones was examined and found to possess a Devil's mark, "a teat, as fresh as if [it] had been newly sucked." This revealed where an imp or animal of the Devil had fastened on to her, a physical affirmation of the reversal of the covenant. Both the Staplies and Knapp cases in Connecticut were concerned with the discovery of witchmarks on Mrs. Knapp's body, and her fate was sealed by seven neighbors who claimed to have seen them. Mrs. Staplies refused to believe Goodwife Knapp was a witch, and suspicion fell on her also. As Mrs. Knapp's body was brought off the gallows, Mrs. Staplies examined it for the alleged witchmarks and found none. Mrs. Lockwood, one of the seven accusers, declared that they had been there; "she had them, and she confessed she was a witch; that is sufficient."

The majority who did withstand the sin of witchcraft did not do so merely as a passive exercise. As the Elect they were presented with Biblical evidence of the existence of witchcraft. They would hardly be good Calvinists if they did not seek out witches, for Calvin stood explicitly by the Old Testament book of Exodus which declared "Thou shalt not suffer a witch to live" and this decree was written into the laws of Massachusetts, Connecticut, New Haven and Plymouth. Upon witchcraft itself Calvin had declared: "now the Bible teaches that there are witches and that they must be slain. God expressly commands that all witches and enchantresses be put to death, and this law of God is a universal law." For this reason the early colonists of New England were good Calvinists precisely because they did search out witches. Witchcraft was not only a "temptation" to resist; it was an evil requiring positive eradication before God.

Consequently, colonial leaders became increasingly concerned during the 1640s with the emergence of witchcraft activity as manifestation of the Devil's desire to subvert God's Commonwealth. Puritan, Anglican, Pilgrim and Catholic alike took steps to arm themselves with legal protection against his agents. In 1636 Plymouth included in its Summary

Offences "lyable to Death," the action of "Solemn Compaction or conversing with the devil by way of Witchcraft, conjuration or the like." The 1641 Massachusetts Bay Body of Liberties and the 1642 Connecticut Capital Code both included, as their second law: "Yf any man or woman be a witch (that is) hath or consulteth with a familiar spirit, they shall be put to death." All three colonies re-enacted these laws in 1646. Rhode Island accepted a witchcraft law on May 19th, 1647, after its charter had been granted. The law stated that "witchcraft is forbidden by this present Assembly to be used in this colony, and the penalty imposed by the authority that we are subjected to, is felony of death." New Haven possessed a law similar to Connecticut's. Armed thus, the colonies were prepared to deal with outbreaks of witchcraft, as well as conform to the laws of England on the subject. By 1662 they had made good use of their legal provisions in a fifteen-year campaign against the Devil's agents in nearly all of the colonies.

While New England laws and religion attempted to undermine the "Great Enemy of God and Mankind," the pressure for an outbreak of witchcraft activity came from overseas. In England, against a background of mounting tension, and later warfare, between King and Parliament, hundreds of witchcraft accusations were made. Between 1645 and 1647 over two hundred witches were executed. The period of greatest slaughter was in the summer of 1645 when Matthew Hopkins, Witch Finder General, was at the height of his campaign to find witches. Altogether, the decade between 1637 and 1647 produced the greatest percentage of hangings per indictment, 42%, of any period in English witchcraft history. Later still, outbreaks were recorded in Scotland, 1643-50; East Anglia, 1645; Newcastle, 1648; Kent, 1652 and Scotland, 1661. In Europe, the Swedish case of bewitched children, sometimes referred to as the possible inspiration for the Goodwin case of 1688 and the Salem episode of 1692, occurred in 1661.

These persecutions undoubtedly troubled the colonists in New England. Certainly the colonial magistrates knew of English methods of examining suspected witches. In their search for "familiars," witch-marks and imps they were adopting the same practices as Matthew Hopkins. In the very first case brought before the bench at Boston, the Court was "desireows that the same course which hath ben taken in England for the discouery of witches, by watchinge, may also be taken here with the witch now in question." Thus for Margaret Jones the

Court ordered that "a strict watch be set about her every night, & that her husband be confined to a priuat roome, & watched also." In Hartford, in 1662, William Ayers and his wife were given the water test, a common European method of determining witchcraft. They failed the test which was sufficient evidence of guilt to warrant execution, and they were in prison after it when they escaped with the aid of friends. The executions at sea in 1654, 1658 and 1659 indicated not only common denominators in the search for witches, but also stimulated witchcraft incidents in the colonies where the vessels landed.

As a series of distressing internal upheavals combined with Old Testament theology in England to generate the witchcraft cases, so too in the colonies did Puritan theology serve as a catalyst to the extraordinary number of distressing events which affected colonial society in the 1640s. A similar state of affairs had prevailed in Salem before the outburst of 1692. Samuel E. Morison has observed that the 1692 episode needed little clerical belief in witchcraft for it arose, "as witchcraft epidemics had usually arisen in Europe, during a troubled period, the *Decennium Luctuosum* of New England History." Morison noted the uneasiness of the people with rebellions, changes of government, fear of Indian attacks, and factional strife within the community. The unsettled state of the colony was further agitated when Increase Mather, after long negotiations, failed to win back the old charter revoked by James II; the colony had to accept a Royal Governor; a boundary dispute broke out with neighboring Topsfield; and the new Governor had to leave for the frontier to lead an expedition against the Indians.

This unrest of the 1692 period was a replica of the distress in the 1640s, particularly in Massachusetts, Connecticut and Plymouth. William Bradford commented upon the wickedness that had grown and broken forth "in a land wher the same was so much witnessed against, and so narrowly looked into, and severly punished." Despite these punishments, Bradford observed "sundrie notorious sins" prevailed in Plymouth, "oftener than once." In analyzing the outbreak of wickedness, he feared that:

> The Divell may carrie a greater spite against the churches of Christ and the gospell hear, by how much the more the indeaour to preserve holynes and puritie amongst them. . . . I would rather thinke thus, then that Satane hath more power in these

heathen lands, as some have thought, then in more Christian nations espetially over God's servants in them.

Even greater evidence of unrest existed in Massachusetts. On September 22, 1642, the year after the colony's promulgation of its witchcraft law, John Winthrop drew attention in his journal to the "unsettled frame of spirit" which had led many people to emigrate to the West Indies, to New Amsterdam, Long Island or even back to England. He blamed the "sudden fall of land and cattle"; the scarcity of money and foreign commodities, and people fleeing from the colony, for the unrest in Massachusetts. From that date forward evidence of Satanic intervention in the colony's affairs fills his pages. The corn crop of 1643 was spoiled by pigeons and mice; a great storm swept over Newberry, darkening the air with dirt on July 5, 1643; lights were seen near Boston and over the North East point in January 1644, at the place where Captain Chaddock's pinnance had been blown up, reputedly by a necromancer. A voice was heard calling across the water several times. At Hingham, a man named Painter, who turned Anabaptist and prevented his wife from baptizing their child, even though she was a member of the church, disturbed the Church leaders sufficiently in July for them to have the man whipped for "reproaching the Lord's ordinance." Out of just such small beginnings arose the great tensions leading to the Half-Way Covenant as a solution for the baptismal problems of the children of non-church members. In 1645 the wife of Hartford's Governor, Mrs. Hopkins, lost her reason and understanding. Externally, preparations were made for a second war against the Pequot Indians, for "Sathan may stir up & combine many of his instruments against the Churches of Christ." The Hingham militia had to be lectured by Winthrop on the meanings of liberty to obey their leaders. On August 28, 1645, a day of fasting and humiliation for troubles in Old and New England was held, the third such day to be set aside since 1643. By 1646 the General Court of Massachusetts was inundated with petitions of grievances. Then came two monumental calamities in 1646-47. The colonies were just struggling back to prosperity after the depression of 1642-43 when the corn, wheat and barley crops were ruined by black worms and caterpillars, which ate the blades and tassels and left the rest to wither. The churches held a day of humiliation. Secondly, in 1647, an epidemic swept the country among Indians, English and Dutch. It weakened the people so much that the gathering of the remaining crops was lost for want of help, even though few died in Massachusetts and Connecticut.

The pessimism that was generated by these plagues was aptly described in the almanacs of a young Harvard intellectual, Samuel Danforth. In 1647 the Harvard "philomathemat" recorded the ordinary occurrences in the colony—the arrival of ships, the coming of winter, and the debilitating effects of the late sickness—in epigrammatic verse. To his first almanac was appended a list of events which optimistically expressed the hopes of the settlers in converting the Indians, and illustrated the expansion of New England towns. In 1648, however, the contents of his verse underwent a marked change. With a painstaking tribute to classical allusion and allegory he ran through all the blessings of the New England scene; a pleasant land in which the Puritan plant, tended by a faithful husbandman, could survive. All of the advantages of Justice, Liberty, Peace, Unity, Truth, Plenty, a Nursery [Harvard College], and the conversion of the Indians, were meticulously spelled out. On the surface this appears to be a hymn of praise to a beneficent providence. But the verses should be examined alongside the chronological table of "some few memorable occurrences" that are listed at the end of the almanac. There Danforth summarized every melancholy event and disaster that had hit the colonies from 1636 to 1647. Nothing was omitted, and the whole checks off exactly with Winthrop's observations. Far from being a hymn of praise, Danforth's verses of 1648 represent an antidote to social, economic and religious distress by referring to classical abstract virtues. With the issue of the 1649 almanac he even removed this escapist cloak. Both his verse content and his table of occurrences list one long series of unhappy events. With intended irony, the young intellectual informed his readers that, even in the midst of their host of troubles, things could still be worse. With England, Ireland, Scotland and Barbadoes racked by war and pestilence, "the worthless Orphan may sit still and blesse, That yet it sleeps in peace and quietness."

In the presence of so many other troubles, the absence of war may have seemed small consolation to New Englanders. For when the synod of 1648 met at Cambridge to settle "such errors, objections, and scruples as had been raised about it by some young heads in the country," the barriers of resistance to the realities of the Devil's work were going down in Connecticut and Massachusetts. While Winthrop glorified the synod as the triumphant representative of the churches of Christ in New England, his fellow magistrates in Boston and Hartford were finding fresh confirmation of the Devil's malignant concern. As Mary Johnson and Margaret Jones went to their respective scaffolds the whole formula of religious ferment added to social distress and natural disasters, which later characterized the Salem episode, was present in 1647.

Once underway, the witchcraft cases of 1647 to 1662 added to the tension from which they sprang. They did this in a steady stream, of cases, year by year, rather than in one frenzied outburst such as occurred in 1692. Yet many of the characteristics of Salem trials were in evidence in the earlier trials. The indictments were often concerned with the bewitchment of children and animals. Mary Johnson and Mary Parsons were accused of killing their own children by witchcraft. The former had smothered her child, and before execution left another baby, born in prison, to the care of Nathaniel Rescew, the jailer. Mary Parsons, after marrying Hugh Parsons on October 27, 1645, had two sons to him, born October 4, 1649, and October 26, 1650. Both died in less than a year of their births, and the evidence suggests that after the death of the second one, on March 1, 1651, the mother lost her reason. Although denunciations of witchcraft were leveled against Hugh Parsons by his neighbors, it was Mary Parsons who was imprisoned at Boston on May 1, and her case came before the General Court six days later. Later still the cases involving Mrs. Kendal and Goodwife Garlick concerned the deaths of other people's children. Mrs. Kendal was executed for bewitching to death a young child belonging to Goodman Genings of Watertown. The child's nurse testified that Mrs. Kendal had fondled the child, that soon afterward it changed color and died. The Court received this evidence without bothering to call the child's parents. After Mrs. Kendal's execution the parents testified that the child had died of exposure caused by the neglect of the nurse. By this time the latter was in prison for adultery, and she died there. The case ended with no further recantations; striking evidence of how the stigma of witchcraft tainted the innocent and muted inquiry. Further afield, in Easthampton, in the winter of 1657-58, Goodwife Garlick escaped from an identical accusation by a fellow servant, who claimed she had bewitched her child. The head of the household, Lion Gardiner, gave evidence that the baby died from the neglect of the mother, yet the magistrates at Easthampton ordered two men, Thomas Baker and John Hand, to go "into Kenicut for to bring us under their government . . . and also to carry Goodwife Garlick, that she may be delivered up into the authorities there for the triall of the cause of witchcraft [of] which she is suspected."

Some of the evidence in many of the cases concerned the illnesses of witnesses and animals, and accidental occurrences. In Maryland, Peter Godson and his wife alleged that he became lame after seeing the wife of Richard Manship. In the first Mrs. Godman case of 1653, in New Haven, she was accused on May 21, of knowing whatever was done at church meetings, muttering to herself, being responsible for the sickness of the Rev. Mr. Hooke's son, and for the "verey strang fitts wch hath continewed at times ever since," of Mrs. Bishop, who had lost her own children. Later Mrs. Godman quarreled with the wife of the Colonial Treasurer, Mrs. Atwater, who then blamed her when she found Betty Brewster, a servant, ill "in a most misserable case, heareing a most dreadful noise wch put her in great feare and trembling, wch put her into such a sweate . . . and in ye morning she looked as one yt had bine allmost dead." Three days later, on May 24, 1653, further depositions were made regarding the cause of Mrs. Bishop's fainting fits. As early as 1648 this type of evidence had brought about the conviction of Margaret Jones, blamed when her neighbor's children fell ill.

Illness among animals was often blamed upon the activities of witches. In New Haven, during the first Mrs. Godman case, Mrs. Thorp swore that after she had refused to sell or give some chickens to Mrs. Godman she feared they would be struck down by witchcraft:

> she thought then that if this woman was naught as folkes suspect, may be she will smite my chickens, and quickly after one chicken dyed, and she remembered she had heard if they were bewitched they would consume wthin, and she opened it and it was consumed in ye gisard to water & wormes, and divers others of them droped, and now they are missing and it is likely dead, and she neuer saw either hen or chicken that was so consumed w'hin wth wormes.

Later, in the second and third Godman cases, the testimonies of new witnesses included similar examples. Allen Ball spoke of strange happenings with his calf; Mrs. Thorp added fresh complaints about her cow; and others mentioned troubles with pigs and calves. In Hartford, the Mary Johnson case involved the frightening of hogs by a goblin. During 1659 a deposition was made before Governor Bradstreet of Massachusetts that the Tyler family in Andover had received a visitation from the Devil in the form of a "Thing like a Bird" six years earlier. In 1665 the Tylers renewed their testimonies. The second case in New Hampshire, involving Eunice Cole, was brought before the courts by Goodman Robe who had lost a cow and a sheep.

Even more trivial evidence was accepted as proof of the Devil's evil influences on his agents. Part of the charges against Mrs. Godman dealt with her ability to smell figs in the pockets of Mrs. Atwater when no one else could. The main evidence against Hugh Parsons was given by his wife after she had confessed to witchcraft in May 1651. Her charges included his knowing all of the secrets that she had revealed only to her intimate friend Mrs. Smith; being out late at night; his arrival in a bad temper; putting out the fire; throwing peas about; talking in his sleep and fighting with the Devil. The Jury convicted him on this testimony, but he was acquitted by the General Court. In the Lydia Gilbert case execution followed evidence that she had caused the accidental death of Henry Stiles, two years previously. Any strange occurrence could thus be laid at the witches' doors. In 1657, Thomas Mullener's use of a witchcraft charge, in an attempt to gain personal revenge upon William Meaker, backfired upon the accuser, but the potentialities of the charge remained. Dissatisfaction with a neighbor could easily be converted into accusations of witchcraft.

As the evidence presented to the courts covered a wide range of accusations it also concerned a large number of people. In the trial of Hugh Parsons 39 testimonies were presented to Edward Rawson, clerk of the court. Only nine of these bore the same surname as other witnesses, and at least 30 families were involved in this case at Springfield in 1651. During 1653 and 1654, the Staplies and Knapp trials recorded the names of at least seven people who had accused Mrs. Knapp and then accused Mrs. Staplies of witchcraft. For the latter case 18 more added their contributions to the evidence. In addition five people went to see Mrs. Knapp in prison. Altogether 30 people were involved in this case, 22 of whom possessed different surnames. Two of the witnesses, Deborah Lockwood and Bethia Brundish were seventeen and sixteen years old respectively. In New Haven, Nicholas Bayly and his wife were called before a court and informed that "sundrie passages taken in writing . . . doth render them both, but especially the woman, very suspitious in poynt of witchcraft. . . ."

With large numbers in small communities that were closely clustered, the news of witchcraft was carried from one region to another on the wings of gossip. This gossip was often sufficient to stimulate a search for other witches. Mary Parsons' charges against her husband included a declaration that "you tould her that you were at a Neighbor's Howse a little before Lecture, when they were speaking of Carrington and his Wife, that were now apprhended for Witches," thus establishing a direct link with the execution of the Carringtons of Wethersfield. In the Staplies' case, Goodwife Sherwood's written testimony against Staplies revealed much of the preoccupation with witchcraft, as well as intercommunity awareness:

> so the next day she went in againe to see the witch with other neighbours, there was Mr. Jones, Mris. Pell & her two daughters, Mris. Ward and goodwife Lockwood . . . Elizabeth [Mrs. Pell's daughter] bid her [Knapp] doe as the witch at the other towne [Bassett] did, that is, discouer all she knew to be witches.

The spread of tragic examples from New England implicated other areas in witchcraft activity. Virginia experienced the first effects of the dangers inherent in gossiping over witches in May 1655. At a private court in Linhaven, the following resolution was passed:

> Whereas divrs dangerous & scandalous speeches have been raised by some psons concerning sevrall women in this Countie, termeing them to be Witches, whereby theire reputacons have been much impaired and their lives brought in question (ffor avoydeing the like offence). It is by this Cort ordered that what pson soever shall hereafter raise any such like scandall, concerninge any partie whatsor, and shall not be able to pve the same, both upon oath, and by sufficient witness, such pson soe offending shall in the first place paie a thousand pounds of tob: and likewise by lyable to further Censure of the Cort.

It was in the face of this resolution that the Rev. David Lindsaye proved his case against William Harding in 1656, and Ann Godby failed to prove her case against Mrs. Nicholas Robinson in 1659. Virginia and Maryland's first cases followed immediately after the excitements of the shipboard hangings that were brought to light in their courts, but the cases resembled New England cases so closely that it is difficult to say which was the major cause of witchcraft spreading to these areas. From the colonists' point of view it was not important. What had occurred was an extension of the Devil's activities. While still interested primarily in Puritan New England, the "Great Enemy" was conducting flanking operations along the shores of Catholic Maryland and Anglican Virginia. He also appeared across the New Hampshire border.

In addition to large numbers of people generating the searches for witches in their own communities, leading to inquiries in other towns, many of these cases reveal a curious comparison with the Salem outburst of 1692. That frenzy had occurred in the absence of the Governor, away fighting the Indians. Similarly, the cases of 1647-62 often developed in the absence of the colonial governors, and were directly connected with the Deputy Governors, leading officials and prominent clergymen. In 1653, all of the eminent citizens of New Haven society were implicated when Elizabeth Godman, a woman possessing a quick temper and the ability to antagonize her own sex, became the subject of malicious gossip by a clique gathered around the wives of Deputy Governor Stephen Goodyeare, Colonial Treasurer, Mr. Atwater, and the Rev. Mr. Hooke. As she was attached to the Goodyeare household, Mrs. Godman was easily accessible as the center of attraction and the rumors spread. After being locked out of the Atwater house one day, Mrs. Godman proceeded to alarm the Rev. Mr. Hooke by maintaining that witches should not be provoked but, instead, brought into the church. This doctrine shocked Hooke, and as he was troubled in his sleep about witches at the time of his son's sickness he centered his uneasiness upon Mrs. Godman. She proved as resourceful as her adversaries, and won the day by carrying the fight to them by summoning all of her tormentors before the magistrates, and complaining of them for suspecting her of being a witch. After reviewing all of the evidence, which included a claim that "Hobbamocke" [the Indian Devil] was her husband, the Court pointed out that Mrs. Godman was known as a liar, and it found the defendants not guilty. Moreover, it warned her that she had "vnjustly called heither the seuerall psons before named, being she can proue nothing against them, and that her cariage doth justly render her suspitious of witchcraft, wch she herselfe in so many words confesseth." The Court warned her to watch her conduct afterward, for in the event of further proof being presented, "these passages will not be forgotten." Credit has been given to the Court of Magistrates for its forbearance in withstanding the force of contemporary pressure, and to Governor Eaton for judiciously distinguishing between "a cross grained temper and possession by a devil," but Mrs. Godman also deserves credit for her astute legal move as opinion began to build against her. It became exceedingly difficult to find her guilty of witchcraft when she was the plaintiff, however much the Court might pass opinions upon her.

The Knapp and Staplies cases developed in New Haven and Connecticut in 1653 when Deputy Governor Roger Ludlow of Connecticut accused the two women. In the course of the trial Ludlow reported that Goodwife Knapp had revealed that Mrs. Staplies was her accomplice. Mrs. Knapp had refused to incriminate anyone, especially when seven of her neighbors constantly placed Mrs. Staplies' name before her. Mrs. Staplies refused to believe that Knapp had witchmarks, or was a witch. When she protested against the searchings for witchmarks she was howled down by the seven old harridans, and then accused by Ludlow. Her husband, Thomas, cross-sued for defamation. Before the court met at New Haven, May 29, 1654, Mrs. Staplies gained an ally, the Rev. Mr. Davenport, who testified that Ludlow had told him that Mrs. Knapp had come down from the gallows and revealed Mrs. Staplies as a witch. Ludlow protested that he had told this to Davenport in strictest confidence, but Davenport testified on oath that he had been careful to make no unlawful promises to Ludlow to keep any confidences and secrets, and that with God's help he would keep only lawful promises. His evidence thus meant that Ludlow had been guilty of defaming Mrs. Staplies. Even though Ludlow marshaled impressive evidence that Mrs. Staplies admitted to possessing witchmarks if Goodwife Knapp did, the Court pressed by Staplies' lawyer, would not accept unsworn testimony for Ludlow, and the case went against him. But it had needed the active intervention of one of the founding fathers of New Haven, invoking the righteousness of his oaths before God, to thwart Ludlow's charges.

In other areas witches were not as fortunate. Deputy Governor Richard Bellingham of Salem was powerless to save his sister, Anne Hibbins, in 1656. But the Hartford case of 1662, when a whole coven of witches was condemned, proved the most disastrous for the accused, when Governor Winthrop was absent in England gaining a charter. The case had a further similarity to Salem in 1692, for the accusations were inspired by two young children. In spring 1662, the eight-year-old daughter of John Kelley cried out in delirium before she died that Goodwife Ayres had bewitched her. William Ayres and his wife were arrested and given the water test. Then James Walkley fled to Rhode Island. The net gathered in Judith Varleth, sister-in-law of the Governor of New Amsterdam, Peter Stuyvesant. On May 13, 1662, Nathaniel Greensmith filed suit against the Ayres for slander of witchcraft, but then the Greensmiths were arrested. Mary Sanford was indicted for the same offense. Nathaniel Greensmith had a criminal record for stealing, and his wife, married twice previously, was described by the Rev. John Whiting as a "lewd, ignorant and considerably aged woman." After the daughter of John Kelley died, the accusations were maintained by Ann Cole, daughter of John Cole, a neighbor of the Greensmiths. She was afflicted with fits, muttering in a Dutch tongue when she did not know the language, and cried out that a company of devils was conspiring to ruin her. She then denounced Goodwife Seager for bewitching her. This woman was indicted for witchcraft three times between 1662 and 1665, and was only released when Governor Winthrop postponed a death sentence upon her, releasing her in 1666. Rebecca Greensmith, under the promptings of the Rev. Mr. Hooke of Farmington, admitted the charges against her, implicated her husband, and set in motion the train of events that led to the executions of four people, the fleeing of several others and the disruption of Hartford society.

Why the Deputy Governors and more prominent religious leaders should be active as participants within the witchcraft cases, and not merely concerned with stamping them out, is difficult to discern. One possibility is that the frustrations attached to a position one level removed from actual power in the colonies concerned may have spilled over into energetic involvement with witch searches. The absence of superior authorities would have given them their chances. Furthermore, they had a compelling desire to prove their worthiness to lead the colonists at a time when the first-generation leaders were dying. They were being called on to lead at a time of spiritual depression. As liberty of conscience was becoming a subject for acrimonious debate, Charles Chauncey complained in 1665 that there was to be found in New England "the contempt of the word of God and his Ordinancies, and listening to lying books & pamphlets, that are brought over into the country whereby multitudes are poysoned amongst us." The next year Thomas Shepherd Jr. worried that "this land which sometimes flourished: Shall in a dying state be found." By 1662, Michael Wigglesworth was ready to condemn, among the hosts who trembled on the day of judgment, those "Witches, Inchanters and Ale-House-haunters" who faced their final doom. In offering reasons for the Truth of the Doctrine of God, John Higginson, pastor at Salem, warned his audience that "Satan from the beginning hath had an old grudge against the seed of the Woman, and he never wanted instruments, who either by force or fraud or both, have done what mischief they could against the Church and cause of God." Well might Edward Johnson declare, therefore, that "now N. E. that had such heaps upon heaps of the riches of Christ's tender compassionate mercies, being turn'd off from his dandling knees, began to read their approaching rod in the bend of his brows and frowns of his former favourable countenance toward them."

From 1647 to 1662 witchcraft incidents and cases spread across the colonies into Maryland, New Hampshire, New Haven, old Plymouth Colony and Virginia, from the original bases in Connecticut and Massachusetts. After 1663 there was still a steady progression of cases, year by year, and they spread still further into New York, Pennsylvania, North and South Carolina. But only two executions took place between 1662 and 1691, and it is evident that the colonial magistrates and governors seriously questioned the wisdom of executions as a remedy for control after 1662. Before 1662, however, it is equally evident that they used executions as a legitimate weapon against the Devil's handmaidens. Their aim was to suppress the work of those covenanting with the Devil. Consequently, this sixteen-year period from 1647 to 1662 produced over 50 indictments and 20 executions, three banishments, three people fleeing to Rhode Island, two water tests, three long-term imprisonments, and at least two whippings, one of which could be prevented by paying a fine. In terms of executions alone, the percentage returns of 40% compare as highly as the witchcraft execution rate in England at the height of the 1637-47 period. By 1662 the English percentage rate was well below that figure.

This period of witchcraft has several obvious similarities with the

Salem episode. But two differences also stand out. By 1692 evidence of witchcraft had been before the public eye for 45 years. The Devil had a solid footing, and to rout him it would require a tremendous effort. In 1647, by contrast, there was no colonial reservoir of cases and prosecutions. The Great Enemy of God and Mankind was then attempting to gain a footing in order to subvert God's Commonwealth in the wilderness, and the early leaders were just as grimly determined that he would not succeed. That they failed is evident from the chain of events culminating in 1692. But in documenting the Devil's advance, the New England ministers, especially the Mathers, went out of their way to record some, though not all, of the earlier cases. To them the urge to provide some background for their own dilemma was compelling. Yet they started out with the Ann Cole case involving the Greensmiths in 1662, in order to illustrate the wonderful providences of the invisible world. Nathaniel Mather chided Increase in 1684 for omitting earlier examples as evidence, but the authors were more concerned with presenting earlier cases merely as evidence that the Devil did exist; thus atheists would be refuted. Consequently, historians relying upon them have accepted their intention and missed an opportunity to demonstrate that their ancestors were faced with an outbreak before 1692, and that they dealt with it severely. Salem should be studied as part of the witchcraft in America, and not as an isolated example. The background, as well as the peculiarities of 1692, is worth examining. Because Salem judges were to deal with their witches in the strange way of hanging those protesting their innocence and releasing those admitting their guilt, the reverse logic of covenant theology applied in 1692 has always attracted historians. The cases of 1647-62 followed a more normal pattern; confession was followed by execution. From that point of view the earlier period of witchcraft was the more orthodox one in the colonies, and Salem was the aberration.

Divide and Rule: Red, White, and Black in the Southeast

WILLIAM S. WILLIS

- *Racial thought is as old as civilized man. It has been a part of European and Oriental culture since antiquity, and its elements have existed in India, China, Egypt, Palestine, and Greece. It is hardly surprising that the United States has always been a racist society; the earliest colonists simply brought with them to the American continent the attitudes and prejudices that prevailed in Europe in their day. The English, for example, considered themselves to be God's chosen people and thought of men of different skin color as being inferior.*

  In the colonial period white settlers found themselves in a minority position with regard to the blacks and the Indians in the Southeast. Fearful that the two groups might combine against them, the whites made every effort to turn Negroes and Indians against each other. In this way, the European settlers hoped to preserve order and retain white supremacy in the New World. That they succeeded in their task we know. Whether their actions were morally justified is another question.

North of Mexico, the Colonial Southeast was the only place where Indians, Whites, and Negroes met in large numbers. Little of the fascinating story of this contact has been told and some crucial parts may be beyond recall for lack of documents. The early attitude of Indians toward Negroes is obviously of great importance. To some extent, it has been dealt with, but conclusions have differed. Laurence

From *Journal of Negro History*, 48 (1962), 157-76. Copyright © 1962 by ASNLH. Reprinted by permission of the Association for the Study of Negro Life and History.

Foster and James Johnston are certain that the early feeling of Indians was one of friendliness. On the other hand, some students, mainly Southern historians, stress hostility. As a matter of fact, a great deal of hostility seems to have existed in the eighteenth century. In 1752, the Catawba Indians showed great anger and bitter resentment when a Negro came among them as a trader. Perhaps the Cherokee had the strongest color prejudice of all Indians. Even the Spaniards were not "White" enough for them. In 1793, Little Turkey, a prominent chief, declared that Spaniards were not "real white people, and what few I have seen of them looked like mulattoes, and I would never have anything to say to them." According to John Brickell, an early eighteenth century reporter, Indians had a "natural aversion to the Blacks." In 1763, George Milligen Johnston, a South Carolina physician, opined that this hostility was mutual and spoke of the "natural Dislike and Antipathy, that subsists between them [Negroes] and our *Indian* Neighbors." But the Southern historians have not explained why Indians disliked Negroes. This paper examines this hostility, and that of Negroes to Indians. The story is the familiar one of divide and rule. Specifically, it will be shown that Whites willfully helped create the antagonism between Indians and Negroes in order to preserve themselves and their privileges.

In the Colonial Southeast, Negro slavery and trade with Indians were more prominent in South Carolina than anywhere else. The province sanctioned slavery from its beginnings in 1670, but South Carolinians brought in few Negroes until the late 1690's. From that time, the steady increase in the number of Negro slaves correlates with the steadily increasing demand for labor. First, there was the expansion of rice production on slave-operated plantations. This occurred at about the same time, near the turn of the eighteenth century, that the general supply of slaves in the New World swelled. In the 1720's, the manufacture of pitch and tar, and in the 1740's the growth of indigo production added to the demand for slave labor. Meanwhile other events conspired to curtail other supplies of labor. Indian slavery dwindled and virtually disappeared after the Yamassee War of 1715-1717. This rebellion of tribes trading with the province produced a widespread notion that South Carolina was a dangerous place and few Whites entered for two decades after the fighting. The demand for Negroes grew in tandem with the mounting political power of the

planters and the government was increasingly responsive to the latter's demands. By the beginning of the eighteenth century, Negroes
outnumbered Whites and they increased their proportion of the population later in the century when various estimates put the ratio at
two or three to one and even higher.

Despite allegations about the submissiveness of Negroes and their
acquiescence to slavery, eighteenth century Whites were afraid of
their slaves. This fear grew as Negroes became more numerous.
Whites especially dreaded slave insurrections; to South Carolinians,
Negro rebels were an "intestine Enemy the most dreadful of Enemies."
The eighteenth century was punctuated by a steady succession of in-
surrectionary plots and actual insurrections. Indeed, the Charles Town
government at times kept half of its soldiers in the capital. Negroes
also struck back at their masters in other ways. They poisoned them,
they set fires, and they committed suicide. They also employed subtle
everyday resistances, such as, malingering and feigned stupidity. They
also ran away. Some went for only short periods to nearby places; others
went permanently to distant hiding places, to the mountains and
swamps, to the Indian country, and to the Spanish in Florida. Running south to Florida became especially common after the Yamassee
War when Spain encouraged more Negroes to come and offered them
freedom. By the late 1720's, Negro subversion had become the main
defense problem of South Carolina.

Indians were also a big problem, and they were feared. The Colonial
Southeast was an arena of an unremitting struggle for empire among
Whites: English, French, Spanish, and later Americans. Indian tribes
were caught in the middle of this struggle; and Whites competed for
their allegiance, for their trade and their warriors. Success in the empire struggle depended upon success in the Indian country. For a
decade at least, the mere survival of South Carolina remained uncertain and the position of the province among Indians was precarious.
But even before the eighteenth century, South Carolina had become
much more secure and had constructed a remarkable system of Indian
alliances. These alliances gave South Carolina sway over the majority
of Indians in the South and forced the Spanish and French to keep
retreating. Through its successes, South Carolina became confident,
perhaps overconfident, of controlling Indians. Then came the Yamassee War. For a time South Carolinians were on the verge of being

driven into the sea; however, in the end they had their victory. But with all the devastation, their province emerged from the war weakened and insecure, with Spain and France stronger than ever. The old confidence of managing Indians was gone, and gone for good. They now believed more than ever that Indians could never be really trusted. From now on, they and all Whites lived in dread of the next Indian uprising—an uprising that would be supported by enemy Whites.

The picture in the Colonial Southeast was this: a frightened and dominant White minority faced two exploited colored majorities. To meet the Negro danger, South Carolina devised a harsh slave code; the police control of slaves was comprehensive, specific, and brutal. To meet the Indian danger, the province had a system of trade regulation that was less brutal than the slave code but of approximately equal thoroughness. That Indian tribes were still independent and had some freedom of choice necessitated their being dealt with somewhat like equals. After the Yamassee War, the province played tribe off against tribe; indeed, village against village. They also watched the munitions trade to prevent any stockpiling of arms. In meeting each danger, South Carolinians were plagued by the discrepancy between what they willed and what they could actually do. This discrepancy became greater with time. It did not take much imagination on the part of Whites to put the two dangers, Indians and Negro slaves, together. As early as 1712, Governor Alexander Spotswood, of Virginia, juxtaposed them. In 1729, the French delayed sending an expedition against the Natchez Indians who had slaughtered French citizens because they feared that New Orleans without troops would be attacked by the Choctaw Indians, and Negroes in order to "free themselves from slavery, might join them." This was the biggest fear of all. In 1775, John Stuart, British Superintendent of Southern Indian Affairs, explained that "nothing can be more alarming to Carolinians than the idea of an attack from Indians and Negroes."

What did South Carolinians do about this nightmare? One answer was, keep Indians and Negroes apart—do not let them mix. In 1757, Captain Daniel Pepper, agent to the Creek Indians, stated that "intimacy" between Indians and Negroes should be avoided. In 1767, Stuart expressed this idea again, perhaps even more strongly: "any Intercourse between Indians and Negroes in my opinion ought to be prevented as much as possible." If this were done, Negroes could not establish personal relations with Indians and learn their languages. This would eliminate the dreaded coordinated blow by Indians and Negroes. But Whites also had other goals in mind. Whites believed that whenever Negro and Indian talked in private the talk was against them. The government believed that Negroes could spread discontent among the tribes and foil its schemes in the Indian country. In 1779, the British Indian Service stated that "Negroes infused many very bad notions into their [Indians] minds." To do this, Negroes need not always lie; as servants, they were sometimes privy to important secrets. Moreover, the government *was* double-dealing with its Indian allies; for instance, stirring up trouble between Creeks and Cherokee. On the other hand, Indians could offer freedom to Negroes and tell them how to get to their villages.

To this end of keeping these colored peoples apart, South Carolinians tried to prevent Indians from coming into the province unless they were on official business. In 1742, a Committee on Indian Affairs warned against frequent visiting by Indians because of the hazard of their associating with slaves, "particularly in regard to their talking, and having too great Intercourse with our Slaves, at the out-plantations, where they camp." Even when on official missions to Charles Town, chiefs were discouraged from bringing too many *aides-de-camp* and were hurried away as quickly as possible. The Settlement Indians, those partially detribalized natives living within the province, presented a special problem. Here again the government opposed contact with Negroes; trading and intermarriage were frowned upon. This determination to prevent Indian-Negro contacts within the White settlements was a main cause for curtailing the enslavement of Indians. Indian slaves got to know Negroes and, since they escaped easily into the hinterland, they might carry Negroes along with them. In 1729, Governor Etienne Perier, of Louisiana, explained that "Indian slaves being mixed with our negroes may induce them to desert."

Keeping Negroes and Indians apart had another aim: keep Negroes out of the Indian country. Eighteenth century legislation consistently prohibited any Negro, slave or free, from going to any Indian tribe either as a trader in his own right or as a White trader's helper. Violations of this prohibition almost always led to hasty action to remove these Negroes. Later in the eighteenth century when the westward movement was getting into high gear, opposition to Whites taking their slaves into Indian country became an important obstruction to White settlement of the interior.

Fugitive Negroes among the Indians were the biggest headache. In 1767, Stuart declared that "to prevent the Indian Country [from] becoming an Asylum for Negroes is a Matter of the Utmost consequence to the prosperity of the provinces." To keep slaves from escaping, South Carolina assigned patrols to watch the roads and countryside; to keep Indian raiding parties out of the province, the government built forts at key approaches and sent rangers out to ride along the frontiers. But Indians were excellent slave catchers. The Settlement Indians in particular were regularly employed to track down fugitive slaves; indeed, slave catching was so profitable to them that they readily agreed in 1727 to move their villages so that they could do a better job. Whites went to great lengths to get their Negroes back. In negotiations, they pressed Indians about these fugitives. They made threats. In 1773, David Taitt, Indian agent, threatened to cut off the Creek trade unless the Indians returned fugitive Negroes. Most treaties stipulated that Indians surrender all Negroes and return all future runaways at an agreed price. Moreover, traders were required to report all Negroes found among Indians and to hold them until they could be sent back to their masters. On their tours of duty, Indian agents also watched for Negroes, and sometimes they made special trips into the Indian country to regain these fugitives.

Keeping Negroes and Indians apart had still another aim: keep Negroes out of the swamps and the mountains. Negroes frequently escaped to these out of the way places. These fugitives, called Maroons, preferred the swamps, especially those in the direction of St. Augustine. Their preference for the southern swamps was dictated by the prospect of freedom among the Spanish in Florida. Meanwhile in these swamps, they could expect help from the Spanish and their Indians. Probably this explains why they went less often to the Southern Appalachians, northwest of Charles Town. But sometimes fugitive Negroes did try for these mountains; for instance, fifteen from Virginia did this in 1729. Large parts of these mountains were impregnable from the east; indeed, South Carolinians realized they could never annihilate the Cherokee in these mountains and they feared that Maroons might team up with these Indians, who were becoming less friendly to the

English and more inclined to the French. If this occurred, the dispersed and almost defenceless White settlers on the Northwest frontier would be at the mercy of a truly formidable antagonist. On the other hand, if the Cherokee were driven from their villages, Maroons might occupy them and become prosperous and secure. These considerations weighed heavily with the Charles Town government, and they were important in leading this government to a policy of appeasing the Cherokee.

Maroons were the most resourceful of all fugitives. They aimed at nothing less than setting up small self-sufficient societies in the most inhospitable places. They had to plan ahead, carefully and secretly. They knew a hard life of hard work and hard fighting awaited them. Those fifteen Virginia Maroons carried guns, ammunition, clothing, furniture, and implements into the mountains; before they were captured, they had started clearing land in order to farm. Once established in their fastnesses, Maroons then lived as banditti; they plundered White settlements, killing masters and rescuing slaves. In 1717, a band under the leadership of one Sebastian terrorized the southern parishes of South Carolina. In the early 1770's, a frightened William Bartram, the noted naturalist, encountered a band of marauders north of Charles Town and later explained that "people [were] . . . frequently attacked, robbed, and sometimes murdered" by Negro bands in this region. These Maroons were dangerous men and women, and they struck out against slavery. No threat, however, was greater than the possibility of their cooperating with hostile Indians and coordinating their attacks against White settlements. Top priority was given by Whites to the immediate destruction of the Maroons. This job was too important to be handled by a local community. Instead the government sent soldiers into the wilderness to eliminate them. Indians were also called upon to help, and they were especially good at ferreting out Maroons from their lurking places.

In addition to keeping Indians and Negroes apart, Whites pitted the colored groups against each other. In 1725, Richard Ludlam, a South Carolina minister, confessed that "we make use of a Wile for our prest. Security to make Indians & Negro's a checque upon each other least by their Vastly Superior Numbers we should be crushed by one or the other." How did Whites go about this? The essential thing was to make bad blood between them: create suspicion, fear, and hatred. In 1758, James Glen, long governor of South Carolina, explained to William Lyttelton, his inexperienced successor, that "it has been allways the policy of this govert to creat an aversion in them [Indians] to Negroes."

It is difficult to show specifically how Whites went about creating this aversion. Eighteenth century Whites, and especially South Carolinians, were reluctant to write about these things. In 1775, when the American Revolution had already made slaveholders in South Carolina insecure, Colonel Stephen Bull wrote Colonel Henry Laurens about a scheme to create Indian-Negro aversion; but first he dismissed his secretary and wrote this part of his letter in his own hand, admonishing Laurens to keep this scheme secret from all South Carolinians except for a few high officials in the government.

Whites sought to convince Indians that Negroes worked against their best interests. In October, 1715, the Cherokee were on the verge of deserting their Indian confederates in the Yamessee War and joining South Carolina in an attack upon the Creeks. They hoped for a better trade with Charles Town and more security in the South. However, two runaway Negroes from South Carolina came to the Cherokee villages and, according to the South Carolinians, told these Indians a "parcell of lies" which dissuaded the Cherokee from joining the South Carolinians. Later in January, 1716, the Cherokee finally went over to the province; on their part, the South Carolinians agreed to specific commitments for a larger trade at cheap prices and for military support against all enemies of the Cherokee. For a while, it seemed that the province really intended to live up to these commitments and the Cherokee were happy with their new friends in Charles Town. During this time, Whites lost no chance of reminding the Indians that Negroes had almost prevented this boon from coming their way. Negroes were also made out to be dangerous people who would bring hardship and suffering to Indians. In 1739, a smallpox epidemic broke out among the Cherokee and about one thousand warriors died from the disease and from suicide because of their disfigurement. These Indians despaired so much that they lost confidence in their gods, and the priests destroyed the sacred objects of the tribe. Whites blamed the epidemic on Negroes, telling the Indians that new slaves from Africa had brought the disease to Charles Town. Since this was not the only epidemic that occurred in the Indian country, we may wonder if Whites had on other occasions also shifted the blame to Negroes.

Whites also contributed to this aversion by using Negro slaves as soldiers against Indians. These slaves were rewarded with goods and sometimes with their freedom. Negroes made good soldiers against other Negroes in rebellion; if they did this against their own people, they certainly had no compunction about fighting Indians. In the Yamassee War, trusted Negroes were drafted and armed and then sent against enemy Indians in the province. Later they were also used against enemy Indians in the interior. When South Carolina invaded the Cherokee country in 1715, Captain Stephen Ford commanded a Negro company. After the Cherokee had come to terms with the province, Ford's company remained in the Cherokee country and took part in attacking the Creeks. In fact, Cherokee chiefs requested this: they said that Negro soldiers would be "very seweasabell [serviceable] to them in Roning after ye Enimy." The French army that invaded the Chickasaw country in 1736 included a company of Negro slaves commanded by a free Negro named Simon; indeed, Simon distinguished himself under fire and was commended by the French. Nevertheless, Whites were reluctant to put muskets in the hands of their slaves; they did not do this until driven by desperation. But in emergencies they were always prepared to do so: legislation was passed in South Carolina in 1747, and renewed from time to time, that authorized the drafting of slaves so long as they did not exceed one third the number of White soldiers. Something besides desperation was behind this: Whites were telling Indians not to count on Negroes in planning another great uprising. This made for Indian antagonism. During the Second Natchez War in 1729, the French accused some Negro slaves of plotting insurrection with the Chouacha Indians, a small harmless tribe living near New Orleans. Although the accusation was unfounded, they armed the Negroes and ordered them to attack this tribe as the sole means of saving their own skins. An on-the-spot reporter tells us that "this expedition rendered the Indians [in Louisiana] mortal enemies of the negroes."

Employing Indians as slave catchers encouraged anti-Negro sentiment among the Indians themselves. Whites paid Indians well for returning fugitive slaves; for instance, at the great Augusta Con-

ference in 1763, the price was set at one musket and three blankets for
each slave brought in. The Indian trade was largely based on deerskins,
and these skins were sold cheaply to the traders; in order to buy a
musket and three blankets, an Indian had to pay about thirty-five skins.
This required several months of hunting. Moreover, the hunting
grounds were dangerous places; enemies were always lurking about.
Hence, an Indian often lost time fighting, if we were lucky enough
not to lose his life. In a word, Indians were usually short of goods
and in debt. The reward for fugitive slaves was, therefore, something
they could rarely afford to turn down. Moreover, the avariciousness of
Indians was proverbial in the South. But Indians knew what slavery
was like among Whites. They saw its cruelty and brutality whenever
they visited the White settlements. They also remembered that Whites
had once enslaved Indians in large numbers and occasionally still did
so. Indeed, the great fear of Indians was that Whites, and especially
South Carolinians, would at some time make slaves of all Indians in
the South. This fear was in the background of all their dealings with
Whites. All of this worked in two contradictory ways on Indians. Self-
interest made the Indian act as an enemy of Negro freedom; but
human feelings made him guilty. Like other men in this ambivalence,
he suppressed his guilt with a convenient hostility.

Since it was important that Negroes should fear and hate Indians,
it is likely that Whites told their slaves many horror stories about
Indians, especially those depicting the terrible things that Indians
did to Negroes. Actually it was not difficult to portray Indians in a
bad light. Indians did kill and they were cruel. Sometimes their raiding parties striking swiftly and with surprise killed Negroes alongside
their White masters. Indians also scalped and otherwise mutilated
their victims regardless of race. Besides, Indians were known in the
early days to subject their male captives to prolonged and deadly tortures; now and then they did this even in the eighteenth century. In
1730, the French gave the Choctaw three Negroes who had helped
the Natchez in 1729. The French expected the Choctaw to torture
these Negroes; moreover, they hoped this would discourage Negroes
from cooperating with Indians. The French were not disappointed.
Father Petit, a Jesuit missionary, reported that these Negroes "have
been burned alive with a degree of cruelty which has inspired all the
Negroes with a new horror of the Savages, which will have a beneficial

effect in securing the safety of the colony." But atrocities were not the main thing. The main thing was that Indians often behaved as real enemies of Negro freedom. To a large extent, Whites encouraged Indians to act this way. As we shall see, this was partly done to make Negroes fear and hate Indians. Given this aim, we assume that Whites publicized these unfriendly acts of Indians among their slaves—and conveniently overlooked their own responsibility. We will now give attention to some situations in which Indians behaved as enemies of Negro freedom.

As we know, Whites employed Indians as slave catchers, and Indians were eager for these jobs. Moreover, Negroes knew that Indians, being expert woodsmen, were better slave catchers than White soldiers and patrols. Negroes also realized that death sometimes awaited the unsuccessful runaway instead of a return to slavery. The Charles Town government executed leaders of fugitive slave parties and those slaves who ran away repeatedly. This government also instructed slave catchers to kill fugitive Negroes when they could not capture them; therefore, dead fugitives were paid for as well as live ones. This encouraged Indians to be more bloodthirsty than White slave catchers: the labor of these fugitives was not going to benefit them. Besides, scalping was more profitable to them than to Whites: Indians could make one scalp look like two or more scalps. To prevent this cheating, the Charles Town government tried to buy only scalps with two ears. Bloodthirstiness was a particular characteristic of Settlement Indians, for slave catching was almost the only opportunity of recapturing the excitement of their old culture. The enthusiasm and violence of Indian slave catchers, as well as the dread Negroes had for them, have been forcibly described by Brickell: "As soon as the Indians have Notice from the *Christians* of their [slaves] being there [in the woods], they disperse them; killing some, others flying for Mercy to the *Christians* . . . rather than fall into the others [Indians] Hands . . . [who] put them to death with the most exquisite Tortures they can invent, whenever they catch them." It is not surprising that a Committee on Indian Affairs in 1727 instructed the Indian Commissioners to have "any Negroe or Negroes Corrected who shall threaten the [Settlement] Indians for Executing any Orders that the said Commissioners shall see fit to give the Indians." Whites did not employ Indians as slave catchers only to recover valuable property and to punish offenders. They also employed them to make their slaves hate Indians. In 1776, some Maroons established themselves on Tybee Island; the Charles Town government secretly arranged for Creek slave catchers to kill these Maroons. Colonel Stephen Bull explained that this would "establish a hatred or aversion between Indians and Negroes."

Indians also permitted and even helped Whites round up Negroes in and about the Indian villages. These Negroes were then conveyed back to slavery. This was a hard blow. These runaways had eluded all the slave catchers and then experienced the intoxication of freedom among the Indians. In either case, Indians betrayed them, blasting villages before moving on to Florida; other runaways settled down in these villages and started making some kind of life for themselves among the Indians. In either case, Indians betrayed them, blasting their hopes. Moreover, these Indians were betraying their own principles of hospitality and sanctuary for strangers—and these principles applied to fugitive Negroes. It seems that Indians, in their greed for trade goods, sometimes betrayed the same fugitives twice. After returning Negroes and collecting their reward, Indians helped these fugitives to escape again before White agents delivered them to their masters. Then these Indians recaptured these fugitives and demanded another full reward from the agents. In time, fugitive Negroes realized that they stayed in jeopardy while among Indians. In 1758, James Beamer, an old Cherokee trader, warned Governor Lyttelton to be discreet in sending for some runaways "for they are always on their Watch and the Least mistrust they have they Will fly Directly to the Woods." In retrieving fugitive slaves from the Indian country, Whites again had the additional motive of making Negroes antagonistic to Indians. Indeed, this motive at times made Whites willingly forego repossessing their slaves. It seems that Whites were pleased when Indians scalped fugitive slaves who lived in Indian villages but would not peaceably surrender. This happened among the Creeks in 1768; Stuart then explained that "this cannot fail of having a very good Effect, by breaking that Intercourse between Negroes & Savages which might have been attended with very troublesome consequences had it continued."

Indians were *bona fide* slave traders. They stole Negroes from White slaveholders in order to sell them to other White slaveholders. Indians had been prepared for this Negro trade by the earlier trade in Indian slaves; for instance, they had learned that male captives were often too valuable to be done away with. Except for raids by Spanish Indians against South Carolina, Indians did not steal too many Negroes in the first half of the eighteenth century. About the only other Indians that regularly raided for Negro slaves were the Chickasaw and other allied tribes of South Carolina living near the Mississippi River. These tribes raided French settlements in Louisiana and French convoys on the Great River. Negroes captured in these raids were sold to Charles Town traders who carried them to South Carolina. This trade did not bring many slaves into the province; the French were always so short of Negroes. For the Negroes, this trade was a calamity. Their capture meant the substitution of one enslavement by a more severe one. Therefore, these Negroes must have been bitter anti-Indian propagandists among the slaves of South Carolina.

After the mid-century, Indians began stealing and selling more and more Negroes. In these years, White settlers increasingly encroached on Indian lands, coming in from almost all sides, and Indians struck back. These years were years of almost continuous warfare between Indians and Whites. Indians made a point of taking Negro slaves from these settlers to discourage their rush into the interior. It was also a fairly easy matter to steal Negroes from slaveholders in transit and in newly established settlements. Moreover, the American Revolution brought a new lawlessness to the South that lasted throughout the century. This meant that more Whites engaged in this Negro trade: these Whites encouraged Indians to steal Negroes and even stole Negroes themselves and disposed of them in the Indian country. British officers during the Revolution had a big part in promoting this Negro stealing: they got Indians, who sided with the British cause, to rob rebel slaveholders. After the Revolution, many White outlaws who were involved in this trade were British sympathizers. In time, this trade became well organized. Negroes were stolen from one part of the Indian frontier and carried into the Indian country and there traded about among Indians, and between Indians and Whites, until they ended up in slavery on another part of the Indian frontier.

Indians had little trouble selling these Negroes. Whites in the frontier settlements never had enough slaves. Moreover, law enforcement was lax. Sometimes Indians sold nearly every Negro they had. In 1784, Alexander McGillivray, the famous half-breed chief, reported that the Creeks were "now pretty well drained of Negroes." This trade extended outside the South. The Cherokee sold Negroes north of the Ohio River and Shawnee traders came from the North into the Creek country to buy Negroes. This trade even extended into the West Indies. In 1783, McGillivray sent Negroes to Pensacola for shipment to Jamaica. It is clear that Indians were avid and heartless slave traders. They looked upon these Negroes as nothing but chattel property. In 1796, John Sevier, Governor of Tennessee and slaveholder, reprimanded the Cherokee for trading Negroes to the Chickasaw for horses: he told them that "you know it is wrong to swop people for horses, for negroes is not horses tho they are black." These were the people Foster and Johnston have made out to be friends of Negroes. We can be sure that eighteenth century Negroes felt differently. We can not say, however, that Whites deliberately fostered this slave trade to create antagonism against Indians. But we can be sure that Whites did not fail to remind Negroes that Indians were slave traders.

Finally, Whites employed Indians to help crush slave insurrections. In the Stono Rebellion of 1739, the most serious insurrection in South Carolina during the eighteenth century, about eighty Negro slaves killed more than thirty Whites. At the outset, the Charles Town government called upon Settlement Indians for help. These Indians pursued those slaves who eluded the militia at Stono; in a few weeks, they managed to capture some of these slaves and to kill a few others. Indians also aided the province in suppressing slave insurrections in 1744 and 1765. Slave insurrections in the eighteenth century were small-scale affairs; South Carolinians did not need many Indians to help them restore order in any particular one. What mattered most was speed in putting them down; otherwise, more timid Negroes might respond to the call of liberty and join the rebel slaves. Therefore, for this job, the Charles Town government turned to Settlement Indians and Eastern Siouans. Although few in numbers, these Indians lived closer to White settlements and could be quickly mustered whenever needed.

The Charles Town government paid Indians high wages for helping suppress slave insurrections. In the Stono Rebellion, each Indian was given a coat, a flap, a pair of stockings, a hat, a gun, two pounds of powder, and eight pounds of bullets. The legislature, dominated by large slaveholders whose eyes were on the future, wanted to increase this payment. It declared that "Indians should be encouraged in such manner as to induce them always to offer their Service whenever this Government may have Occasion for them." In 1744, the Natchez, now living as scattered Settlement Indians in South Carolina after their defeat by the French in 1729, informed Governor Glen that they wanted to be "together to be ready to assist the Government in case of any Insurrection, or Rebellion of the Negroes." We can be certain that Negroes knew how eager Indians were to help keep them in slavery.

The Charles Town government did not wait for an uprising before calling on Indians. This government tried to anticipate trouble and then prevent it by using Indians to intimidate Negroes. On November 10, 1739, less than two months after Stono, the legislature ordered its Committee on Indian Affairs to cooperate with its special committee investigating this insurrection in "finding the most effectual means for preventing of such Dangers throughout the province." South Carolinians feared insurrections especially at Christmas, Negroes having so much more free time during these holidays. During the Christmas of 1716, the Charles Town government ordered Settlement Indians to move nearer White settlements to terrorize the slaves. Moreover, the government made a practice of locating Settlement Indians near places at which slaves might become troublesome. In the summer of 1716, it maintained the Wineau Indians around the Santee settlements "for keeping ye Negroes in awe." But South Carolinians did not rely only on Settlement Indians to prevent insurrections. These tribes and even the Catawba were not large enough to intimidate all Negroes in the province; there were not enough Settlement Indians to station at every danger point. As we know, South Carolinians saw the danger of a big insurrection in every little one. For intimidating all slaves, South Carolina needed at least one big inland tribe. Therefore, the government turned to its most trusted ally and probably the tribe most hostile to Negroes: the Cherokee. In 1737, Lieutenant-Governor Thomas Broughton reported that he was sending for Cherokee warriors "to come down to the settlements to be an awe to the negroes." Thus, a special effort was made after the Yamassee War to keep Negroes isolated from the Cherokee. In

1741, the legislature requested that Broughton purchase two Negro slaves owned by a Cherokee chief so that they could be shipped to the "West Indies or Northern Colonies to prevent any Detriment that they might do this Province by getting acquainted with the Cherokees." It is clear that this intimidation by Indians helped prevent slave insurrections.

CONCLUSIONS

Hostility between Indians and Negroes in the Colonial Southeast was more pronounced than friendliness. Southern Whites were afraid of these two colored races, each of which outnumbered them. Whites were especially afraid that these two exploited races would combine against them. To prevent this combination, Whites deliberately maintained social distance between Indians and Negroes and created antagonism between them. To maintain this social distance, Whites segregated Indians and Negroes from each other. They did this by keeping Indians out of White settlements as much as possible and by trying to keep Negroes out of the Indian country and other out of the way places where these colored races might meet. To create antagonism, Whites deliberately played Indians and Negroes against each other. They pointed out to these races that each was the enemy of the other. To this end of mutual hostility, Whites also used Negroes as soldiers against Indians; on the other hand, they used Indians to catch runaway slaves and to suppress slave insurrections. In the eyes of Negroes, Indians were enemies of Negro freedom. At times, Whites encouraged Indians and Negroes to murder each other. In these ways, Whites created much of the hostility between Indians and Negroes in the eighteenth century.

From the King's Peace to the Patrol Car:
The Origins of the City Police

JONATHAN RUBINSTEIN

• Americans are fond of recalling an urban past when neighborhoods were quiet and friendly, schools were havens of learning, parks were clean and safe, and public services were cheap and efficient. Actually, such visions are erroneous because neither our city problems today nor our attempted solutions are unique. Even in the colonial period, streets were choked with mud and dust, and the air was rancid with the odors of decaying garbage and fecal waste. By the nineteenth century, urban slums, venal municipal governments, overpopulation, and windfall speculators matched anything the twentieth century has yet produced. The current urban crisis can best be understood against a background of undesirable conditions in the past.

Law enforcement has always been an ill-defined and elusive goal of cities. The reformer Josiah Strong proclaimed that "the first city was built by the first murderer, and crime and vice and wretchedness have festered in it ever since." In the colonial period, the larger towns relied on the "watch" to secure tranquility and keep the drunks off the streets. But riots, gangs, and confidence men overwhelmed such informal arrangements in the nineteenth century, and by 1865 every important city had organized a professional and full time constabulary. In these endeavors they often profited from the experience of London.

Unfortunately, the murders, rapes, and thefts continued even after the police were fully operative, and the happy vision of a city free from vice and crime was never fulfilled. In fact, the dangers of the wicked cities were heavily emphasized by rural spokesmen like Hamlin Garland, who entertained

*lurid dreams of the pitfalls attendant upon a callow youth
who might venture to walk across downtown Chicago even
at midday.*

The preservation of public order in towns, the protection of property,
and the safekeeping of good manners and morals have never been left
to chance or to the whims of city people. Long before city police, as
we know them, were first established in London in the nineteenth
century, townspeople were subject to the scrutiny either of the military or local property owners who were obliged to serve terms as watchmen. Their principal concern was to protect the walls and gates which
continued to enclose most English and European towns until the sixteenth century, but they also had obligations to police the manners
and public behavior of those who lived in the cities. The English constables were charged generally with "maintaining the King's Peace,"
and "for the better preventing that nothing be done against the Peace
any of these officers may take (or arrest) suspected persons which walk
in the night, and sleep in the day: or which do haunt any house, where
is suspicion of bawdie."

During the day the constables and the watchmen they supervised
had the responsibility of enforcing regulations designed to protect the
towns from the very real dangers of plague and fire as well as commercial fraud, "in all which, be it matter of corrupting air, water or
victuals, stopping, straitening, or indangering of passages, or general
deceits, in weights, measures, sizes or counterfeiting wares and things
vendible. . . ."

London watchmen were armed with clubs and swords and occasionally did battle with the gangs of marauding toughs who roamed the
darkened streets, but generally they did not patrol their territories in
search of suspicious persons. Each city ward appointed its own constables and watchmen and there was no coordination of their efforts.
The watchmen wore no uniforms but were distinguished only by the
lanterns they carried and their staffs. They stayed at fixed posts, frequently congregating together for comfort and safety. Each citizen was
ultimately responsible for his own security, and everyone who could
afford it lived in a stout house closely guarded by servants, who acted

as bodyguards for their masters when they went out of their houses. The obligation to serve as a watchman or a constable which had been customary since before the Norman invasion began to weaken as the city grew larger and the threat of external attack lessened. More and more property owners sought to evade their service by hiring substitutes to serve for them. Inevitably, the wealthiest withdrew first, and gradually what had been a voluntary service organized by property owners to protect what they had became a paid service employing poor and often aged men.

During the sixteenth and seventeenth centuries, there was no question in the minds of Londoners that they lived in a dangerous place which was ill-protected by their watchmen, who were generally considered to be incompetent and cowardly. By the mid-seventeenth century they had acquired the derisive name of "Charlies." It was a common sport of rich young men of the time to taunt and terrorize them, to wreck their watch-houses and occasionally to murder them. The large rattles they carried to signal for help were little comfort since they knew their colleagues were not dependable; the watchmen spent a good deal of their time discreetly concealed from the public. Whether people were troubled by these conditions is unclear, but there was no public effort to make any improvements. As for the poor, who were then as now the principal victims of crimes, nobody cared. This indifference changed with the invention of gin.

Until "geneva," as it was then called, was invented in the seventeenth century by a Dutch chemist, only the rich regularly drank the powerful and expensive brandies which were the only kind of hard liquor available. The distillation of alcohol from grain may have originated in Scotland many centuries before the invention of gin, but Scotch whiskey was consumed only locally. It was not introduced into England until the mid-eighteenth century. Most people drank beer, ale, and wine, which could produce drunkenness but hardly had the potency of strong drink. The near-monopoly the rich had on hard liquor may help to explain their attachment to brawling, fighting, and killing —habits which most people today associate exclusively with the poor. Gin democratized drunkenness and brought new terrors to London and then to all cities. Henry Fielding wrote in his *Enquiry into the Causes of the Late Increase of Robbers* (1751), one of the first (and certainly the best written) essays in criminology:

A new kind of drunkenness, unknown to our ancestors, is lately sprung up amongst us, and which if not put a stop to, will infallibly destroy a great part of the inferior people. The drunkenness I here intend is . . . by this Poison called Gin . . . the principal sustenance (if it may be so called) of more than a hundred thousand People in this Metropolis.

The agricultural interests which dominated the House of Commons saw in gin the opportunity to dispose profitably of the grain surpluses which the country produced, and every encouragement was given to its manufacture. Within a few decades, London was awash in an orgy of drinking which has probably not been matched in history. By 1725 there were more than 7,000 gin shops in London, and drink was sold as a sideline by numerous shopkeepers and retailers. For a penny anyone could drink all day in any "flash house" and get a straw pallet in a back room to sleep it off. The sale of gin (mainly in London) rose from three and one-half million gallons in 1727 and then soared to over eight million in 1743. Public drunkenness became a commonplace sight, and drink-crazed mobs often roamed through the city.

The government responded to the increase in crime and disorder by improving street lighting, hiring more watchmen, and greatly increasing the severity of punishment for all kinds of crimes. People privately responded by arming themselves with pistols and avoiding the streets at night unless accompanied by a "linkman," a private guard who carried a sword and a large torch to light the way. The rich, who until this time continued to live among the poor, began to move away, initiating the residential segregation of people by income which dominates most cities today.

In 1736 a law was passed requiring every gin seller and manufacturer to purchase a license for a fee set so high it was hoped that most gin shops would have to close. To enforce this law, the government offered a reward to every informer who gave information leading to the successful prosecution of an unlicensed retailer or distiller. The law did not stanch the flow of gin, but it greatly increased the corruption of the constables who had traditionally proven themselves willing to exploit their duties for graft.

The London watchmen had always been responsible for regulating the morals of townspeople, which, from early times, provided opportunities to extort money and accept payoffs. Any person suspected of maintaining a house of ill repute could be lawfully harassed and threatened by the watchmen. Failing a reformation of the owner's manners (or a bribe), the watch was empowered to break open the house, remove all the windows and doors, and make it uninhabitable. These Draconian measures did not discourage prostitution, and in the thirteenth century the city sought to regulate the trade by confining all whores to the "stews of Southwark," the steam baths which were situated across the Thames River from the city. Again, this measure did not eliminate prostitution, although it made it easier for some city magistrates to collect a rakeoff for protecting the bathhouses.

During the seven years the Gin Act of 1736 was in force, there were almost 10,000 prosecutions for violations of its provisions in London, but only three licenses under the Gin Act were sold in the city, and there was no reduction in the consumption of gin.

The government wisely abandoned its efforts to eradicate drinking and instead successfully reduced the rate of consumption over a period of several decades by increasing taxation to raise the price of gin and by easing the licensing system. Although the gin craze abated, the fear of crime and the belief that it continued to increase did not. Members of Parliament continued to be accompanied to and from sessions by linkmen, and bulletproof coaches were advertised to thwart the highwaymen who plagued travelers on the roads to the city. In 1776 the Lord Mayor of London was robbed at gunpoint, and within the decade two of England's great nobles, the Duke of York and the Prince of Wales, were mugged as they walked in the city during the day. Parliament paid rewards to any man who successfully prosecuted a criminal, and private "thief-takers" prospered, as did those who were hired by religious organizations. At mid-century, Henry Fielding, who earned his living as a magistrate, proposed that the system be centralized and constables organized to patrol the streets rather than remain at their watch boxes. For a brief time he organized a mounted patrol to guard the highways. It languished when he died, but for the first time the ideas of a mobile police had been advanced.

By the turn of the century, active supporters of the idea of a preventive police, as it was termed, were arguing that a police force constantly patrolling the city would greatly reduce and ultimately eliminate most crime. The novelty of the New Police—as the Metropolitan Police of London, established in 1829, were called—resided in the territorial character of their purpose and organization. For the first time the entire city was to be continuously patrolled by men who were assigned specific territories and whose courses (or beats) were prescribed by their superiors. Past experience had demonstrated clearly that without strict supervision there was no guarantee that the patrolmen, unless they were highly motivated men of great dedication, would actually perform their duties. The founders of the police sought to inspire the men by imposing the principles of military organization and service on what had always been a civilian force.

But as the first commissioner of police, Colonel Charles Rowan, discovered on his first day, the policeman is not a soldier. He spent months carefully selecting candidates, then held an inaugural parade-ground ceremony. It was a rainy day and many of the constables arrived bearing umbrellas. Quite a few were unable to stand at attention because they had been celebrating the historic occasion by getting drunk. Rowan's first general regulation forbade any man to carry an umbrella with him on duty; the second forbade drinking. Umbrellas never again posed a serious problem. The military enforced discipline by imposing severe punishments for even minor infractions, but the police could not whip delinquent constables. The only way to punish them was by firing them. In the first years the London police discharged more than one-third of the force annually.

Despite the defects of the New Police, their organization and principles quickly attracted attention abroad, mainly in America, where the policing of the towns had closely followed the English pattern. Like their English counterparts, the American police did not patrol their territories regularly with the purpose of preventing crime and capturing suspects. They were responsible for enforcing liquor laws and controlling the prostitution which was common in most towns. They, too, were held in low regard by most people, and they were not very successful in rooting out vice or preventing crime.

Between 1830 and the Civil War, every important American town adopted the territorial organization and strategy of the preventive police. In Boston, New York, Brooklyn, and Philadelphia, the local watch committees were abolished and a central police force established. Everywhere the men strenuously objected to wearing uniforms. It was argued that a uniform was a kind of livery which demeaned the freedom and equality of the man who had to wear it, but these objections were overridden by the argument that the discipline and dignity required of policemen made the uniform a necessity. But Americans also learned that the uniform was not sufficient to assure the proper bearing of the man who wore it as the recurrence of scandal and complaints about his ineffectiveness testified.

Despite the various names given to different police tactics today, they all continue to rely on the basic strategy initiated by Henry Fielding and Colonel Rowan, requiring each man to patrol his entire area continuously. In order to make supervision easier, Rowan ordered each man to walk a prescribed route at a specific pace so that his supervisor could know where he was at any time. This was also beneficial to anyone interested in evading the constable's attention and was soon abandoned. But if the men responsible for assuring the correct performance of the patrolmen did not know exactly where they were, how could they properly supervise them? And how could a citizen in need of a policeman find him promptly?

When city police were first established, the only way contact could be maintained was in face-to-face meetings or by messengers. In Philadelphia and Brooklyn it was customary for the captains to meet every morning with their commissioner before proceeding to their districts. This was the only opportunity they had to receive orders.

Once the men were dismissed from roll call, their supervisors had no certain way of controlling what they did during their tour of work. The sergeants, who were called roundsmen in Philadelphia and Brooklyn during the early nineteenth century, frequently assigned men "meets," prearranged times and places where the supervisors could visually check on them. The only way a roundsman had of discovering what his men were doing was to follow them around and make inquiries among the people who lived and worked on the beats. The men were also isolated from each other, and their only way of attracting attention in moments of distress was by swinging the large rattles which city policemen had been carrying since the sixteenth century.

During the 1850s, the establishment of telegraph networks first linked police headquarters directly with their districts, making unnecessary the daily morning meetings between the captains and the commissioner. Several decades later, a modified telegraph system was invented which linked the patrolman directly to his station. The fire-alarm system that had been introduced in Boston was adapted for police use and the call box became a feature on city street corners. Since it was impractical to teach every man Morse code, the boxes were outfitted with a simple lever which signaled the station that the officer (or whoever pulled the lever) was at his post. A bell system was soon added that enabled the patrolman to tell his district by means of a few simple signals whether he needed a "slow wagon" for routine duties, or a "fast wagon" for emergencies.

The introduction of the telephone into the call box in 1880 made it a genuine two-way communication system. A "pulling system" was devised which obliged each man to contact his district every hour. If there were any messages for him, the operations clerk gave him a special signal to open the locked inner box containing the telephone. This double-box system reserved part of the equipment for exclusive police use, leaving the outer part for the public, since people still had no sure way of gaining the quick attention of the police. Local merchants and bankers were given keys that activated an emergency signal at the station house.

The pulling system greatly improved the ability of sergeants to supervise their men, but it did not eliminate the basic problem. It was possible to neutralize the system, and the easily learned tricks were quickly acquired by the men. Like all methods of evasion, the most effective was the simplest. One officer was given the keys to the boxes, and while he walked the district "pulling" on schedule, the others were free to do as they pleased. The transformation from signal boxes to telephone contact required that the collusion be extended to the men inside the station house who worked the phones. But the technology also provided the men with new means of evasion if they could not gain the cooperation of their operators. Because of the prohibitive costs of wiring each box individually, the phones were hooked in series, so that if one was left off the hook, the entire line was interrupted. A squad of men could agree to unhook a phone at the far end of their territory, putting the entire network out of service. Even under normal circumstances, the call boxes required substantial maintenance (they often shorted out in the rain), and this was increased by deliberate sabotage. It was not uncommon for some men to cut the wires or short them out by splashing water on the cables.

The weaknesses of the new system obliged the supervisors to continue what had already become an acknowledged "game" in police work—finding your men. Some departments sought to aid their sergeants by maximizing the number of "straight beats," which required an officer to walk along a single street for a number of blocks, checking only the alleys on either side. The patrolman's absence from a beat which could be observed by standing in the middle of the street and looking its length was not easy to explain; it was hoped that this would deter men from seeking out their "holes" or "coops." But straight beats required hiring additional men for which few cities were willing to pay. Some supervisors informally acknowledged the existence of holes, since this made it easier for them to find someone when he was needed in a hurry. Barber shops were frequently favored as "legitimate" holes because they allowed the patrolmen to sit comfortably and to observe the street. (In many neighborhoods barber shops used to be local centers of petty gambling, which may have been an inducement to barbers to treat policemen with kindness.)

Sergeants developed methods for discovering unacknowledged hiding places and for surprising their men to discourage unauthorized loafing. A sergeant could order a man to meet him night after night at a specific place. Arriving early, he could watch from a concealed place the direction of the man's approach. Each day he would pick the man up a bit closer to his hole, or if he was skillful and the patrolman incautious, he might follow him. In winter, some supervisors would put their arm about a man's shoulder in a friendly and "accidentally" touch his tin badge, whose temperature would reveal immediately whether the man had been walking his beat or had just come outside. Some men wore two badges or left their badge outside when they went inside.

The call box and the pull system greatly improved the contact between the station and the men in the street but it offered the policeman little solace if he was in personal trouble. Even if he could reach it, there was no guarantee that help would arrive quickly. Since his sense of isolation was one reason why he sought relief from the street in holes, this inclination could be checked only if the supervisors had a way of monitoring him constantly or of reducing his insecurity.

The call box system was not even very useful to the public. As suggested, some businessmen received extra protection by having keys which allowed them to give alarms or make phone calls when public telephones were still a rarity. But most people had no way of quickly attracting a policeman's attention other than running into the street and yelling. Experiments with open call boxes were quickly abandoned when the number of crank calls overwhelmed the operators and the cost of repairing acts of vandalism became too great.

The introduction of the patrol car and the development of the wireless radio were heralded as the way to resolve all of the problems created by the territorial strategy of the New Police. When the two-way radio was first successfully used in a patrol car in 1929, it meant that a cruiser could be informed immediately of a call for help, greatly enhancing the chances of capturing suspects and deterring further crime. Some thought this delevopment would finally enable the police to eliminate city crime entirely. The radio cruiser also offered police supervisors a way of knowing where the patrolman was. He could be checked on frequently and without warning. In addition the radio placed the patrolman in continuous contact with his colleagues, improving his sense of security.

Having found an effective means of placing their services at the disposal of the public, the police set about actively to encourage business. In recent years large police departments have tied their radio systems directly into the telephone networks and, following the lead of the British and the Belgian police, created emergency numbers which place callers in direct contact with a police dispatcher. These efforts have been so successful that they threaten to overturn the traditional conceptions of police work and to undermine the efficiency and purpose of street patrols. Since New York City introduced its emergency number—911—in July, 1968, the average number of calls each day to the police has risen from 12,000 to 17,000, and it is still climbing. During peak periods, patrolmen are often unable to handle all of their assignments. They are so busy answering calls that they have no time to patrol their territories. Despite the tremendous increase in the amount of "work" policemen do, the crime rates continue to grow, and harried police administrators are being forced to seek ways of reducing the demand they have encouraged without arousing bitterness and hostility among those people who will be deprived of "free" services.

Despite the introduction of technology, the basic strategy of city police has not been altered. While the changes have reduced the policeman's inclinations to avoid work, they have obviously not made him the fearsome presence who can extinguish crime.

The present crime wave that grips the metropolitan areas of the United States is causing cities to improve their street lighting, increase the number of policemen on the streets, and demand more severe punishment for convicted criminals. Privately, people are protecting themselves and protecting their homes with a variety of locks and alarm systems that they hope will deter burglars. But the belief persists that there is a police solution to the crime problem, that more policemen—how many more?—will assure the safety of a city. But what difference will more policemen make if they continue to do the same things policemen have been doing for the last century and a half?

England's Vietnam:
The American Revolution

RICHARD M. KETCHUM

• Whether used by labor organizers, college students, or
statesmen, the word "revolution" arouses misgivings and even
terror in the minds of most people. Perhaps this is due to the
normal human preference for the comfort of the tried and the
true rather than the uncertainty of a new situation. The idea
of revolution was also disturbing to the founders of the
United States. They believed in John Locke's notion of natural right, that just governments rested on the consent of the
governed, and that the colonial cause was just. But a large
portion of the citizenry, including Benjamin Franklin, hoped
for some kind of settlement, short of an open break, of their
quarrel with the mother country. This is contrary to the popular stereotype of a people united from the beginning in a
desire for independence from England and imbued with the
vision of a continental destiny.

From the British perspective, war with the colonies was a
frustrating experience, not unlike that encountered by the
United States in Vietnam almost two centuries later. In both
instances the conflict pitted the most powerful country in
the world against a weak and undeveloped foe. King George
III and his advisers felt that if the American colonies gained
independence, then the whole British Empire might fall
away like a series of dominos. Once the battle had been
joined at Lexington and Concord and Bunker Hill, the English discovered the difficulties of fighting a distant wilderness
war, where it was difficult to tell the friendly natives from the
rebels. And at every important juncture, Lord North and his
sovereign had to weigh the consequences of possible inter-

From *American Heritage*. © 1971, American Heritage Publishing Company,
Inc. Reprinted by permission of the publisher (June 1971).

vention by hostile powers. The reasons for their ultimate
failure are discussed in this perceptive essay by Richard M.
Ketchum.

If it is true that those who cannot remember the past are condemned
to repeat it, America's last three Presidents might have profited by
examining the ghostly footsteps of America's last king before pursuing
their adventure in Vietnam. As the United States concludes a decade
of war in Southeast Asia, it is worth recalling the time, two centuries
ago, when Britain faced the same agonizing problems in America that
we have met in Vietnam. History seldom repeats itself exactly, and it
would be a mistake to try to equate the ideologies or the motivating
factors involved; but enough disturbing parallels may be drawn between those two distant events to make one wonder if the Messrs.
Kennedy, Johnson, and Nixon had their ears closed while the class was
studying the American Revolution.

Britain, on the eve of that war, was the greatest empire since Rome.
Never before had she known such wealth and power; never had the future seemed so bright, the prospects so glowing. All, that is, except the
spreading sore of discontent in the American colonies that, after fes-
tering for a decade and more, finally erupted in violence at Lexington
and Concord on April 19, 1775. When news of the subsequent battle
for Bunker Hill reached England that summer, George III and his
ministers concluded that there was no alternative to using force to put
down the insurrection. In the King's mind, at least, there was no
longer any hope of reconciliation—nor did the idea appeal to him. He
was determined to teach the rebellious colonials a lesson, and no
doubts troubled him as to the righteousness of the course he had
chosen. "I am not sorry that the line of conduct seems now chalked
out," he had said even before fighting began; later he told his prime
minister, Lord North, "I know I am doing my Duty and I can never
wish to retract." And then, making acceptance of the war a matter of
personal loyalty, "I wish nothing but good," he said, "therefore anyone who does not agree with me is a traitor and a scoundrel." Filled
with high moral purpose and confidence, he was certain that "when
once these rebels have felt a smart blow, they will submit . . ."

In British political and military circles there was general agreement
that the war would be quickly and easily won. "Shall we be told,"
asked one of the King's men in Commons, "that [the Americans] can
resist the powerful efforts of this nation?" Major John Pitcairn, writing home from Boston in March, 1775, said, "I am satisfied that one
active campaign, a smart action, and burning two or three of their
towns, will set everything to rights." The man who would direct the
British navy during seven years of war, the unprincipled, inefficient
Earl of Sandwich, rose in the House of Lords to express his opinion
of the provincial fighting man. "Suppose the Colonies do abound in
men," the First Lord of the Admiralty asked, "what does that signify?
They are raw, undisciplined, cowardly men. I wish instead of forty or
fifty thousand of these *brave* fellows they would produce in the field
at least two hundred thousand; the more the better, the easier would
be the conquest; if they did not run away, they would starve themselves into compliance with our measures. . . ." And General James
Murray, who had succeeded the great Wolfe in 1749 as commander
in North America, called the native American "a very effeminate thing,
very unfit for and very impatient of war." Between these estimates of
the colonial militiaman and a belief that the might of Great Britain
was invincible, there was a kind of arrogant optimism in official quar-
ters when the conflict began. "As there is not common sense in pro-
tracting a war of this sort," wrote Lord George Germain, the secretary
for the American colonies, in September, 1775, "I should be for exerting the utmost force of this Kingdom to finish the rebellion in one
campaign."

Optimism bred more optimism, arrogance more arrogance. One
armchair strategist in the House of Commons, William Innes, outlined for the other members an elaborate scheme he had devised for
the conduct of the war. First, he would remove the British troops from
Boston, since that place was poorly situated for defense. Then, while
the people of the Massachusetts Bay Colony were treated like the mad-
men they were and shut up by the navy, the army would move to one
of the southern colonies, fortify itself in an impregnable position, and
let the provincials attack if they pleased. The British could sally forth
from this and other defensive enclaves at will, and eventually "success
against one-half of America will pave the way to the conquest of the
whole. . . ." What was more, Innes went on, it was "more than prob-

able you may find men to recruit your army in America." There was a good possibility, in other words, that the British regulars would be replaced after a while by Americans who were loyal to their king, so that the army fighting the rebels would be Americanized, so to speak, and the Irish and English lads sent home. General James Robertson also believed that success lay in this scheme of Americanizing the combat force: "I never had an idea of subduing the Americans," he said, "I meant to assist the good Americans to subdue the bad."

This notion was important not only from the standpoint of the fighting, but in terms of administering the colonies once they were beaten; loyalists would take over the reins of government when the British pulled out, and loyalist militiamen would preserve order in the pacified colonies. No one knew, of course, how many "good" Americans there were; some thought they might make up half or more of the population. Shortly after arriving in the colonies in 1775, General William Howe, for one, was convinced that "the insurgents are very few, in comparison with the whole of the people."

Before taking the final steps into full-scale war, however, the King and his ministers had to be certain about one vitally important matter: they had to be able to count on the support of the English people. On several occasions in 1775 they were able to read the public pulse (that part of it, at least, that mattered) by observing certain important votes in Parliament. The King's address to both Houses on October 26, in which he announced plans to suppress the uprising in America, was followed by weeks of angry debate; but when the votes were counted, the North ministry's majority was overwhelming. Each vote indicated the full tide of anger that influenced the independent members, the country gentlemen who agreed that the colonials must be put in their place and taught a lesson. A bit out of touch with the news, highly principled, and content in the belief that the King and the ministry must be right, none of them seem to have asked what would be best for the empire; they simply went along with the vindictive measures that were being set in motion. Eloquent voices—those of Edmund Burke, Charles James Fox, the Earl of Chatham, John Wilkes, among others—were raised in opposition to the policies of the Crown, but as Burke said, ". . . it was almost in vain to contend, for the country gentlemen had abandoned their duty, and placed an implicit confidence in the Minister."

The words of sanity and moderation went unheeded because the men who spoke them were out of power and out of public favor; and each time the votes were tallied, the strong, silent, unquestioning majority prevailed. No one in any position of power in the government proposed, after the Battle of Bunker Hill, to halt the fighting in order to settle the differences; no one seriously contemplated conversations that might have led to peace. Instead the government—like so many governments before and since—took what appeared to be the easy way out and settled for war.

George III was determined to maintain his empire, intact and undiminished, and his greatest fear was that the loss of the American colonies would set off a reaction like a line of dominoes falling. Writing to Lord North in 1779, he called the contest with America "the most serious in which any country was ever engaged. It contains such a train of consequences that they must be examined to feel its real weight. . . . Independence is [the Americans'] object, which every man not willing to sacrifice every object to a momentary and inglorious peace must concur with me in thinking this country can never submit to. Should America succeed in that, the West Indies must follow, not in independence, but for their own interest they must become dependent on America. Ireland would soon follow, and this island reduced to itself, would be a poor island indeed."

Despite George's unalterable determination, strengthened by his domino theory; despite the wealth and might of the British empire; despite all the odds favoring a quick triumph, the problems facing the King and his ministers and the armed forces were formidable ones indeed. Surpassing all others in sheer magnitude was the immense distance between the mother country and the rebellious colonies. As Edmund Burke described the situation in his last, most eloquent appeal for conciliation, "Three thousand miles of ocean lie between you and them. No contrivance can prevent the effect of this distance in weakening government. Seas roll, and months pass, between the order and the execution; and the want of a speedy explanation of a single point is enough to defeat a whole system." Often the westerly passage took three months, and every soldier, every weapon, every button and gaiter and musket ball, every article of clothing and great quantities of food and even fuel, had to be shipped across those three thousand miles of the Atlantic. It was not only immensely costly and time consuming, but there was a terrifying wastefulness to it. Ships sank or were blown hundreds of miles off course, supplies spoiled, animals died en route. Worse yet, men died, and in substantial numbers: returns from regiments sent from the British Isles to the West Indies between 1776 and 1780 reveal that an average of 11 per cent of the troops was lost on these crossings.

Beyond the water lay the North American land mass, and it was an article of faith on the part of many a British military man that certain ruin lay in fighting an enemy on any large scale in that savage wilderness. In the House of Lords in November, 1775, the Duke of Richmond warned the peers to consult their geographies before turning their backs on a peaceful settlement. There was, he said, "one insuperable difficulty with which an army would have to struggle"—America abounded in vast rivers that provided natural barriers to the progress of troops; it was a country in which every bush might conceal an enemy, a land whose cultivated parts would be laid waste, so that "the army (if any army could march or subsist) would be obliged to draw all its provisions from Europe, and all its fresh meat from Smithfield market." The French, the mortal enemies of Great Britain, who had seen a good deal more of the North American wilds than the English had, were already laying plans to capitalize on the situation when the British army was bogged down there. In Paris, watchfully eyeing his adversary's every move, France's foreign minister, the Comte de Vergennes, predicted in July, 1775, that "it will be vain for the English to multiply their forces" in the colonies; "no longer can they bring that vast continent back to dependence by force of arms." Seven years later, as the war drew to a close, one of Rochambeau's aides told a friend of Charles James Fox: "No opinion was clearer than that though the people of America might be conquered by well disciplined European troops, the country of America was unconquerable."

Yet even in 1775 some thoughtful Englishmen doubted if the American people or their army could be defeated. Before the news of Bunker Hill arrived in London, the adjutant general declared that a plan to defeat the colonials militarily was "as wild an idea as ever controverted common sense," and the secretary-at-war, Lord Barrington, had similar reservations. As early as 1774 Barrington ventured the opinion that a war in the wilderness of North America would cost Britain far more than she could ever gain from it; that the size of the country and the

colonials' familiarity with firearms would make victory questionable—
or at best achievable only at the cost of enormous suffering; and finally,
even if Britain should win such a contest, Barrington believed that the
cost of maintaining the colonies in any state of subjection would be
staggering. John Wilkes, taunting Lord North on this matter of military conquest, suggested that North—even if he rode out at the head of
the entire English cavalry—would not venture ten miles into the countryside for fear of guerrilla fighters. "The Americans," Wilkes promised, "will dispute every inch of territory with you, every narrow pass,
every strong defile, every Thermopylae, every Bunker's Hill."

It was left to the great William Pitt to provide the most stirring
warning against fighting the Americans. Now Earl of Chatham, he was
so crippled in mind and body that he rarely appeared in the House of
Lords, but in May, 1777, he made the supreme effort, determined to
raise his voice once again in behalf of conciliation. Supported on
canes, his eyes flashing with the old fire and his beak-like face thrust
forward belligerently, he warned the peers: "You cannot conquer the
Americans. You talk of your numerous friends to annihilate the Congress, and of your powerful forces to disperse their army, but I might
as well talk of driving them before me with this crutch. . . . You
have been three years teaching them the art of war, and they are apt
scholars. I will venture to tell your lordships that the American gentry
will make officers enough fit to command the troops of all the European powers. What you have sent there are too many to make peace,
too few to make war. You cannot make them respect you. You cannot
make them wear your cloth. You will plant an invincible hatred in
their breast against you . . ."

"My lords," he went on, "you have been the aggressors from the beginning. I say again, this country has been the aggressor. You have
made descents upon their coasts. You have burnt their towns, plundered their country, made war upon the inhabitants, confiscated their
property, proscribed and imprisoned their persons. . . . The people
of America look upon Parliament as the authors of their miseries. Their
affections are estranged from their sovereign. Let, then, reparation
come from the hands that inflicted the injuries. Let conciliation succeed chastisement. . . ." But there was no persuading the majority;
Chatham's appeal was rejected and the war went on unabated.

It began to appear, however, that destruction of the Continental

Army—even if that goal could be achieved—might not be conclusive. After the disastrous campaign around Manhattan in 1776, George Washington had determined not to risk his army in a major engagement, and he began moving away from the European battle style in which two armies confronted each other head to head. His tactical method became that of the small, outweighed prizefighter who depends on his legs to keep him out of range of his opponent and who, when the bigger man begins to tire, darts in quickly to throw a quick punch, then retreats again. It was an approach to fighting described by Nathanael Greene, writing of the campaign in the South in 1780: "We fight, get beat, rise, and fight again." In fact, between January and September of the following year, Greene, short of money, troops, and supplies, won a major campaign without ever really winning a battle. The battle at Guilford Courthouse, which was won by the British, was typical of the results. As Horace Walpole observed, "Lord Cornwallis has conquered his troops out of shoes and provisions and himself out of troops."

There was, in the colonies, no great political center like Paris or London, whose loss might have been demoralizing to the Americans; indeed, Boston, New York, and Philadelphia, the seat of government, were all held at one time or another by the British without irreparable damage to the rebel cause. The fragmented political and military structure of the colonies was often a help to the rebels, rather than a hindrance, for it meant that there was almost no chance of the enemy striking a single crushing blow. The difficulty, as General Frederick Haldimand, who succeeded Carleton in Canada, saw it, was the seemingly unending availability of colonial militiamen who rose up out of nowhere to fight in support of the nucleus of regular troops called the Continental Army. "It is not the number of troops Mr. Washington can spare from his army that is to be apprehended," Haldimand wrote, "it is the multitude of militia and men in arms ready to turn out at an hour's notice at the shew of a single regiment of Continental Troops. . . ." So long as the British were able to split up their forces and fan out over the countryside in relatively small units, they were fairly successful in putting down the irregulars' activities and cutting off their supplies; but the moment they had to concentrate again to fight the Continentals, guerrilla warfare burst out like so many small brush fires on their flank and rear. No British regular could tell if an

American was friend or foe, for loyalty to King George was easy to at-
test; and the man who was a farmer or merchant when a British battalion marched by his home was a militiaman as soon as it had passed
by, ready to shoulder his musket when an emergency or an opportunity
to confound the enemy arose.

Against an unnumberable supply of irregular forces the British could
bring to bear only a fixed quantity of troops—however many, that is,
they happened to have on the western side of the Atlantic Ocean at
any given moment. Early in the war General James Murray had foreseen the difficulties that would undoubtedly arise. Writing to Lord
Barrington, he warned that military conquest was no real answer. If
the war proved to be a long one, their advantage in numbers would
heavily favor the rebels, who could replace their losses while the British could not. Not only did every musket and grain of powder have to
be shipped across the ocean; but if a man was killed or wounded, the
only way to replace him was to send another man in full kit across the
Atlantic. And troop transports were slow and small: three or four were
required to move a single battalion.

During the summer of 1775 recruiting went badly in England and
Ireland, for the war was not popular with a lot of the people who
would have to fight it, and there were jobs to be had. It was evident
that the only means of assembling a force large enough to suppress the
rebellion in the one massive stroke that had been determined upon
was to hire foreign troops. And immediately this word was out, the
rapacious petty princes of Brunswick, Hesse-Cassel, and Waldeck, and
the Margrave of Anspach-Bayreuth, generously offered up a number of
their subjects—at a price—fully equipped and ready for duty, to serve
His Majesty George III. Frederick the Great of Prussia, seeing the plan
for what it was, announced that he would "make all the Hessian
troops, marching through his dominions to America, pay the usual
cattle tax, because, although human beings, they had been sold as
beasts." But George III and the princes regarded it as a business deal,
in the manner of such dubious alliances ever since: each foot soldier
and trooper supplied by the Duke of Brunswick, for instance, was to
be worth seven pounds, four shillings, fourpence halfpenny in levy
money to his Most Serene Highness. Three wounded men were to
count as one killed in action, and it was stipulated that a soldier killed

in combat would be paid for at the same rate as levy money. In other words the life of a subject was worth precisely seven pounds, four shillings, fourpence halfpenny to the Duke.

As it turned out, the large army that was assembled in 1776 to strike a quick, overpowering blow that would put a sudden end to the rebellion proved—when that decisive victory never came to pass—to be a distinct liability, a hideously expensive and at times vulnerable weapon. In the indecisive hands of men like William Howe and Henry Clinton, who never seemed absolutely certain about what they should do or how they should do it, the great army rarely had an opportunity to realize its potential; yet, it remained a ponderous and insatiable consumer of supplies, food, and money.

The loyalists, on whom many Englishmen had placed such high hopes, proved a will-o'-the-wisp. Largely ignored by the policy makers early in the war despite their pleas for assistance, the loyalists were numerous enough but were neither well organized nor evenly distributed throughout the colonies. Where the optimists in Britain went wrong in thinking that loyalist strength would be an important factor was to imagine that anything like a majority of Americans *could* remain loyal to the Crown if they were not continuously supported and sustained by the mother country. Especially as the war went on, as opinions hardened, and as the possibility increased that the new government in America might actually survive, it was a very difficult matter to retain one's loyalty to the King unless friends and neighbors were of like mind and unless there was British force nearby to safeguard such a belief. Furthermore, it proved almost impossible for the British command to satisfy the loyalists, who were bitterly angry over the persecution and physical violence and robbery they had to endure and who charged constantly that the British generals were too lax in their treatment of rebels.

While the problems of fighting the war in distant America mounted, Britain found herself unhappily confronted with the combination of circumstances the Foreign Office dreaded most: with her armies tied down, the great European maritime powers—France and Spain—vengeful and adventurous and undistracted by war in the Old World, formed a coalition against her. When the American war began, the risk of foreign intervention was regarded as minimal, and the decision to fight was made on the premise that victory would be early and complete and that the armed forces would be released before any threatening European power could take advantage of the situation. But as the war continued without any definite signs of American collapse, France and Spain seized the chance to embarrass and perhaps humiliate their old antagonist. At first they supported the rebels surreptitiously with shipments of weapons and other supplies; then, when the situation appeared more auspicious, France in particular furnished active support in the form of an army and a navy, with catastrophic results for Great Britain.

One fascinating might-have-been is what would have happened had the Opposition in Parliament been more powerful politically. It consisted, after all, of some of the most forceful and eloquent orators imaginable, men whose words still have the power to send shivers up the spine. Not simply vocal, they were highly intelligent men whose concern went beyond the injustice and inhumanity of war. They were quick to see that the personal liberty of the King's subjects was as much an issue in London as it was in the colonies, and they foresaw irreparable damage to the empire if the government followed its unthinking policy of coercion. Given a stronger power base, they might have headed off war or the ultimate disaster; had the government been in the hands of men like Chatham or Burke or their followers, some accommodation with America might conceivably have evolved from the various proposals for reconciliation. But the King and North had the votes in their pockets, and the antiwar Opposition failed because a majority that was largely indifferent to reason supported the North ministry until the bitter end came with Cornwallis' surrender. Time and again a member of the Opposition would rise to speak out against the war for one reason or another: "This country," the Earl of Shelburne protested, "already burdened much beyond its abilities, is now on the eve of groaning under new taxes, for the purpose of carrying on this cruel and destructive war." Or, from Dr. Franklin's friend David Hartley: "Every proposition for reconciliation has so constantly and uniformly been crushed by Administration, that I think they seem not even to wish for the appearance of justice. The law of force is that which they appeal to. . . ." Or, from Sir James Lowther, when he learned that the King had rejected an "Olive Branch Petition" from the provincials: "Why have we not peace with a people who, it is evident, desire peace with us?" Or this, from General Henry Seymour Conway, inviting Lord North to inform members of the House of Commons about his overall program: "I do not desire the detail; let us have general outline, to be able to judge of the probability of its success. It is indecent not to lay before the House some plan, or the outlines of a plan. . . . If [the] plan is conciliation, let us see it, that we may form some opinion of it; if it be hostility and coercion, I do repeat, that we have no cause for a minute's consideration; for I can with confidence pronounce, that the present military armament will never succeed." But all unavailing, year after year, as each appeal to reason and humanity fell on ears deafened by self-righteousness and minds hardened against change.

Although it might be said that the arguments raised by the Opposition did not change the course of the war, they nevertheless affected the manner in which it was conducted, which in turn led to the ultimate British defeat. Whether Lord North was uncertain of that silent majority's loyalty is difficult to determine, but it seems clear that he was sufficiently nervous about public support to decide that a bold policy which risked defeats was not for him. As a result the war of the American Revolution was a limited war—limited from the standpoint of its objectives and the force with which Britain waged it.

In some respects the aspect of the struggle that may have had the greatest influence on the outcome was an intangible one. Until the outbreak of hostilities in 1775 no more than a small minority of the colonials had seriously contemplated independence, but after a year of war the situation was radically different. Now the mood was reflected in words such as these—instructions prepared by the county of Buckingham, in Virginia, for its delegates to a General Convention in Williamsburg: ". . . as far as your voices are admitted, you [will] cause a free and happy Constitution to be established, with a renunciation of the old, and so much thereof as has been found inconvenient and oppressive." That simple and powerful idea—renunciation of the old and its replacement with something new, independently conceived—was destined to sweep all obstacles before it. In Boston, James Warren was writing the news of home to John Adams in Philadelphia and told him: "Your Declaration of Independence came on Saturday and diffused a general joy. Every one of us feels more important than ever; we now congratulate each other as Freemen." Such winds of change were strong, and by contrast all Britain had to offer was a return to the status quo. Indeed, it was difficult for the average Englishman to comprehend the appeal that personal freedom and independence held for a growing number of Americans. As William Innes put it in a debate in Commons, all the government had to do to put an end to the nonsense in the colonies was to "convince the lower class of those infatuated people that the imaginary liberty they are so eagerly pursuing is not by any means to be compared to that which the Constitution of this happy country already permits them to enjoy."

With everything to gain from victory and everything to lose by defeat, the Americans could follow Livy's advice, that "in desperate matters the boldest counsels are the safest." Frequently beaten and disheartened, inadequately trained and fed and clothed, they fought on against unreasonably long odds because of that slim hope of attaining a distant goal. And as they fought on, increasing with each passing year the possibility that independence might be achieved, the people of Britain finally lost the will to keep going.

In England the goal had not been high enough, while the cost was too high. There was nothing compelling about the limited objective of bringing the colonies back into the empire, nothing inspiring about punishing the rebels, nothing noble in proving that retribution awaited those who would change the nature of things.

After the war had been lost and the treaty of peace signed, Lord North looked back on the whole affair and sadly informed the members of the House of Commons where, in his opinion, the fault lay. With a few minor changes, it was a message as appropriate to America in 1971 as to Britain in 1783: "The American war," he said, "has been suggested to have been the war of the Crown, contrary to the wishes of the people. I deny it. It was the war of Parliament. There was not a step taken in it that had not the sanction of Parliament. It was the war of the people, for it was undertaken for the express purpose of maintaining the just rights of Parliament, or, in other words, of the people of Great Britain, over the dependencies of the empire. For this reason, it was popular at its commencement, and eagerly embraced by the people and Parliament. . . . Nor did it ever cease to be popular until a series of unparalleled disasters and calamities caused the people, wearied out with almost uninterrupted ill-success and misfortune, to call out as loudly for peace as they had formerly done for war."

The Unprofessional Soldier

DANIEL J. BOORSTIN

• Despite tales of valor and glory which punctuate American history textbooks—especially at the elementary levels—Americans have rarely been overly eager to march off to war or to accept the discipline of military life.

During the War of 1812 bounties of money, land, and clothing were promised to recruits to stimulate voluntary enlistments, but the army was consistently short of men. Although the free population of the United States outnumbered that of Canada by twelve to one, two months after the initiation of hostilities Henry Adams reported that Canadian forces outnumbered the Americans "at every point of danger on the frontier."

Before the advent of national conscription on March 3, 1863, the reluctance of American men to arise to the call of the Union was frequently evident. On July 2, 1862, President Abraham Lincoln appealed to the states to raise "three hundred thousand more," yet state-wide drafts and other inducements produced only 88,000. Soon after the draft laws went into effect, Irish mobs in New York City gave expression to their resentment by burning buildings and attacking free blacks. The rioters objected to the fact that well-to-do citizens could and did avoid military duty either by paying fees or hiring substitutes. During the first four months of the application of the law, ninety-eight registrars were killed by indignant citizens. The Confederacy also permitted the hiring of substitutes for a time and exempted the owners of twenty or more slaves from military duty.

The Spanish-American War and World Wars I and II were probably the most widely supported American wars. In World War I, for example, desertions were less common than in any previous American military action. But even then, when conscientious objection was not recognized by draft law, men used marriage and other less severe measures to escape the draft.

Once in combat, Americans have been as courageous and effective as the soldiers of any other nation. In World War II German prisoners testified "to the fear of these silent soldiers moving remorselessly forward that grew in the ranks of the German divisions." Yet Americans anxiously returned to their civilian roles as soon as hostilities ended. The tradition of the citizen-soldier, of the man who goes to war unwillingly but with the firm expectation of victory, is a long one in American history. Daniel J. Boorstin explains the role of the militia in the Revolutionary War and suggests that military leaders have often been popular in American society precisely because they were expected to be "Unprofessional soldiers."

The belief that American wars would always be fought by "embattled farmers" was rooted in the earliest facts of American life. Military men were to be simply citizens in arms. The military caste, the Man-on-Horseback, the Palace Revolution, the Coup d'État, the tug of war between army and civil government—these recurring motifs in continental European political life did not appear on the American scene. Civilian control over the army, clearly asserted in the Federal Constitution, merely declared what was already one of the firmest institutions of colonial life.

The typical American view of the military appeared in Doddridge's description of the backwoodsmen who "formed the cordon along the Ohio river, on the frontiers of Pennsylvania, Virginia and Kentucky, which defended the country against the attacks of the Indians during the revolutionary war. They were the janizaries of the country, that is, they were soldiers when they chose to be so, and when they chose laid down their arms. Their military service was voluntary, and of course received no pay."

Long before the end of the colonial period, British politicians and professional soldiers had learned that they could not rely on Americans to fill the ranks of the regular army stationed in America. While the backwoodsman with his sharpshooting rifle was ready and able to defend his home, he was intractable within a European-type professional army. The armed civilians of the separate colonies, which in their intense localism refused to cooperate in any large strategy, were inadequate to the large tasks of colonial defense. If the British government hoped to protect the colonies by preventing the accumulation of offensive French military strength, they had to send in a professional army from the outside. The capture of Louisbourg by New Englanders in 1745 was the only instance in the colonial period of a successful large-scale military operation by provincial fighters—and even that was the product not of wise planning but of lucky coincidence.

When General Braddock made his preparations for the disastrous campaign of 1755, he put relatively small reliance on American troops. Even at that he was expecting too much. The nucleus of his army was soldiers of regular regiments of the British Army, supposed to be brought up to full strength by American recruits, to be supported by voluntary financial aid from the colonial assemblies, and to be partly provisioned by the colonies. But Braddock was disappointed: few recruits were raised, the assemblies refused substantial assistance, and wagons and supplies were offered only at exorbitant rates. Characteristically, the northern colonies voted instead to set up a wholly provincial army under a general of their own choosing. This foreshadowed the difficulties which Lord Loudoun would meet on a larger scale a few years later and which would dramatize the divergence of American from European ways of war.

Loudoun's activities comprised the greatest British effort before the Revolution to control and centralize American military activities. According to plans made in advance, he arrived in America in 1756 carrying a broad commission to organize a force against the French and Indians; he was supposed to command a regular army of nearly fourteen thousand men (two-thirds of the privates besides replacements to be colonials). During two years of recruitment, the British, using dubious methods, managed to enlist about 7500 Americans; during the same period the British Isles supplied only about 4500. The year 1757 showed a decided reversal of proportions: in that year only about 1200 men were recruited in the colonies, while 11,000 came from England. Loudoun, with the hoped-for acquiescence of the separate colonial governments, was supposed to be supreme commander of all local forces, including, of course, their militia. But the more Loudoun learned of colonial troops and colonial ways, the less he came to rely on them—whether as recruits for the ranks of his regular regiments or as supporting forces organized in their own militia. "The King must trust in this country to himself and those he sends," Lord Loudoun wrote back from America as early as September 1756, ". . . for this Country will not run when he calls."

Everything that Loudoun, with the experienced eye of a professional soldier, saw of the American provincial militias appalled him. Upon his arrival, there were about seven thousand militiamen occupying the colonies' northern forts. These men had been raised, and their officers commissioned, each by his separate province; for all practical purposes each group was responsible only to its own distinct government. When Loudoun and his subordinates inspected the camp commanded by General John Winslow (who had been commissioned by the Governors of Massachusetts, Connecticut, and New York), they were horrified by the absence of decent military order or even rudimentary sanitation. They saw a hundred graves dug in a day for men dead of disease. "The fort stinks enough to cause an infection," Loudoun heard from Fort William Henry, "they have all their sick in it. The camp nastier than anything I could conceive, their necessary houses, kitchens, graves and places for slaughtering cattle, all mixed through their encampment." Deserters were only mildly punished. Loudoun was shocked to see men firing their guns at random after drill, sleeping on post, and taking pot shots at game while they were on the march. But the elected officers would seldom risk unpopularity by punishing offenders.

No commander in his right mind would admit men with such a conception of an army into a regiment of well-disciplined regulars. And why, indeed, should any American put himself under the strict discipline of the British Army? Everything was better in the provincial militias: a Massachusetts private soldier received all of 10¼d sterling a day while a British regular private received no more than 4d; in addition, the provincial soldier received an annual bounty for reënlistment. Supplies for the provincials looked like luxuries to the regulars. The militiaman not only received a greater staple allowance, but after one summer's service, he was allowed to keep his hatchet, blanket, and knapsack—and he soon established the profitable custom of taking his musket home with him. He could count on his sugar, ginger, rum, and molasses; and his marching allowance was three times that of a British regular.

This life of a provincial militiaman was free-and-easy compared to that of the regular, who might be punished with flogging, or be forced to enlist for life in the West Indies. It was so free-and-easy in fact that the commander of provincial troops never really knew how many men he had at his disposal. The militiaman preferred to stay close to home, so that he could return to his family in case of need. When the General Court of Massachusetts voted troops for the expedition to Crown Point in northeastern New York, they expressly provided that the men "shall not be compelled to march southward of Albany, or westward of Schenechtedy." "The Troops are constantly coming & going," an observer wrote of General Johnson's New York army, "ill arm'd, ill cloath'd & worse disciplined, some having served their time out, as they phrase it, and some commencing fresh men. Never to be sure was such a motly Herd, almost every man his own master & a General."

The "leveling spirit" of the Americans was notorious among British officers. "Our Militia is under no kind of discipline. . . ." complained Cadwallader Colden to Lord Halifax in 1754. "The Inhabitants of the Northern Colonies are all so nearly on a level, and a licentiousness, under the notion of liberty, so generally prevails, that they are impatient under all kind of superiority and authority." "The Officers of the Army with very few Exceptions," a colonial observer noted of such provincial troops, "are utter Strangers to Military Life and most of them in no Respect superior to the Men they are put over, They are like the heads and indeed are the heads of a Mob." Such "officers" had long been snubbed by British regulars. In 1741 in the expedition against Cartagena in the Caribbean, officers from Virginia, including even the experienced and highly competent Governor Gooch, had been passed over for promotion and brazenly mistreated. George Washington himself had traveled alone half-way across the colonies to settle just such a question concerning his own military rank. The established policy repeated by the Duke of Cumberland in 1754 ordered "that all Troops serving by Commissions signed by Us, or by Our General Commanding in Chief in North America, shall take Rank before all Troops which may serve by Commission from any of the Governors or Councils of Our Provinces in North America: And It is Our further Pleasure, that the Generals and Field Officers of the Provincial Troops shall have no Rank with the Generals & Field Officers who serve by Commissions from Us." Loudoun brought with him to America a modified order allowing colonial officers more rank, but by then it was too late.

There was not a single problem that plagued Loudoun in the French and Indian War that did not also trouble Washington in the War of Independence. Washington, trying to raise a unified Continental Army from unmilitary Americans, now stood in the shoes of Lord Loudoun. Although the "cause" was different, the difficulties were the same. The Continental Army, like the British Regular Army twenty years earlier, had to compete for men against the separate state militias, and Washington had only slightly more success. Had the American cause been forced to depend on an American regular army, the outcome would have been even more doubtful and drawn-out. Washington, however, took wise advantage of his opportunity to fight the war seriatim—first in New England, then in the Middle Colonies, then in the South—rather than all-at-once, as the French and Indian Wars had been fought. This made the dispersed militia more useful and his smaller army more effective.

The unseemly disputes over rank and precedence, in which regular British officers had lorded it over mere militiamen, were reënacted with the officers of the Continental line now assuming the old airs of the regulars. The Congress and the States showed democratic prodigality; they lavished military titles on mere able-bodied citizens, regardless of competence. "My blacksmith is a captain," De Kalb reported in amazement. To avoid offense, it was always safer to assume that anybody was entitled to be addressed as a high officer. "Not an hour passes," Washington wrote to the President of the Continental Congress (Aug. 3, 1778), "without new applications and new complaints about rank. . . . We can scarcely form a Court Martial or parade a detachment in any instance, without a warm discussion on the subject of precedence." When Colonel Crafts of the militia and Colonel Jackson of the Continental army arrived to act as pall-bearers at the funeral of a fellow-officer, Crafts as the older man claimed the right to walk first, but Jackson argued that as a Continental officer he was entitled to precedence. Neither gave in, and Crafts and his friends walked out on the funeral.

Even Washington's patience wore thin; but since local prides were not to be overcome, he learned to live with them and somehow to harness them in the common cause. "I have labored, ever since I have been in the service," Washington wrote at the end of 1776, "to discourage all kinds of local attachments and distinctions of country [i.e. of State], denominating the whole by the greater name of *American*, but I have found it impossible to overcome prejudices; and, under the new establishment, I conceive it best to stir up an emulation; in order to do which would it not be better for each State to furnish, though not to appoint, their own brigadiers?" In 1780, to the inquiries of the Congress about his problems of promotion and rank, he replied: "If in all cases ours was *one* army, or *thirteen* armies allied for the common defence, there would be no difficulty in solving your question; but we are occasionally both, and I should not be much out if I were to say, that we are sometimes *neither*, but a compound of *both*."

All the American armies were competing against each other for men, for officers, for rank, and for glory. Privates from New England were being offered higher pay than those from the Middle States. Massachusetts even offered to pay its men by lunar rather than calendar months in order to secure a competitive advantage. This particular trick Washington stigmatized as the "most fatal stab to the peace of this Army, that ever was given. . . . Lord North himself could not have devised a more effectual blow to the recruiting Service." Problems were compounded by the familiar "leveling" tendencies of the Americans; by their refusal to allow a sufficiently higher pay to officers, they stirred discontent and bred an unmilitary familiarity between officers and men.

The widespread fear of a permanent professional army increased the difficulties. John Adams declared it safer in the long run to put public faith in a temporary though less effective militia. "Although it may cost us more, and we may put now and then a battle to hazard by the method we are in, yet we shall be less in danger of corruption and violence from a standing army, and our militia will acquire courage, experience, discipline, and hardiness in actual service. I wish every man upon the continent was a soldier, and obliged, upon occasion, to fight and determined to conquer or to die. Flight was unknown to the Romans. I wish it was to Americans." Proposals to offer long-term pensions to officers, in order to attract better men and to raise their morale, were widely opposed. Elbridge Gerry listed the reasons (Jan. 13, 1778): "the infant state of the country, its aversion to placemen and pensioners, whereby Great Britain is likely to lose her liberty, the equality of the officers and soldiers of some States, before the war."

Short-term enlistments (sometimes for as little as three months) expressed both the widespread fear of a professional standing army and the assumption that an army would be superfluous the day after the war was won. Washington repeatedly complained that this was the core of his problem. For example, in a circular (Oct. 18, 1780) to the several States from his headquarters near Passaic, he said:

> I am religiously persuaded that the duration of the war, and the greatest part of the Misfortunes, and perplexities we have hitherto experienced, are chiefly to be attributed to temporary inlistments. . . . A moderate, compact force, on a permanent establishment capable of acquiring the discipline essential to military operations, would have been able to make head against the Enemy, without comparison better than the throngs of Militia, which have been at certain periods not in the feild, but on their way to, and from the feild: for from that want of perseverance which characterises all Militia, and of that coercion which cannot be exercised upon them it has always been found impracticable to detain the greatest part of them in service even for the term, for which they have been called out; and this has been commonly so short, that we have had a great proportion of the time, two sets of men to feed and pay, one coming to the Army, and the other going from it.

Men went home just as they were beginning to understand their duties, and it was often necessary to recruit a new army in the face of the enemy. More than one American military defeat can be explained by the transient character of the army. General Richard Montgomery rushed into his disastrous assault on Quebec in late December 1775 because the enlistments of all his New England troops would expire at midnight on December 31, and he was sure they would not stay with him a day longer.

The unreliability and lack of discipline of the American armed citizenry, which had been so hastily gathered into military ranks, haunted brave Revolutionary commanders from Washington down to lieutenants in the field, and made large-scale planning mere wishful thinking. Time after time militia fled the battlefield, spreading defeatism as they went. "America," warned Washington, "has been almost amused out of her Liberties" by the proponents of the militia. "I solemnly declare I never was witness to a single instance, that can countenance an opinion of Militia or raw Troops being fit for the real business of fighting. I have found them useful as light Parties to skirmish in the woods, but incapable of making or sustaining a serious attack. . . . The late battle of Camden is a mancholly comment upon this doctrine. The Militia fled at the first fire, and left the Continental Troops surrounded on every side, and overpowered by numbers to combat for safety instead of victory." "Great god," exclaimed Daniel Morgan on Feb. 1, 1781, only a few days after his victory over Tarleton, "what is the reason we cant Have more men in the field— so many men in the country Nearby idle for want of employment." At this critical moment in the War, when Greene was retreating before Cornwallis, Edward Stevens vainly appealed to his troops.

> After crossing the Yadkin we could not have Paraded a greater Force than Eight Hundred for Action if even that Including Militia and all and a great part of the number was the Militia under me whose times were out. I saw the greatest necessity of these men remaining a few days till the Troops from General Greens Camp could get up, and this the General requested of me to endeavour to bring about. I had them paraded and addressed them on the Subject. But to my great mortification and astonishment scarce a man would agree to it, And gave for answer he was a good Soldier that Served his time out. If the Salvation of the Country had depended on their staying Ten or Fifteen days, I dont believe they would have done it. Militia wont do. Their greatest Study is to Rub through their Tower [Tour] of Duty with whole Bones.

But many militiamen were not this scrupulous of their duty; they often went home before their term was up. Desertions were commonplace. It is hard to assess the military tactics of some battles because one can never be sure how many of the "losses" of the Revolutionary army were due to desertion rather than to death or capture. Within a few weeks before the Battle of Bennington on August 16, 1777, more than four hundred men deserted—or, more accurately, disappeared. At the siege of Newport, about the same time, five thousand militiamen deserted within a few days, so weakening Sullivan's forces that he had to abandon any idea of attack. On many occasions—for example, near Savannah in March 1779, at Johnstown in October 1781, and at other places too numerous to mention—large numbers of militia fled in panic. Although the Americans had outnumbered the British by more than fifty per cent at Guilford Court House on March 15, 1781, the wholesale flight of the militia to the woods gave victory to the British. The experienced General Daniel Morgan had shrewdly foreseen just this when he warned General Nathanael Greene against the "great number of militia" and advised, "If they fight, you beat Cornwallis, if not, he will beat you." "Put the . . . militia in the centre, with some picked troops in their rear with orders to shoot down the first man that runs." Greene followed Morgan's advice, but the anxiety of the North Carolina and Virginia militia prevailed.

How could such an ill-assorted, ill-disciplined, and ill-supplied army succeed against the well-organized forces of one of the great military powers? How, indeed, can we account for the final victory? Many acts of heroism, courage, and sacrifice embellished the records of the fighting Americans. The unorthodox imagination of amateur American generals, in sharp contrast to the professional rigidity of the British command, gave the colonials an unexpected advantage. But it is still hard to explain why the British surrendered so quickly after Yorktown. Today the most persuasive answer is not that the Americans won but that the British lost—or perhaps that they simply gave up, having seen the long-run hopelessness of their cause. The American terrain (together with the colonial dispersion, which meant that there was no jugular vein to be cut by British force) led the British to realize that to subdue America was beyond their means. Within the first four years of the Revolution, every one of the most populous towns—Boston, New York, Philadelphia, and Charleston—had fallen to the British and had been occupied by their regular troops, but always without decisive effect. The American center was everywhere and nowhere—in each man himself. In addition, the French brought crucial aid to the American militia and irregulars, and the spectre of a permanent American alliance with France haunted the British Empire.

Perhaps the most typical and most ominous of the military events of the war was the abrupt disbanding of the army. In January, 1781— ten months before Cornwallis' surrender at Yorktown—mutiny shook the army in Pennsylvania; again, on the brink of peace in June 1783, mutinous soldiers, in control of the powder magazines and public officers at the seat of the Continental Congress in Philadelphia, threatened to use force to get their wages. It was in the shadow of such disorder that the Continental Army was hastily dispersed and that General Washington on December fourth bade a tearful farewell to his officers. Nothing was more American about the Revolution than this conclusion of it, when armed citizens impatiently dissolved themselves back into the populace. In this, as in later wars in American history, "the end of the war" and the end of the army were substantially, and disastrously, synonymous.

In American folklore it is fitting that the first call to arms, the rousing of "embattled farmers," the sudden appearance of Minute Men, together with Washington's Farewell and the last dispersion of the army, should remain the most permanent and the most moving symbols. The story of the actual administration of the Army is dismal and discreditable—almost unprecedented in the annals of war.

Yet the very weaknesses of the professional army had already foreshadowed strengths in American institutions. Unmilitary Americans freely chose a general for their first President. Washington might become "first in war, first in peace, and first in the hearts of his countrymen," but the political power given to a military leader meant something very different here from what it might have meant elsewhere. The American military ideal was not Caesar but Cincinnatus, not the skilled general glorying in the tasks of warfare to which he gave his life, but the planter who had unwillingly left his tobacco fields.

When, near the end of the war, American officers tried to set up an organization to perpetuate their comradeship, their memories, and their tradition (and perhaps their political influence), they significantly chose to call themselves the Society of the Cincinnati. Washington assumed its leadership—though only with the greatest reluctance, for he was suspicious of the organization and hoped to see it soon dissolved. Among the people at large it aroused violent fears of a military caste; they saw in such a hereditary military society a dangerous center of aristocracy, a focus of monarchic conspiracy. The Society was so congenial to the monarchic spirit that King Louis XVI of France authorized his officers to form a branch chapter and to wear the Order of the Cincinnati as a military decoration.

Long after the Society of the Cincinnati had faded from the public memory, another American military institution reached into many American homes. This was the Purple Heart Badge of Military Merit, which Washington established by a general order of Aug. 7, 1782:

> The General ever desirous to cherish a virtuous ambition in his soldiers, as well as to foster and encourage every species of Military merit, directs that whenever any singularly meritorious action is performed, the author of it shall be permitted to wear on his facings over the left breast, the figure of a heart in purple cloth or silk, edged with narrow lace or binding. Not only instances of unusual gallantry, but also of extraordinary fidelity and essential Service in any way shall meet with a due reward. . . . Men who have merited this last distinction to be suffered to pass all guards and sentinels which officers are permitted to do.

> The road to glory in a patriot army and a free country is thus open to all—this order is also to have retrospect to the earliest stages of the war, and to be considered as a permanent one.

Even though the Federal Constitution later gave the power to wage war to the central government, the American army was never fully unified. State militias, under their later guise of the "national guard," remained important; they helped keep alive a spirit of local allegiance and a variety of practice and military standards which eventually created all kinds of problems. The peacetime regional nucleus of the militia or "national guard" stayed together through a Civil War and two World Wars, so that many men continued to fight beside their neighbors.

Starting with Washington himself, American history would offer again and again—especially after the decline of the Virginia Dynasty —examples of men whose fame on the battlefield eventually led them to the highest civil office. Even in Great Britain, where there was little fear of military coups d'état during the 18th and 19th centuries, military men rarely became prime ministers; turning military success into a political career was almost unheard of there. But in America this became common: the prominent examples—Jackson, William Henry Harrison, Taylor, Grant, Theodore Roosevelt, and Eisenhower—come quickly to mind. Some of these men had begun, not in the ranks of the regular army, but in the local militia. And their military exploits —far from seeming mere success in a specialized profession— actually attested their success as undifferentiated Americans. Precisely because there was no military caste, the citizen-soldier easily found a place in American political life.

Watermelon Armies and Whiskey Boys

GERALD CARSON

• Although Americans hold ambivalent views about alcoholic beverages, it cannot be denied that whiskey has played an important role in our culture from its very inception. The Pilgrims carried liquor with them on the Mayflower, and Congress itself voted to provide supplies of spirits to the American army during Revolutionary times. During the 1700's whiskey was said to be vital to the workers in the southern states because of the hot climate.

To the Scotch-Irish of Pennsylvania, whiskey was not only an economic commodity but as necessary to their lives as Bibles and plows. Thus, when Alexander Hamilton proposed an internal revenue tax on distilled liquors, rumblings of dissatisfaction arose from the western Pennsylvania frontier. Because they based their livelihood on distilling grain rather than transporting the crop across the mountains, the farmers regarded the tax as discriminatory and leveled their shotguns at the revenue agents who came to collect. Public protests erupted, thousands marched on Pittsburgh, and there were talks of secession from the United States. Ultimately, President George Washington sent in federal troops.

Alexander Hamilton thought that the use of the army would illustrate the power of the newly created government to enforce the law. As you read Carson's witty and colorful account of the Whiskey Rebellion of 1794, consider the question of the use of federal troops to force compliance with a locally unpopular national policy. Does the use of military force, as Hamilton suggested, increase the citizen's respect for and adherence to the national laws? What similarities, if any, do you find between the quelling of the Whiskey Rebellion of 1794 and the use of the military to enforce integrated edu-

cation in Little Rock, Arkansas, in 1957 and to dispel youth-
ful protesters at the Democratic National Convention in
Chicago in August 1968?

When one recalls that the President of the United States, the Secretary of War, the Secretary of the Treasury and the governors of four
states once mobilized against the farmers of western Pennsylvania
almost as large an army as ever took the field in the Revolutionary
War, the event appears at first glance as one of the more improbable
episodes in the annals of this country. Thirteen thousand grenadiers,
dragoons, foot soldiers and pioneers, a train of artillery with six-
pounders, mortars and several "grasshoppers," equipped with mountains of ammunition, forage, baggage and a bountiful stock of tax-
paid whiskey, paraded over the mountains to Pittsburgh against a
gaggle of homespun rebels who had already dispersed.

Yet the march had a rationale. President George Washington and
his Secretary of the Treasury, Alexander Hamilton, moved to counter
civil commotion with overwhelming force because they well understood that the viability of the United States Constitution was involved.
Soon after he assumed his post at the Treasury, Hamilton had proposed, to the astonishment of the country, that the United States
should meet fully and promptly its financial obligations, including the
assumption of the debts contracted by the states in the struggle for
independence. The money was partly to be raised by laying an excise
tax upon distilled spirits. The tax, which was universally detested in
the West—"odious" was the word most commonly used to describe
it—became law on March 3, 1791.

The news of the passage of the measure was greeted with a roar
of indignation in the back country settlements. The duty was laid
uniformly upon all the states, as the Constitution provided. If the
West had to pay more, Secretary Hamilton explained, it was only
because it used more whiskey. The East could, if it so desired,
forgo beverage spirits and fall back on cider and beer. The South
could not. It had neither orchards nor breweries. To Virginia and
Maryland the excise tax appeared to be as unjust and oppressive as

the well-remembered Molasses Act and the tea duties of George III. "The time will come," predicted fiery James Jackson of Georgia in the House of Representatives, "when a shirt shall not be washed without an excise."

Kentucky, then thinly settled, but already producing its character-istic hand-made, whole-souled liquor from planished copper stills, was of the opinion that the law was unconstitutional. Deputy revenue collectors throughout the Bluegrass region were assaulted, their papers stolen, their horses' ears cropped and their saddles cut to pieces. On one wild night the people of Lexington dragged a stuffed dummy through the streets and hanged in effigy Colonel Thomas Marshall, the chief collector for the district.

Yet in no other place did popular fury rise so high, spread so rapidly, involve a whole population so completely, express so many assorted grievances, as in the Pennsylvania frontier counties of Fayette, Al-legheny, Westmoreland and Washington. In these counties, around 1791, a light plume of wood smoke rose from the chimneys of no less than five thousand log stillhouses. The rates went into effect on July first. The whiskey maker could choose whether he would pay a yearly levy on his still capacity or a gallonage tax ranging from nine to eleven cents on his actual production.

Before the month was out, "committees of correspondence," in the old Revolutionary phrase, were speeding horsemen over the ridges and through the valleys to arouse the people to arm and assemble. The majority, but not all, of the men who made the whiskey decided to "forbear" from paying the tax. The revenue officers were thoroughly worked over. Robert Johnson, for example, collector for Washington and Allegheny counties, was waylaid near Pigeon Creek by a mob disguised in women's clothing. They cut off his hair, gave him a coat of tar and feathers and stole his horse.

The Pennsylvania troubles were rooted in the economic importance and impregnable social position of mellow old Monongahela rye whiskey. In 1825, for instance, when the Philadelphia Society for Promoting Agriculture offered a gold medal to the person in Pennsyl-vania who carried on large-scale farming operations without providing ardent spirits for his farm workers, the medal could not be awarded. There were no entries for the uncoveted honor.

The frontier people had been reared from childhood on the

family jug of farmer whiskey. They found the taste pleasant, the effect agreeable. Whiskey was usually involved when there was kissing or fighting. It beatified the rituals of birth and death. The doctor kept a bottle in his office for his own use under the deceptive label "Arsenic —Deadly poison." The lawyer produced the bottle when the papers were signed. Whiskey was available in the prothonotary's office when the trial-list was made up. Jurors got their dram, and the constable drew his ration for his services on election day. The hospitable barrel and the tin cup were the mark of the successful political candidate. The United States Army issued a gill to a man every day. Ministers of the gospel were paid in rye whiskey, for they were shepherds of a devout flock, Scotch Presbyterians mostly, who took their Bible straight, especially where it said: "Give strong drink unto him that is ready to perish, and wine unto those that be of heavy hearts."

With grain the most abundant commodity west of the mountains, the farmers could eat it or drink it, but they couldn't sell it in distant markets unless it was reduced in bulk and enhanced in value. A Pennsylvania farmer's "best holt," then, was whiskey. A pack-horse could move only four bushels of grain. But it could carry twenty-four bushels if it was condensed into two kegs of whiskey slung across its back, while the price of the goods would double when they reached the eastern markets. So whiskey became the remittance of the fringe settlements for salt, sugar, nails, bar iron, pewter plates, powder and shot. Along the western rivers where men saw few shilling pieces, a gallon of good, sound rye whiskey was a stable measure of value.

The bitter resistance of the western men to the whiskey tax involved both practical considerations and principles. First, the excise payment was due and must be paid in hard money as soon as the water-white distillate flowed from the condensing coil. The principle concerned the whole repulsive idea of an internal revenue levy. The settlers of western Pennsylvania were a bold, hardy, emigrant race who brought with them bitter memories of oppression under the excise laws in Scotland and Ireland, involving invasion of their homes, confiscation of their property and a system of paid informers. Revenue collectors were social outcasts in a society which warmly seconded Doctor Samuel Johnson's definition of excise: "a hateful tax levied upon commodities, and adjudged not by the common judges of property, but wretches hired by those to whom excise is paid."

The whiskey boys of Pennsylvania saw it as simply a matter of sound Whig doctrine to resist the exciseman as he made his rounds with Dicas' hydrometer to measure the proof of the whiskey and his marking iron to brand the casks with his findings. Earlier, Pennsylvania had taxed spirits. But whiskey produced for purely private use was exempt. William Findley of Westmoreland County, a member of Congress at the time and a sympathetic interpreter of the western point of view, looked into this angle. To his astonishment, he learned that all of the whiskey distilled in the west was for purely personal use. So far as the state's excise tax was concerned, or any other tax, for that matter, the sturdy Celtic peoples of the Monongahela region had cheerfully returned to nature: they just didn't pay. About every sixth man made whiskey. But all were involved in the problem, since the other five took their grain to the stillhouse where the master distiller turned it into liquid form.

The state had been lenient. But now matters had taken a more serious turn. The new federal government in Philadelphia was dividing the whole country up into "districts" for the purpose of collecting the money. And the districts were subdivided into smaller "surveys." The transmontane Pennsylvanians found themselves in the grip of something known as the fourth survey, with General John Neville, hitherto a popular citizen and leader, getting ready to enforce the law, with a reward paid to informers and a percentage to the collectors, who appeared to be a rapacious set.

The first meeting of public protest against the 1791 federal tax was held at Redstone Old Fort, now Brownsville. The proceedings were moderate on that occasion, and scarcely went beyond the right of petition. Another meeting in August, more characteristic of others which were to follow, was radical in tone, disorderly, threatening. It passed resolves to the effect that any person taking office under the revenue law was an enemy of society.

When warrants were issued in the affair of Robert Johnson, the process server was robbed, beaten, tarred and feathered and left tied to a tree in the forest. As the inspectors' offices were established, they were systematically raided. Liberty poles reappeared as whiskey poles. The stills of operators who paid the tax were riddled with bullets in attacks sardonically known as "mending" the still. This led to a popular description of the Whiskey Boys as "Tom the Tinker's Men," an ironical reference to the familiar, itinerant repairer of pots and kettles. Notices proposing measures for thwarting the law, or aimed at coercing the distillers, were posted on trees or published in the *Pittsburgh Gazette* over the signature, "Tom the Tinker," nom de plume of the insurgent John Holcroft and other anti-tax agitators. Findley, who tried to build a bridge of understanding between the backwoodsmen and the central government, described the outbreak as not the result of any concerted plan, but rather as a flame, "an infatuation almost incredible."

An additional grievance grew out of the circumstance that offenders were required to appear in the federal court at Philadelphia, three hundred miles away. The whiskey-makers saw this distant government as being no less oppressive than one seated in London, and often drew the parallel. The Scotch-Irish of western Pennsylvania were, in sum, anti-federalist, anti-tax, and it may be added, anti-Indian. West of Pittsburgh lay Indian country. The men of the west held to a simple concept of how to solve the Indian problem: extermination. The Indians had the same program, in reverse, and were getting better results. The bungling campaigns, which generals Hamar and St. Clair had conducted in the early 1790's made the people of the fringe settlements despair of the ability of the Union to protect them.

Congress amended the excise tax law in 1792 and again in 1794 to lighten the burden on country distillers. A further conciliatory step was taken. To ease the hardships of the judicial process, Congress gave to the state courts jurisdiction in excise offenses so that accused persons might be tried in their own vicinity. But some fifty or sixty writs already issued and returnable at Philadelphia resulted in men being carried away from their fields during harvest time. This convinced the insurgents that the federalist East was seeking a pretext to discipline the democratic West.

One day in July, while the papers were being served, William Miller, a delinquent farmer-distiller, and political supporter of General Neville, saw the General riding up his lane accompanied by a stranger who turned out to be a United States marshal from Philadelphia. The marshal unlimbered an official paper and began to read a summons. It ordered said Miller peremptorily to "set aside all manner of business and excuses" and appear in his "proper person" before a Philadelphia judge. Miller had been planning to sell his property and remove to Kentucky. The cost of the trip to Philadelphia and the fine for which he was liable would eat up the value of his land and betterments. The farm was as good as gone.

"I felt my blood boil at seeing General Neville along to pilot the sheriff to my very door," Miller said afterward. "I felt myself mad with passion."

As Neville and the marshal rode away, a party from the county militia which was mustered at Mingo Creek fired upon them, but there were no casualties. When the General reached Bower Hill, his country home above the Chartiers Valley, another party under the command of John Holcroft awaited him there and demanded his commission and official papers. The demand was refused and both sides began to shoot. As the rebels closed in on the main house, a flanking fire came from the Negro cabins on the plantation. The Whiskey Boys were driven off with one killed and four wounded.

The next day, Major James McFarlane, a veteran of the Revolution, led an attack in force upon Neville's painted and wall-papered mansion, furnished with such marvels as carpets, mirrors, pictures and prints and an eight-day clock. The house was now defended by a dozen soldiers from Fort Fayette at Pittsburgh. A fire-fight followed during which a soldier was shot and McFarlane was killed—by treachery, the rebels said, when a white flag was displayed. The soldiers surrendered and were either released or allowed to escape. Neville was not found, but his cabins, barns, outbuildings and finally the residence were all burned to the ground. Stocks of grain were destroyed, all fences leveled, as the victors broke up the furniture, liberated the mirrors and clock, and distributed Neville's supply of liquor to the mob.

The funeral of McFarlane caused great excitement. Among those present were Hugh Henry Brackenridge, author, lawyer and one of the western moderates, and David Bradford, prosecuting attorney for Washington County. The former wished to find ways to reduce the tension; the latter to increase it. Bradford was a rash, impetuous Marylander, ambitious for power and position. Some thought him a second-rate lawyer. Others disagreed. They said he was third-rate. But he had a gift for rough mob eloquence. Bradford had already robbed the United States mails to find out what information was being sent east against the conspirators. He had already called for the people to make a choice of "submission or opposition . . . with *head, heart, hand* and *voice*."

At Major McFarlane's funeral service Bradford worked powerfully upon the feelings of his sympathizers as he described "the murder of McFarlane." Brackenridge also spoke, using wit and drollery to let down the pressure and to make palatable his warning to the insurgents that they were flirting with the possibility of being hanged. But the temper of the throng was for Bradford, clearly revealed in the epitaph which was set over McFarlane's grave. It said "He fell . . . by the hands of an unprincipled villain in the support of what he supposed to be the rights of his country."

The high-water mark of the insurrection was the occupation of Pittsburgh. After the fight and the funeral, Bradford called out the militia regiments of the four disaffected counties. They were commanded to rendezvous at Braddock's Feld, near Pittsburgh, with arms, full equipment and four days' rations. At the field there was a great beating of drums, much marching and counter-marching, almost a holiday spirit. Men in hunting shirts practiced shooting at the mark until a dense pall of smoke hung over the plain, as there had been thirty-nine years before at the time of General Braddock's disaster. There were between five and seven thousand men on the field, many meditating in an ugly mood upon their enemies holed up in the town, talking of storming Fort Fayette and burning Pittsburgh as "a second Sodom."

Bradford's dream was the establishment of an independent state with himself cast as a sort of Washington of the West. Elected by acclaim as Major General, he dashed about the field on a superb horse in a fancy uniform, his sword flashing, plumes floating out from his hat. As he harangued the multitude, Bradford received applications for commissions in the service of—what? No one quite knew.

Marching in good order, strung out over two and a half miles of road, the rebels advanced on August first toward Pittsburgh in what was hopefully interpreted as a "visit," though the temper of the whiskey soldiers was perhaps nearer to that of one man who twirled his hat on the muzzle of his rifle and shouted, "I have a bad hat now, but I expect to have a better one soon." While the panic-stricken burghers buried the silver and locked up the girls, the mob marched in on what is now Fourth Avenue to the vicinity of the present Baltimore and Ohio Railroad station. A reception committee extended nervous hospitality in the form of hams, poultry, dried venison, bear meat, water and whiskey. They agreed to banish certain citizens obnoxious to the insurrectionists. One building on a suburban farm was burned. Another attempt at arson failed to come off. The day cost Brackenridge four barrels of prime Monongahela. It was better, he reflected, "to be employed in extinguishing the fire of their thirst than of my house." Pittsburgh was fortunate in getting the main body in and then out again without a battle or a burning.

All through the month of August armed bands continued to patrol the roads as a "scrub Congress," in the phrase of one scoffer, met at Parkinson's Ferry, now Monongahela, to debate, pass resolutions and move somewhat uncertainly toward separation from the United States. Wild and ignorant rumors won belief. It was said that Congress was extending the excise levy to plows at a dollar each, that every wagon entering Philadelphia would be forced to pay a dollar, that a tax was soon to be established at Pittsburgh of fifteen shillings for the birth of every boy baby, and ten for each girl.

With the terrorizing of Pittsburgh, it was evident that the crisis had arrived. The President requisitioned 15,000 militia from Pennsylvania, New Jersey, Virginia and Maryland, of whom about 13,000 actually marched. Would the citizens of one state invade another to compel obedience to federal law? Here one gets a glimpse of the larger importance of the affair. Both the national government and the state of Pennsylvania sent commissioners to the West with offers of pardon upon satisfactory assurances that the people would obey the laws. Albert Gallatin, William Findley, Brackenridge and others made a desperate effort to win the people to compliance, though their motives were often questioned by both the rebels and the federal authorities. The response to the offer of amnesty was judged not to be sufficiently positive. Pressed by Hamilton to have federal power show its teeth, Washington announced that the troops would march.

The army was aroused. In particular, the New Jersey militia were ready for lynch law because they had been derided in a western newspaper as a "Water-mellon Army" and an uncomplimentary estimate was made of their military capabilities. The piece was written as a take-off on the kind of negotiations which preceded an Indian treaty.

Possibly the idea was suggested by the fact that the Whiskey Boys were often called "White Indians." At any rate, in the satire the Indians admonished the great council in Philadelphia: ". . . Brothers, we have that powerful monarch, Capt. Whiskey, to command us. By the power of his influence, and a love to *his person* we are compelled to every great and heroic act. . . . We, the Six United Nations of White Indians . . . have all imbibed his principles and passions— that is a love of whiskey. . . . Brothers, you must not think to frighten us with . . . infantry, cavalry and artillery, composed of your water-mellon armies from the Jersey shores; they would cut a much better figure in warring with the crabs and oysters about the Capes of Delaware."

Captain Whiskey was answered hotly by "A Jersey Blue." He pointed out that "the water-melon army of New Jersey" was going to march westward shortly with "ten-inch howitzers for throwing a species of mellon very useful for curing a *gravel occasioned by whiskey!*" The expedition was tagged thereafter as the "Watermelon Army."

The troops moved in two columns under the command of General Henry (Light Horse Harry) Lee, Governor of Virginia. Old Dan Morgan was there and young Meriwether Lewis, five nephews of President Washington, the governors of Pennsylvania and New Jersey, too, and many a veteran blooded in Revolutionary fighting, including the extraordinary German, Captain John Fries of the Bucks County militia and his remarkable dog to which the Captain gave the name of a beverage he occasionally enjoyed—Whiskey.

The left wing marched west during October, 1794, over General Braddock's old route from Virginia and Maryland to Cumberland on the Potomac, then northwest into Pennsylvania, to join forces with the right wing at Union Town. The Pennsylvania and New Jersey corps proceeded via Norristown and Reading to Harrisburg and Carlisle. There, on October 4th, President Washington arrived, accompanied by Colonel Hamilton. The representatives of the disaffected counties told the President at Carlisle that the army was not needed but Hamilton convinced him that it was. Washington proceeded with the troops as far as Bedford, then returned to Philadelphia for the meeting of Congress. Hamilton ordered a roundup of many of the rebels and personally interrogated the most important ones. Brackenridge, incidentally, came off well in his encounter with Hamilton, who declared that he was satisfied with Brackenridge's conduct.

By the time the expedition had crossed the mountains, the uprising was already coming apart at the seams. David Bradford, who had been excluded from the offer of amnesty, fled to Spanish Louisiana. About two thousand of the best riflemen in the West also left the country, including many a distiller, who loaded his pot still on a pack horse or a keel boat and sought asylum in Kentucky where, hopefully, a man could make "the creature" without giving the public debt a lift.

The punitive army moved forward in glorious autumn weather, raiding chicken coops, consuming prodigious quantities of the commodity which lay at the heart of the controversy. Richard Howell, governor of New Jersey and commander of the right wing, revived the spirits of the Jersey troops by composing a marching song, "Dash to the Mountains, Jersey Blue":

> To arms once more, our hero cries,
> Sedition lives and order dies;
> To peace and ease then did adieu
> And dash to the mountains, Jersey Blue.

Faded diaries, old letters and orderly books preserve something of the gala atmosphere of the expedition. At Trenton a Miss Forman and a Miss Milnor were most amiable. Newtown, Pennsylvania, was ticketed as a poor place for hay. At Potts Grove a captain of the cavalry troop got kicked in the shin by his horse. Among the Virginians, Meriwether Lewis enjoyed the martial excitement, wrote to his mother in high spirits of the "mountains of beef and oceans of Whiskey"; sent regards "to all the girls" and announced that he would bring "an Insergiant Girl to se them next fall bearing the title of Mrs. Lewis." If there was such a girl, he soon forgot her.

Yet where there is an army in being there are bound to be unpleasant occurrences. Men were lashed. Quartermasters stole government property. A soldier was ordered to put a Scotch-Irish rebel under guard. In execution of the order, he ran said insurgent through with his bayonet, of which the prisoner died. At Carlisle a dragoon's pistol went off and hit a countryman in the groin; he too died. On November 13, long remembered in many a cabin and stump-clearing as "the dismal night," the Jersey horse captured various citizens whom they described grimly as "the whiskey pole gentry," dragging them out of bed, tying them back to back. The troopers held their prisoners in a damp cellar for twenty-four hours without food or water, before marching them off at gun point to a collection center at Washington, Pennsylvania.

In late November, finding no one to fight, the army turned east again, leaving a volunteer force under General Morgan to conciliate and consolidate the position during the winter. Twenty "Yahoos" were carried back to Philadelphia and were paraded by the Philadelphia Horse through the streets of the city with placards marked "Insurrection" attached to their hats, in an odd federalist version of a Roman triumph. The cavalry was composed, as an admirer said, of "young men of the first property of the city," with beautiful mounts, uniforms of the finest blue broadcloth. They held their swords elevated in the right hand while the light flashed from their silver stirrups, martingales and jingling bridles. Stretched over half a mile they came, first two troopers abreast, then a pair of Yahoos, walking; then two more mounted men, and so on.

The army, meditating upon their fatigues and hardships, called for a substantial number of hangings. Samuel Hodgson, Commissary-general of the army, wrote to a Pittsburgh confidant, "We all lament that so few of the insurgents fell—such disorders can only be cured by copious bleedings. . . ." Philip Freneau, friend and literary colleague of Brackenridge, suggested in retrospect—ironically, of course —the benefits which would have accrued to the country "If Washington had drawn and quartered thirty or forty of the whiskey boys. . . ." Most of the captives escaped any punishment other than that of being held in jail without a trial for ten or twelve months. One died. Two were finally tried and sentenced to death. Eventually both were let off.

Gradually the bitterness receded. In August, 1794, General Anthony Wayne had crushed the Indians at the Battle of Fallen Timbers. A treaty was concluded with Spain in October, 1795, clearing the Mississippi for western trade. The movement of the army into the Pennsylvania hinterland, meanwhile, brought with it a flood of cash which furnished the distillers with currency for paying their taxes. These events served to produce a better feeling toward the Union.

If the rising was a failure, so was the liquor tax. The military adventure alone, without ordinary costs of collection, ran up a bill of $1,500,000, or about one third of all the money that was realized during the life of the revenue act. The excise was quietly repealed during Jefferson's administration. Yet the watermelon armies and the Whiskey Boys made a not inconsiderable contribution to our constitutional history. Through them, the year 1794 completed what 1787 had begun; for it established the reality of a federal union whose law was not a suggestion but a command.

II THE EMERGING REPUBLIC
1800–1877

The Great Jefferson Taboo

FAWN M. BRODIE

• One of the most talented individuals ever to sit in the White House, Thomas Jefferson is the only American president who may be honestly classified as a Renaissance Man. Exceptionally gifted in a wide spectrum of activities, he not only authored the Declaration of Independence and the classic *Notes on Virginia* but also mastered Greek and Latin, conversed in French and Italian, designed his own estate at Monticello, became an accomplished horticulturist and violinist, founded the University of Virginia, and still made time to participate dramatically in the politics of his era. He distinguished himself as Governor of Virginia, as Ambassador to France, as George Washington's first Secretary of State, as a founder of the Democratic-Republican Party, as a spokesman for individual freedom in the Kentucky Resolutions of 1798, and of course as President of the United States. In his inaugural address of 1801, he proclaimed: "We are all Republicans, we are all Federalists." But in his performance as president he displayed a unique talent for mobilizing the members of his party into a cohesive unit.

Jefferson's personal and private life was almost as fascinating as his public career. He was tall and slender with a sunny disposition and excellent health. At the age of thirty-nine, he was widowed by the premature death of his wife Martha, for whom he felt a deep and lasting affection. The question posed in the following essay by Professor Fawn Brodie is whether Jefferson then took as a mistress a beautiful slave girl by the name of Sally Hemings. According to Professor Brodie, they did in fact have an affair and their love making resulted in as many as seven children. Others scholars dispute this inevitably controversial case, and the long and bitter argument on this taboo subject is likely to continue.

From *American Heritage.* © 1972, American Heritage Publishing Company, Inc. Reprinted by permission of the publisher (June 1972).

Thomas Jefferson spent his earliest years on a plantation in Tuckahoe, Virginia, where the blacks outnumbered the whites ten to one. Here he learned about the hierarchies of power and saw early that a white child could tyrannize over a black adult. Here his basic sympathy with emancipation, which we see in him as a young man, had its roots in what he called, in his *Notes on the State of Virginia*, the "daily exercise in tyranny." But along with a pervasive anger at slavery, there also developed in Jefferson at some period a conviction he could never wholly escape, that blacks and whites must be carefully kept separate. Emancipation of the blacks, he said in his *Notes*, should be accompanied by colonization, whether in Africa, in the West Indies, or in a separate state in the West.

At age seventy-one he wrote privately, and with some bitterness, that "amalgamation" of blacks and whites "produces a degradation to which no lover of his country, no lover of excellence in the human character can innocently consent." And at seventy-seven, in his unfinished *Autobiography*, he wrote, "Nothing is more certainly written in the book of fate, than that these people are to be free; nor is it less certain that the two races, equally free, cannot live in the same government."

Yet, ironically, one of the stories that clings tenaciously to Jefferson is that he actually had a family by a slave woman. The so-called Sally Hemings story broke into the press in great detail in 1802; public scoldings and bawdy ballads humiliated President Jefferson well into 1805. Throughout the 1830's and 1840's abolitionists elaborated the story to suggest that Jefferson had had a whole seraglio of black women and that one of his black mistresses and two of his daughters had been sold at a slave auction in New Orleans. Jefferson biographers, on the other hand, have almost unanimously denounced the stories as libellous.

On March 13, 1873, there appeared in an obscure Ohio newspaper, the *Pike County Republican*, a memoir by one of Sally Hemings' sons, Madison. The account was lucidly written, suggesting considerable education; when checked with Jefferson's *Farm Book*, the details were remarkably but not totally accurate. Madison Hemings wrote simply, even drily, that his mother had indeed borne Jefferson several children of whom he was one and that she was his only "concubine." This revelation caused a shudder among Jefferson scholars. Since its publication the memoir has been cited often for various details of life at Monticello, but its basic claim of paternity has been totally rejected almost without exception. Curiously, the piece itself has never been reprinted.

Although today's biographers still repudiate the Sally Hemings story, comment on the great Jefferson taboo does not disappear. Instead, we have the spectacle of ever-increasing numbers of pages devoted to its refutation. Merrill Peterson, in *The Jefferson Image in the American Mind*, looked at the documentation with some care, and in his recent biography, *Thomas Jefferson and the New Nation*, he writes:

> The evidence, highly circumstantial, is far from conclusive, however, and unless Jefferson was capable of slipping badly out of character in hidden moments at Monticello, it is difficult to imagine him caught up in a miscegenous relationship. Such a mixture of the races, such a ruthless exploitation of the master-slave relationship, revolted his whole being.

Dumas Malone devotes a whole appendix in his recent volume, *Jefferson the President, First Term 1801-1805*, to a refutation of the charge. He writes:

> . . . it is virtually inconceivable that this fastidious gentleman whose devotion to his dead wife's memory and to the happiness of his daughters and grandchildren bordered on the excessive could have carried on through a period of years a vulgar liaison which his own family could not have failed to detect.

And Professor Malone suggests that Sally Hemings may have told her children that Jefferson was their father out of "vanity."

Certain black historians, on the other hand, including Lerone Bennett, believe that the miscegenation was real and that Jefferson's descendants dot the country from Cambridge, Massachusetts, to San Francisco. Any defense of this thesis causes anguish and outrage among Jefferson admirers. Why does this story nevertheless persist? Does it touch some chord in fantasy life? Or do people feel that the scholars protest too much? Jefferson, after all, was a widower at thirty-nine. Defenders of Jefferson assure us again and again that miscegenation was out of character for him. But the first duty of a historian is to ask not "Is it out of character?" but "Is it true?"

What one might call "the family's official denial," begun by Jefferson's grandson, Thomas Jefferson Randolph, holds, first, that Jefferson was not at Monticello when Sally Hemings' children were conceived and, second, that they were fathered by Jefferson's nephews, Peter and

Samuel Carr. This denial has been gratefully accepted by Jefferson bi-ographers, his admirers, and his heirs. Still, one must note the fact, as Winthrop Jordan has done in his *White Over Black, American Atti-tudes Toward the Negro, 1550-1812*—and he was the first to say it in print—that Jefferson actually was at Monticello nine months before the births of each of Sally Hemings' children that are recorded in the *Farm Book*. And there is no evidence that she ever conceived a child when he was not there. Moreover, it takes very little research in the enormous file of family letters at the University of Virginia to demon-strate that Peter and Samuel Carr were elsewhere, managing planta-tions with slaves of their own, during most of the years that Sally Hem-ings was bearing children at Monticello.

Professor Jordan is the first white historian in our own time to describe dispassionately evidence for the Sally Hemings liaison, as well as the case against it, writing on the one hand that it was unlikely, a "lapse from character unique in his mature life," but noting on the other that it could have been evidence of deep ambivalence and that Jefferson's "repulsion" toward blacks may have hidden a powerful at-traction. Jordan finds the story distasteful, however, and regrets that the charge is "dragged after Jefferson like a dead cat through the pages of formal and informal history. . . ." Still, he calls for an "unexcited" discussion of the facts.

It is possible to keep such a discussion "unexcited," though the ma-terial is dramatic and, at times, tragic. There are many facts that Jeffer-son scholars have overlooked, and some that have been ignored, ap-parently because they were too painful to consider. This is not uncommon with biographers, especially those whose sense of iden-tification with their subject is almost total. In all fairness to Sally Hemings, as well as to Jefferson, whether one believes the story or not, phrases like "vulgar liaison," "ruthless exploitation of the master-slave relationship," and even "dragged after Jefferson like a dead cat" simply do not apply.

As everyone knows, Jefferson was a man of very great gifts and spe-cial sensibility. Yet we know little about Sally Hemings except that she was a quadroon of considerable beauty and that she was the half sister of his wife. Several of her brothers could read and write, and one may assume that this was true also of Sally. But no letter from her has been preserved, nor any by Jefferson to her.

Still, if it is true that Sally's seven children were also his children, this already illuminates the length and steadiness of their affection for each other and suggests that there may have been much suffering because it could not publicly be honored. A careful marshalling of the facts surely helps to throw light on Jefferson's life and character, and discovering a liaison does not degrade him or her. It may help explain some mysteries, such as why he never married again, and why he lapsed in his later years into ever-increasing apathy toward emancipation of slaves. For it may well be that this special involvement peculiarly incapacitated him for action in helping to change the national pattern of white over black. In any case, the facts may serve to illuminate his general ambivalence—his mixture of love and hate—concerning race.

Jefferson knew and revered two men who had children by slave women. One was his law teacher, George Wythe, whom he called his second father. Wythe, having no children of his own by two white wives, took a black mistress, Lydia Broadnax, whom he had freed. She bore a son, whom he raised with affection, teaching him Greek and Latin and promising him an inheritance in his will. Wythe even named Jefferson in his will as trustee in charge of the boy's education. But this provision was never to be fulfilled. An envious grandnephew of Wythe's named Sweney forged Wythe's name on several checks; seeking to avoid prosecution and also to win the total inheritance, Sweney put arsenic in the coffee and on some strawberries at Wythe's house. The mulatto child died quickly; Wythe lived long enough to disinherit Sweney. Lydia Broadnax, though very ill, survived. But because the only people who could testify against the murderer were blacks, he was acquitted.

Almost as close to Jefferson as George Wythe, at least for a time, was Jefferson's father-in-law, John Wayles. Wayles had had three white wives, who bore him four daughters. When his third wife died, he turned to Elizabeth Hemings, a slave on his plantation and the daughter of an English sea captain and an African slave woman. "Betty" Hemings bore Wayles six children, the youngest a girl named Sally, all of whom came to Monticello with their mother in the inheritance of Jefferson's wife, Martha Wayles. So it can be seen that although Jefferson may have been intellectually opposed to miscegenation, he grew up seeing it close at hand, and in his adult life he had two important models. He could hardly have believed it to be a grave sin.

Jefferson was greatly blessed in his marriage. He loved his wife passionately, and described their union in his *Autobiography* as "ten years of unchecquered happiness." Still, it was full of tragedy. Three of their six children died in infancy. After the birth of their sixth child, on May 8, 1782, Martha Jefferson hovered between life and death for months. When she finally died, on September 6, 1782, Jefferson fainted and, according to his oldest daughter, who was then ten, "remained so long insensible that they feared he never would revive."

> He kept his room for three weeks and I was never a moment from his side. He walked almost incessantly night and day only lying down occasionally when nature was completely exhausted on a pallet that had been brought in during his long fainting fit. My Aunts remained constantly with him for some weeks, I do not remember how many. When at last he left his room he rode out and from that time he was incessantly on horseback rambling about the mountain in the least frequented roads and just as often through the woods; in those melancholy rambles I was his constant companion, a solitary witness to many a violent burst of grief. . . .

Most Jefferson biographers believe that he never again felt any deep or lasting affection for any woman. Gilbert Chinard wrote in 1928 that "there is no indication that he ever fell in love again," and in one fashion or another Jefferson scholars have adhered to the tradition that he became essentially passionless, monastic, and ascetic. Yet this view has had to be reconciled with the fact that Jefferson had a romance in Paris in the 1780's with an Englishwoman, Maria Cosway. One solution has been to describe it as "superficially frantic," temporary, and playful rather than passionate. But the episode resulted in what are certainly the greatest love letters in the history of the American Presidency—letters whose copies were carefully preserved by Jefferson (and mostly kept hidden by his heirs until 1945), despite the fact that he is thought to have destroyed all his correspondence with both his wife and his mother. Moreover, passion does not usually disappear in a man's life unless his capacity for passion is constricted and warped from the beginning. When at forty-three, four years after his wife's death, he met the enchanting artist-musician and sensed at once the unhappiness of her marriage to the decadent and foppish Richard Cosway, he fell in love in a single afternoon. They saw each other alone many times during five happy weeks in the autumn of 1786, and in August, 1787, she returned to Paris for a second visit, without her husband. She remained four months. The story of this romance, told in AMERICAN HERITAGE in August, 1971, need not be repeated here, except as it relates in a subtle fashion to the Sally Hemings story.

Jefferson had taken his eldest daughter Martha (Patsy) with him to Paris, leaving Maria (Polly) and baby Lucy with his wife's sister. When Lucy died of whooping cough, Jefferson in a frenzy of anxiety insisted that Polly be sent to Paris. He ordered that a middle-aged slave woman accompany her, one who had had the smallpox. But when Abigail Adams met the ship in London, she saw with some consternation that the maid accompanying the eight-year-old Polly was a young slave girl of striking beauty. It was Sally Hemings. Though Sally was only fourteen, Abigail believed her to be "about 15 or 16" and described her unhappily in a letter to Jefferson as "quite a child . . . wanting even more care" than Polly, and "wholly incapable" of looking after her young charge properly by herself.

It had been a lively voyage, with no other females on the ship, and Captain John Ramsay had quite won Polly's affection. She had become, Abigail reported grimly, "rough as a little sailor." The captain readily agreed with Abigail that Sally Hemings would be of "little Service" to Jefferson and suggested that "he had better carry her back with him." It takes no special imagination to see why, for quite different reasons, Abigail Adams and Captain Ramsay agreed that it would be better if Sally Hemings did not go on to Paris. But Jefferson sent his trusted French servant Petit to fetch them, and they arrived in July, 1787.

Sally Hemings was later described by a Monticello slave as "very handsome" and "mighty near white" with "long straight hair down her back." Jefferson's grandson, Thomas Jefferson Randolph, said she was "light colored and decidedly good looking," and at Monticello she was described as "Dashing Sally." If she resembled her half sister Martha Wayles Jefferson in any fashion, there is no record of it. But certainly she brought to Paris the fresh, untainted aura of Jefferson's past, the whole untrammeled childhood with the quantities of slave children, the memory of the easy, apparently guiltless miscegenation of his father-in-law, the many-faceted reality of black and white in Virginia.

Sally Hemings arrived in Paris shortly before Maria Cosway returned for her second visit, without her husband. There are some indications that Maria was troubled and guilt-ridden, and there were many reasons why such an affair could not continue. She was a devout Catholic, and besides, divorce was virtually impossible for an Englishwoman, even a Protestant. Her husband, increasingly restive in London, became nastier in his letters. She went back to England in December, 1787, and Jefferson was again left lonely and bereft. Earlier he had written to her, "I am born to lose everything I love."

Sally Hemings was now fifteen. She was learning French, as was her older brother James, who was in Paris as Jefferson's personal servant. We know from Jefferson's account books that he paid 240 francs to a Dr. Sutton on November 6, 1787, for Sally's smallpox inoculation, and that by January, 1788, he had begun for the first time to pay wages to both James and Sally Hemings, thirty-six francs a month to James and twenty-four to his sister. The French servants received fifty and sixty francs. By French law both were free if they chose to make an issue of it, and they knew it.

The circumstances were propitious for an attachment. Sally Hemings must certainly have been lonely in Paris, as well as supremely ready for the first great love of her life. She was thrown daily into the presence of a man who was by nature tender and gallant with women. He was, moreover, the man whom all the children at Monticello, whether white or black, had looked upon as a kind of deity. What is more, if Jefferson had a model in the person of his father-in-law, who had turned to a slave woman after the death of his third wife, Sally Hemings, too, had a model in her mother, that Betty Hemings who had apparently dominated the private life and passions of John Wayles until his death.

In his *Notes on the State of Virginia* Jefferson had described blacks as more "ardent" than whites, a preconception that could have served only to heighten an interest in Sally at this moment, whatever dilemma it might produce. Moreover, he liked warmly domestic women. Though he took pleasure in intellectual female companions, enjoying the sharp, witty, and inquiring minds of Abigail Adams and several talented Frenchwomen, he did not fall in love with them. In this respect he resembled Goethe and Rousseau, both of whom loved and lived with unlettered women for many years before marrying them. Furthermore, during this Paris sojourn, Jefferson wrote to an American friend, the beautiful Anne Bingham, deploring the new preoccupation of Frenchwomen with politics:

> Society is spoilt by it. . . . You too, have had your political fever. But our good ladies, I trust have been too wise to wrinkle their foreheads with politics. They are contented to soothe and calm the minds of their husbands returning ruffled from political debate. . . . Recollect the women of this capital, some on foot, some on horses, and some in carriages hunting pleasure in the streets, in routs and assemblies, and forgetting that they have left it behind them in their nurseries; compare them with our own countrywomen occupied in the tender and tranquil amusements of domestic life, and confess that it is a comparison of Amazons and Angels.

Maria Cosway was no Amazon. Nor, it can be assumed, was Sally Hemings. Her son Madison tells us nothing of his mother's education or temperament. But he does write of what happened to her in Paris:

> Their stay (my mother and Maria's) was about eighteen months. But during that time my mother became Mr. Jefferson's concubine, and when he was called home she was *enceinte* by him. He desired to bring my mother back to Virginia with him but she demurred. In France she was free, while if she returned to Virginia she would be re-enslaved. So she refused to return with him. To induce her to do so he promised her extraordinary privileges, and made a solemn pledge that her children should be freed at the age of twenty-one years. In consequence of his promises, on which she implicitly relied, she returned with him to Virginia. Soon after their arrival, she gave birth to a child, of whom Thomas Jefferson was the father.

Is there any evidence other than Madison Hemings' memoir that a liaison between Jefferson and Sally Hemings began in Paris? If a man is in love, in however clandestine an affair, he must tell someone, if only unconsciously and with inadvertence. This is what happened to Jefferson. In March, 1788, he went to Holland on a diplomatic mission and then continued as a tourist into Germany. Not usually a diary keeper, he did write an almost daily journal of this seven-week trip. It is a matter of great curiosity that in this twenty-five-page document he uses the word *mulatto* eight times:

"The road goes thro' the plains of the Maine, which are mulatto and very fine. . . ."

"It has a good Southern aspect, the soil a barren mulatto clay. . . ."

"It is of South Western aspect, very poor, sometimes grey, sometimes mulatto. . . ."

"These plains are sometimes black, sometimes mulatto, always rich. . . ."

". . . the plains are generally mulatto. . . ."

". . . the valley of the Rhine . . . varies in quality, sometimes a rich mulatto loam, sometimes a poor sand. . . ."

". . . the hills are mulatto but also whitish. . . ."

"Meagre mulatto clay mixt with small broken stones. . . ."

This appears to be evidence of both a preoccupation and a problem. If, moreover, one contrasts this journal with another he kept when touring southern France in the spring of 1787, before Sally Hemings' disturbing mulatto presence had come to trouble him, one will see that in that account, numbering forty-eight pages, he uses the word *mulatto* only once. The rest of the time he describes the hills, plains, and earth as dark, reddish-brown, gray, dark-brown, and black.

There is another quotation, too, in Jefferson's Holland journal that bears repeating:

> The women here [in Holland], as in Germany, do all sorts of work. While one considers them as useful and rational companions, one cannot forget that they are also objects of our pleasures. Nor can they ever forget it. While employed in dirt and drudgery some tag of ribbon, some ring or bit of bracelet, earbob or necklace, or something of that kind will shew that the desire of pleasing is never suspended in them. . . . They are formed by nature for attentions and not for hard labour.

This is all very tender, and suggests that he was thinking not at all of the splendidly dressed Maria Cosway when he wrote it.

Upon his return to Paris, Jefferson found a letter from Maria Cosway reproaching him for not writing, which he had not done for three months. His reply was affectionate; he described his trip to Germany, and in mentioning the art gallery at Düsseldorf, he made what would seem to be a wholly unconscious confession of his new love:

> At Dusseldorpf I wished for you much. I surely never saw so precious a collection of paintings. Above all things those of Van der Werff affected me the most. His picture of Sarah delivering Agar

> to Abraham is delicious. I would have agreed to have been Abra-
> ham though the consequence would have been that I should
> have been dead five or six thousand years.

Hagar the Egyptian, it will be remembered, was Abraham's concubine,
given to him by his wife Sarah when she could not bear a child. Known
through legend as mother of the Ishmaelites, she was depicted by art-
ists as having a dark skin.

Jefferson continued in this letter to Maria Cosway: "I am but a son
of nature, loving what I see & feel, without being able to give a reason, nor caring much whether there be one." Shortly afterward he formulated what became the most provocative of all his moral directives
to society: "The earth belongs to the living and not to the dead." He
wrote this in a famous letter to James Madison on September 6, 1789,
repeating it in slightly different fashion: "The earth belongs always to
the living generation. . . . They are masters too of their own persons,
and consequently may govern them as they please."

In another fascinating letter, written to Maria Cosway on January
14, 1789, he described himself as "an animal of a warm climate, a
mere Oran-ootan." In 1789 the word *orang-utan* meant for most people not one of the great apes but "wild man of the woods," the literal
translation of the Malay words from which it is derived. There was
much confusion about the relation of the great apes to man; even the
gorilla was as yet unknown in Europe and America. In his *Notes on
the State of Virginia*, published only a few months before Sally Hemings' arrival, Jefferson had indiscreetly written that blacks preferred
white women, just as "the Oran-ootan" preferred "the black woman
over those of his own species." We do not know exactly what Jefferson conceived an "Oran-ootan" to be in 1787, but we do know that in
Paris on October 2, 1788, he sent away to his London bookseller for
a list of books which included E. Tyson's *Oran-outang, or an anatomy
of a pigmy* (1699), a work that tried to clarify the problem of whether
an orang-utan was an ape or a man. All of this would indicate that
Jefferson was suddenly uncomfortable about what he had written in
his book. And well he might be. For when the Federalist press in
America later heard rumors about his slave paramour, it needled Jefferson mercilessly on this very passage. For example, on September 29,
1802, the editor of the Frederick-Town, Virginia, *Herald* quoted from

Jefferson's *Notes*, adding that "by the same criterion he might be making himself out to be an 'Oranootan.' . . . there is merriment on the subject. . . ."

There is also what one might call "hard," as well as psychological, evidence that Jefferson was treating Sally Hemings with special consideration. A curious item for April 29, 1789, in Jefferson's Paris account book reads as follows:

$$
\begin{array}{r}
\text{pd Dupré 5 weeks board of Sally} \quad 105'' \\
\text{washing \&c} \quad \underline{41\text{-}9} \\
146\text{-}9
\end{array}
$$

This suggests the possibility that when Jefferson went to Holland and Germany he saw to it that Sally was properly chaperoned in a French home and not left as prey to the French servants in his ministry on the Champs Elysées. Jefferson's account book shows, too, that in April, 1789, he spent a surprising amount of money on Sally Hemings' clothes. His figures for that month include ninety-six francs for "clothes for Sally on April 6," seventy-two more on the sixteenth, and an additional twenty-three francs on the twenty-sixth for "making clothes for servts," which might also apply to her wardrobe. The total, including the last, was 191 francs, almost as much as the 215 francs he had spent on his daughter Martha the previous June.

The basic "proof" of the liaison, of course, would be Sally Hemings' pregnancy in Paris at age sixteen. To support this, we have the statement of her son Madison, who could have learned it only from his mother and who, perhaps, learned from her at the same time the French word for pregnant, *enceinte*. But there is additional evidence, for which one must jump ahead almost thirteen years to 1802, when Jefferson was President. Madison Hemings tells us that the child was born "soon after" their arrival back in America, which was in late October, 1789. On September 2, 1802, James T. Callender, co-editor of the Richmond *Recorder*, published the following:

> It is well known that the man, *whom it delighteth the people to honor*, keeps and for many years has kept, as his concubine, one of his slaves. Her name is SALLY. The name of her oldest is Tom. His features are said to bear a striking though sable resemblance to the president himself. The boy is ten or twelve years of age.

Most Jefferson biographers give the impression that Callender was a lying renegade who was determined to destroy Jefferson politically. It is true that he was obsessively a defamer of the great, and that after calling Jefferson a hero for some years he had turned against him venomously. But while Callender repeated and exaggerated scandal, he did not invent it. He had been the first to publish the story of Alexander Hamilton's affair with Mrs. Reynolds, which Hamilton later admitted. He was also the first to publish the ancient rumor that Jefferson before his own marriage had tried to seduce Betsey Walker, the wife of one of his best friends. Poor Jefferson, terribly besieged, and even threatened by Walker with a challenge to a duel in 1803, finally in 1805 admitted privately in a now-famous letter, "when young and single I offered love to a handsome lady; I acknolege its incorrectness."

Callender in 1802 was told by Jefferson's neighbors that Sally Hemings by then had borne Jefferson five children, and he reported this additional scandal in the *Recorder* on September 15. Though Jefferson's *Farm Book* records are scanty up to 1794, we know from scattered entries after that date that Sally Hemings bore four children from 1795 to 1802, and that two of them, both daughters, died in infancy. Once Callender broke the story, other newspapermen felt free to join the attack, and it soon became evident that some of them had been quietly circulating among themselves since 1800 the rumors that Jefferson had a slave mistress. Now those who had not heard of it began checking on their own.

The editor of the Lynchburg, Virginia, *Gazette*, who scolded Jefferson like an indignant parish vicar for not marrying a nice white girl, said that he had waited two months for a Presidential denial of Callender's charges, and then made inquiries and found "nothing but proofs of their authenticity." The Frederick-Town *Herald* editor wrote that he had waited three months before personally checking, and then concluded:

> Other information assures us that Mr. Jefferson's Sally and their children are real persons, and that the woman herself has a room to herself at Monticello in the character of semstress to the family, if not as house-keeper, that she is an industrious and orderly creature in her behaviour, but that her intimacy with her master is well known, and that on this account she is treated by the rest of his house as one much above the level of his other servants. Her son, whom Callender calls president Tom, we are assured, bears a strong likeness to Mr. Jefferson.

This description of Sally's position is very like that given by Madison Hemings:

> We were always permitted to be with our mother, who was well used. It was her duty all her life which I can remember, up to the time of father's death, to take care of his chamber and wardrobe, and look after us children and do such light work as sewing &c.

Jefferson's stauch editor friend, Meriwether Jones, in defending the President in the Richmond *Examiner* on September 25, 1802, made a rare and astonishing public admission that mulatto children were born by the thousands on southern plantations. He admitted also that there was a "mulatto child" at Monticello but denied that Jefferson was the father:

> That this servant woman has a child is very true. But that it is M. Jefferson's, or that the connection exists, which Callender mentions, *is false*—I call upon him for his evidence. . . .
> In gentlemen's houses everywhere, we know that the virtue of the unfortunate slaves is assailed with impunity. . . . Is it strange therefore, that a servant of Mr. Jefferson's at a house where so many strangers resort, who is daily engaged in the ordinary vocations of the family, like thousands of others, should have a mulatto child? Certainly not. . . .

John Adams, one of the few statesmen of the time who could testify firsthand about Sally Hemings' beauty, fully believed the Callender story. He said, privately, that it was "a natural and almost unavoidable consequence of that foul contagion in the human character—Negro slavery." But he found circulation of the story saddening. It is said that young John Quincy Adams wrote a ballad about the President and Sally, as did a great many other bad poets at the time.

Jefferson, despite enormous public and private pressure, made no public denial of either the Sally Hemings or the Mrs. Walker story. He insisted that he would not dignify calumny by answering it in the press, though actually he did delegate friends, to whom he supplied material, quietly, to write defenses on his behalf. We know he wrote at least one article during the crisis of these scandals and published it under the pseudonym Timoleon, but curiously it answered only one charge, both obscure and false, namely, that he had paid one Gabriel Jones a debt of £50 in depreciated currency.

There were other defenses made, however, that touched on Sally Hemings. William Burwell, Jefferson's private secretary in 1805, in an unpublished memoir now in the Library of Congress, tell us that at Jefferson's request he wrote a series of articles for the Richmond *Enquirer* in 1805 in reply to accusations of a Virginia plantation owner, Tom Turner, in the Boston *Repertory*. Turner had accused Jefferson of a whole list of misdemeanors, including the favorite Federalist canard that he had acted as a coward when, during the Revolution, the British invaded Virginia while he was governor of the state. Turner had also insisted that the Sally Hemings story was "unquestionably true." The Burwell articles, called "Vindication to Mr. Jefferson," appeared serially in the Richmond *Enquirer* in August and September of 1805. They consisted chiefly of a vigorous defense of Jefferson's wartime governorship. But of the slave-paramour charge Burwell, on September 27, 1805, said only that it was "below the dignity of a man of understanding."

Finally, in 1805, apparently under great pressure, Jefferson wrote a private letter, now missing, to his Attorney General, Levi Lincoln. In it, presumably, he answered more, possibly all, of the many charges being heaped upon him in the venomous Federalist press. He sent a copy to Robert Smith, Secretary of the Navy, on July 1, 1805, with a covering letter, part of which we have already quoted, in which he acknowledged offering love to Betsey Walker. But he then added that this story was "the only one founded in truth among all their allegations against me." Because of that statement, some Jefferson scholars believe that this covering letter is "a categorical denial" by Jefferson of the Sally Hemings story.

And yet the original letter to Levi Lincoln, the copy to Robert Smith, and presumably the letterpress copy Jefferson almost always made of his letters have all inexplicably disappeared. One wonders why. If this letter contained the denial Jefferson's friends had been hoping to see for almost three years, what became of it and the copies? The covering letter to Robert Smith is very ambiguous. Who knows exactly which "allegations against me" Jefferson had chosen to list in the missing letter? It is conceivable that this letter and its copies disappeared because there was something essentially and inadvertently damaging to Jefferson in them.

The story of the abuse heaped upon Jefferson during his Presidency

in regard to his intimate life has never been told in full detail. Nor
have the evidences of his anguished reaction to this abuse ever been
pieced together in such a fashion that one can see the extent of his
humiliation and his suffering. Nevertheless, despite the savagery of the
attacks, despite the dozen or so published pornographic ballads, Jefferson kept Sally Hemings and her children at Monticello. In 1805 and
1808 she bore two more sons.

Years later Thomas Jefferson Randolph, Jefferson's favorite grandson, who was born in 1792 and spent many summers at Monticello, in
effect growing up with Sally Hemings' children, talked to biographer
Henry Randall confidentially about the controversy. Randall reported
privately that Randolph described one of the children as looking so
much like Jefferson that "at some distance or in the dusk the slave,
dressed in the same way, might have been mistaken for Mr. Jefferson."
Since he was a house servant, Randall noted, "the likeness between
master and slave was blazoned to all the multitudes who visited this
political mecca." When Randall asked Randolph why Jefferson did not
send this family away from Monticello to another of his plantations,
the grandson replied that though "he had no doubt his mother would
have been very glad to have them thus removed," still "all venerated
Mr. Jefferson too deeply to broach such a topic to him," and "he never
betrayed the least consciousness of the resemblance."

One is reminded here of Tolstoi, also a great egalitarian, who had an
illegitimate son by a serf on his estate before marrying the Countess
Sophia. This son became Tolstoi's coachman—similarly visible for
everyone to see. But he was never educated like Tolstoi's numerous
legitimate children nor made part of the inner family.

Both Thomas Jefferson Randolph and his sister, Ellen Randolph
Coolidge, blamed their uncles, Peter and Samuel Carr, instead of their
grandfather, for the paternity of Sally Hemings' children. Randolph
told Randall in all seriousness that he himself had "slept within sound
of his [Jefferson's] breathing at night," and "had never seen a motion,
or a look, or a circumstance" that was suspicious. Still, in an article
about his grandfather, he wrote that Jefferson's bedroom-study was his
sanctum sanctorum, and that even his own daughters never sat in it.

In the end, much evidence is contained in the history of Sally Hemings' seven children. Despite the strenuous "family denial" and the
secrecy Jefferson himself, not surprisingly, seems to have encouraged,

a considerable amount of information is available about them. Ellen Randolph Coolidge, in discussing the "yellow children" at Monticello in an unpublished letter, wrote that she knew of her "own knowledge" that Jefferson permitted "each of his slaves as were sufficiently white to pass for white to withdraw quietly from the plantation; it was called running away, but they were never reclaimed." "I remember," she wrote, "four instances of this, three young men and a girl, who walked away and staid away—their whereabouts was perfectly known but they were left to themselves—for they were white enough to pass for white."

Tom

There are three runaways listed in Jefferson's *Farm Book*. Jamy, son of Critta Hemings, born in 1787 when Jefferson was still in Paris, ran away in April, 1804. Beverly and Harriet, two children of Sally Hemings, ran away in 1822. It is possible that the fourth runaway referred to by Ellen Coolidge was the oldest son of Sally Hemings, the one Callender derisively called "president Tom." Though he is described in the newspapers of 1802 as resembling Jefferson, in one respect he remains the most mysterious of all Sally Hemings' children because he is not listed in the *Farm Book* under the name of his mother, as are the others. Since there are at least six different slaves named Tom recorded at various times in the *Farm Book*, only one listed with a birth year, absolute identification of "Tom Hemings" in this old record is not possible.

Jefferson listed his slaves first in 1774, again in 1783, but not again till 1794. During his Presidency, 1801 through March, 1809, he neglected his *Farm Book* altogether. Almost all his slaves are listed by first name only except Betty, Peter, and John Hemings and two or three others, including an old slave, Tom Shackleford. Sally Hemings is easily identified, both by her birth year, 1773, and by the names of her children, listed and indented under her own, at least when they were small. Of the several slaves in the *Farm Book* named Tom, one appears frequently among the Hemings family slaves, which are usually listed together. He does not appear on the official inventories of 1794, 1798, and 1810, but shows up consistently on the food and clothing distribution lists from 1794 to 1801. It can be argued that this "Tom" represents Tom Shackleford without his last name. If true, then it would seem that Jefferson did not choose to list Sally Hemings' oldest son regularly among his slaves and may have considered him free from birth.

Martha Jefferson Randolph mentions a "Tom" in a letter to her father on January 22, 1798, describing an epidemic of sickness in the neighborhood:

> Our intercourse with Monticello has been almost *daily*. They have generally been well there except Tom and Goliah who are both *about* again and poor little Harriot who died a few days after you left us.

This "Harriot," we know from *Farm Book* entries, was Sally Hemings' daughter, and the "Tom" may have been her son. There were two slaves named Goliah at Monticello, one an old man and the other a child of seven.

There are no listings in the *Farm Book* between 1801 and 1810. By this time Tom Shackleford had died, but there are several listings of a "hired" Tom in 1810 and 1811. One can speculate that this was "Tom Hemings," and that he was by then old enough for regular wages. Since no slave named Tom appears after 1811 in the *Farm Book*, it is possible that Sally Hemings' son left Monticello in that year, when he was twenty-one. This would have been a fulfillment of Jefferson's promise to Sally, as described by her son Madison.

Madison Hemings, who was born in 1805, makes no mention of an older brother Tom. It is possible that the "president Tom" who was the subject of all the ribald publicity from 1802 through 1805 was persuaded to leave the shelter of Monticello after he became old enough to make the transition into white society on his own. Even in 1805 he would have been fifteen, old enough to leave. He could have returned for the summers of 1810 and 1811, long enough to appear in various distribution lists. Madison Hemings wrote that the child his mother conceived in France "lived but a short time." Here he is obviously confusing him with the two small daughters who died in 1796 and 1797. It is conceivable that Sally Hemings, burned by the scandal-mongering publicity of 1802–5, chose not to discuss this son with anyone after his departure and made every effort to protect his identity in the white society by a mantle of silence. Such behavior is common even today among relatives of a black who "passes."

HARRIET AND EDY

Jefferson was in political semiretirement at Monticello from January 16, 1794, to February 20, 1797. He wrote to Edward Rutledge on November 30, 1795, "Your son . . . found me in a retirement I doat on, living like an Antediluvian patriarch among my children & grandchildren, and tilling my soil. . . ." The celebrated French rationalist, Comte de Volney, a fugitive from the French Revolution, visited Jefferson in Monticello in 1796. He noted in his journal some astonishment at seeing slave children as white as himself: *"Mais je fus étonné de voir appeler noirs et traiter comme tels des enfants aussi blancs que moi."* They resulted, he said, from miscegenation between mulatto slave women and the white workmen Jefferson hired. But were some of these children in fact Jefferson's?

Two daughters were born to Sally Hemings during this temporary retirement: Harriet, on October 5, 1795, and Edy, whose name is listed twice in 1796 in the *Farm Book* under Sally's name and then disappears. Edy, it can be assumed, died in 1796, since she appears in no slave listings under her mother's name thereafter. We know that Harriet died in 1797, not only because she disappears from *Farm Book* listings after that year, but also by Martha Jefferson's report in January, 1798, already quoted. If Jefferson wrote a letter of sympathy to Sally Hemings, there is no record of it. What has been preserved is his reply to Martha, a letter of such melancholy that it suggests something more than peripheral involvement. He said in part:

> Indeed I feel myself detaching very fast, perhaps too fast, from every thing but yourself, your sister, and those who are identified with you. These form the last hold the world will have on me, the cords which will be cut only when I am loosened from this state of being. I am looking forward to the spring with all the fondness of desire to meet you all once more. . . .

BEVERLY

Beverly, a son, was born to Sally Hemings on April 1, 1798, eight months and twenty days after Jefferson's arrival in Monticello from Philadelphia on July 11, 1797. We know nothing of Beverly's youth except a tantalizing reference in the reminiscences of the Monticello slave named Isaac, who referred to "the balloon that Beverley sent off," and the fact that he is listed as a runaway at age twenty-four. Madison Hemings wrote that "Beverly left Monticello and went to Washington as a white man. He married a white woman in Maryland, and their only child, a daughter, was not known by the white folks to have any colored blood coursing in her veins. Beverly's wife's family were people in good circumstances." All of this suggests that Beverly had some schooling at Monticello and could have had some financial assistance from Jefferson, as did his sister Harriet.

HARRIET (No. 2)

A second Harriet, named after the child that died in 1797, was born in May, 1801, and it must be noted that Jefferson was in Monticello from May 29 to November 24, 1800. Harriet was listed as a runaway in the *Farm Book* in 1822. Edmund Bacon, an overseer at Monticello, said later of this slave girl:

> He [Jefferson] freed one girl some years before he died, and there was a great deal of talk about it. She was nearly as white as anybody and very beautiful. People said he freed her because she was his own daughter. She was not his daughter: she was _____'s daughter. I know that. I have seen him come out of her mother's room many a morning when I went up to Monticello very early. When she was nearly grown, by Mr. Jefferson's direction I paid her stage fare to Philadelphia and gave her fifty dollars. I have never seen her since and don't know what became of her. From the time she was large enough, she always worked in the cotton factory. She never did any hard work.

Bacon, however, did not come to Monticello as overseer till 1806, after six of Sally's seven children were born, and he never lived in the big house.

Madison Hemings wrote of his sister Harriet with a touch of irony:

> Harriet married a white man in good standing in Washington City, whose name I could give, but will not, for prudential reasons. She raised a family of children, and so far as I know they were never suspected of being tainted with African blood in the community where she lived or lives. I have not heard from her for ten years, and do not know whether she is dead or alive.

MADISON

Madison Hemings, named after James Madison, was born January 19, 1805. Jefferson was not in Monticello at his birth, but had been there from April 4 to May 11, 1804. Madison's reminiscences, on the whole remarkable for their accuracy of detail concerning Monticello, show evidence of considerable education, though he insists he learned to read "by inducing the white cihldren to teach me." Of his relations with Jefferson he writes in his memoir:

> He was uniformly kind to all about him. He was not in the habit of showing partiality or fatherly affection to us children. We were the only children of his by a slave woman. He was affectionate toward his white grandchildren, of whom he had fourteen, twelve of whom lived to manhood and womanhood.

The slave Isaac in his reminiscences reported that "Sally had a son named Madison, who learned to be a great fiddler," but we do not know whether it was Jefferson, himself an able violinist, who taught the young slave who claimed to be his son. Freed by Jefferson in his will, Madison lived for a time with his mother (by then also free) in Albermarle County, Virginia, married a free black woman in 1834, and after his mother's death in 1835 went west to Ohio, where he made his living as a carpenter.

ESTON

Jefferson was in Monticello from August 4 to October 1, 1807. Eston Hemings was born May 21, 1808. As with Beverly, Harriet, and Madison, his name appears many times in the *Farm Book* under the name of Sally Hemings. He was one of the five slaves freed in Jefferson's will, all of whom were members of the Hemings family. Madison Hemings wrote that Eston married a free black woman, immigrated to Ohio, and then went on to Wisconsin.

Jefferson's will contained the request that the Virginia legislature be petitioned to permit Madison and Eston Hemings to stay in the state if they so chose. Otherwise, by Virginia law, which barred free Negroes, they would automatically have been banished. Still, it must be noted, by Jefferson's own reckoning, based on Virginia's legal definitions of the time, these youths were white. When a friend wrote to him in 1815 asking at what point a black man officially changes into a white man, Jefferson replied explicitly, "Our canon considers two crosses with the pure white, and a third with any degree of mixture, however small, as clearing the issue of negro blood. . . ."

And what, in the end, was "the condition" of Sally Hemings? Jefferson did not free her in his will, but left this service for his daughter Martha to perform, which she did two years after Jefferson's death in 1826. Had Jefferson freed her during his lifetime and made the necessary request from the Virginia legislature that she be allowed to remain in the state, the news would have been trumpeted over the nation. This publicity he was probably unwilling to subject himself to, and it is conceivable that Sally Hemings never requested it. Still, it is a melancholy discovery to find her listed on the official inventory of Jefferson's estate, made after his death, as an "old woman" worth thirty dollars. She was then fifty-three.

Madison Hemings wrote that his mother lived with him and Eston Hemings in a rented house until her death in 1835. The U.S. Census of Albermarle County in 1830 listed Eston Hemings as head of a family, and as a white man. The other members of this family are listed under his name by age and sex only, as was traditional at the time. There is a listing of a woman—fifty to sixty years of age—described as white. This is Sally Hemings. So the census taker, in making this small descriptive decision, underlined the irony and tragedy of her life.

As for Jefferson, he had watched with increasing despair over the years as Virginia permitted slavery to expand and as the laws controlling slaves became ever more repressive. He had seen the social degradation imposed upon Sally Hemings' five living children by the taboos and rituals of the slave society in which he was inextricably enmeshed. So rigid were these taboos that he could not admit these children to be his own, even when they passed into white society, without social ostracism and political annihilation. Whether one believes they were his children or not, one cannot deny that he paid dearly for their presence on that enchanted hill. He could not abandon the slave society in Virginia if he would, and he would not if he could. Overwhelmed at the end with a crushing burden of debt—$107,000—he could not find his way to free in his will more than five of his hundred-odd slaves. He had lived almost half of his life, in the phrase he used to describe himself to Maria Cosway at age seventy-seven, "like a patriarch of old." And so his ambivalence—which may well have served to lessen for him the sense of the tragedy of it all—was continually compounded.

How They Built the Erie Canal

LYNWOOD MARK RHODES

• Founded in 1625 by the Dutch, New York (or New Amsterdam as it was then called) was the first "city" to be established in the thirteen original colonies. But Manhattan was soon overshadowed by Boston, which was founded by John Winthrop and the Puritans in 1630, and by Philadelphia, which was founded by William Penn in 1682. Not until about 1800 did New York re-establish itself as the first city of the New World.

The Hudson River metropolis owed its national primacy to its magnificent port, which soon became the busiest in the world, and to the energy of its entrepreneurs, who introduced the concept of regularly scheduled packet service to Europe and to other ports along the Atlantic Coast. By 1830, New York was already uniquely a city of business and had acquired an international reputation as a center of frenetic hustle and bustle.

An important contributor to the growth of New York, which by 1860 had almost a million inhabitants and was one of the largest cities on earth, was the Erie Canal. Financed by commercial interests in Manhattan and sponsored by the state of New York, the canal stretched 364 miles through the wilderness between Albany and Buffalo and connected with the Hudson River thereby providing New York City with an all water route to the west. Almost immediately after its opening in 1825 it showed profits, and, ultimately, the Erie Canal exerted a greater influence on the economic development of the United States than any other single public improvement. Not surprisingly, other cities and states launched similar projects in the next generation, and the country as a whole experienced a speculative craze for canal construction

From *The American Legion Magazine* (June 1974), pp. 10–15, 38, 40, 42. Copyright 1974. Reprinted by permission.

that fostered urban growth and expanded the national economy.

To build a canal in 1817 connecting the Hudson River at Albany with Lake Erie at Buffalo—a span of 363 miles—was as momentous an undertaking as going to the moon in the 1960's. In some ways it was a greater challenge, since we lacked the supplies, the knowledge, the manpower, the equipment, some of the raw materials and the engineers. Each challenge was met only after work on the canal was under way.

The results of building the Erie Canal were immeasurable. It opened the West to large-scale east-west commerce and passenger traffic in a roadless, railless era. It guaranteed the supremacy of New York City as the largest port and commercial capital of the country.

In its time, the Erie Canal was the greatest engineering feat ever known in America. The chief tools were picks, shovels and the muscle of a working force which was virtually immobilized at one point by malaria. A great deal of the work was let out to farmers along the route. In a nation of farmers and tradesmen, every man was his own engineer. The only engineering school in the land was the U.S. Military Academy at West Point, which had been charged in 1802 with teaching cadets to create the budding Army Corps of Engineers.

The chief engineer of the Erie canal was Benjamin Wright, an Oneida county judge who'd been interested in canals for 25 years and who was also a competent surveyor. He was assisted by James Geddes and Charles Broadhead, whose qualifications were similar. No plans were drawn for the canal—Wright had them in his head. After the canal had been started, a stretch was filled with water and it leaked. When it came time to plan the locks, it was discovered that cement would be needed. There was none in America. Rivers and creeks ran directly across the path of the canal. At the western end its route faced the 1,100-foot Niagara Escarpment—through which the Niagara River tumbles from Lake Erie to Lake Ontario. This obstacle was almost twice as high as the 565 feet the canal had to rise from the level of the Hudson to that of Lake Erie. When the project began, it wasn't clear how the rivers would be crossed or how the Niagara obstacle would be surmounted.

Nevertheless, New York Governor DeWitt Clinton was determined that the canal should proceed. Clinton had three things going for him —he combined guts with the qualities of a shrewd politician and a visionary. He dinned it into the New York legislature and all of the business heads of New York State that when the early trickle of western commerce floated down the Great Lakes to Buffalo and was wagonned around Niagara to Lake Ontario, it was proceeding down the St. Lawrence to Montreal, and thence to Europe. This commerce would grow forever, he warned, yet it could easily be enticed away from the Canadian winter ices and the overland haul around Niagara if a canal should provide an easier, cheaper, all-water route through New York to Albany and thence down the Hudson to New York City.

This was extremely persuasive. But the appraisal offered by Benjamin Wright, after surveying the route for the N.Y. Joint Commission on Canals, was frightening for those times.

There were less than a dozen canals in the young republic. The longest was the 27-mile Middlesex canal between Boston harbor and the Merrimack River. The Middlesex took nine years to build and cost Massachusetts a cool million dollars—more like a billion in today's money. Wright and Clinton were talking about 363 miles and a $5 million price tag. Some legislators said that Clinton and his Commission were "exalted in the head," or just plain nuts. The $5 million was staggering, yet seemed a gross underestimate—for the Erie would be nearly 14 times as long as the Middlesex and quite possibly more expensive per mile. It ought to cost more than $14 million in 1817 money.

Nevertheless, Clinton said it wouldn't and the commercial promise of the canal carried the day. On April 15, 1817, the state assembly passed the canal bill by 64 to 36, and before sunset the state senate approved it by 18 to 9. It was by far the biggest and costliest public project yet undertaken in the United States. One law-maker called it "a monument to folly that will mortgage us forever," but Clinton promptly promised that it would be finished in less than ten years— or as fast as the Middlesex had been built. Cynics called it "Clinton's Ditch" and Wright was astonished at the timetable the governor had "volunteered" for him.

Bids went out for excavating the channel before the end of April and the first contracts were awarded in May. From a canal basin at Albany, where boats would enter the Hudson, the proposed channel— 40 feet wide at the surface, 28 at the bottom, and four feet deep— pointed northward a few miles to Troy, then struck out westward up the Mohawk Valley for Schenectady, Amsterdam, Canajoharie, Little Falls, Herkimer, Utica, Rome, Syracuse, the Montezuma marshes, Lyons and Rochester before finally terminating at Buffalo. To overcome the 565-foot difference in level between the Hudson and Lake Erie would require 83 locks, each 90 feet long and 15 feet wide—27 of them in the first 15 miles just to get around Cohoes Falls. The canal could simply mingle its waters with many smaller streams, letting them flow in one side and out the other, while borrowing such water from them as might be needed. But it would have to bridge larger rivers 18 times, to cross them in masonry aqueducts the way modern freeways bridge other highways. The Niagara problem would be faced when necessary.

Clinton and his supporters wanted as much ditch as they could get as fast as possible. They were of no mind to let the legislature and the public get cold feet while locks and aqueducts were slowly being constructed. So they began to dig close to the middle, where the going was easiest.

On July 4, 1817, contractor John Richardson ceremoniously broke the first ground at Rome, N.Y., while cannon boomed and a cornet band played. Rome was about mid-point of the Long Level, one of the two soft-earth stretches, each about 62 miles long, which needed no locks or extensive cutting through rock. With a little bit of luck, Clinton knew he would have something to show the voters by year's end.

Many of the contractors were local farmers who hoped to improve their slack season by excavating a portion of the canal. The idea was to spread the work—always good politics. Some contracts were let for sections as short as a quarter of a mile. "While my contract may not make me a millionaire-man," one Rome farmer noted, "I look to touch a pretty profit on it."

The state paid ten cents (sometimes more, sometimes less, depending on the terrain and the obstacles along the way) for every cubic yard of earth excavated—which meant that one could earn roughly

$3,000 for finishing a mile of canal. He furnished his own tools and hired his own labor, but farm hands jumped at the chance to work "on the line" for $8 per month, maybe as high as $12 for an extra muscular shovel-slinger. To country boys used to being paid $10 a month in anything but cash for farm work, the very thought of digging a ditch for real money was mind-boggling.

Fifteen miles of canal with a towpath ten feet wide and retaining banks, called "berms," were done when an early winter halted work in October. This wasn't bad, considering that nobody on the job knew much about canal building. But it meant that 30 miles a year (beginning in April instead of July) was par for the course for the easiest construction.

If it were all that easy it would take 12 years to finish the job. Add lock and aqueduct construction plus digging in more difficult terrain ahead, and Clinton's Ditch would never be ready in "less than ten years." It was obvious that more workers and more experience were needed to finish the job on schedule. Wright sent 26-year-old Canvass White to Britain to study English canal techniques, especially lock construction. He'd noticed that White, a surveyor from Oneida County, had a flair for things mechanical. It was one of the wisest decisions he ever made.

A potato famine in Ireland solved the labor problem. Rich Irish contractors of Tammany Hall brought over hordes of penniless, half-starved young Irishmen. As indentured men, they paid for their passage by putting their sweat and muscle into the Erie in the spring of 1818—for 50¢ a day plus board and lodging.

"'Mohawks and Senecas we have survived," a Rome housewife told her diary, "but these strange people look fitter for crime than for honest work. I mis-doubt that we shall find ourselves murdered in our beds one fine morning." The newcomers probably did look strange to American eyes. Their speech certainly sounded strange to American ears, but edgy farmers soon put their shotguns away. It was the immigrants who were scared. Owl and wildcat music echoing from the woods— "the devil's own choir," some said—kept them awake at night and the story goes that the whole lot almost deserted when the first snake wiggled into camp. "The ould sod" this wasn't.

Work in 1818 proceeded in both directions, one crew aiming east from Syracuse while another dug west from Frankfort. Sunrise to sunset, six days a week, dirt flew and berms rose out of the ground as 3,000 sweating, cursing men narrowed the gap during the long, hot summer. More and more New Yorkers left their farms and flocked to the canal, eager for some of the hard cash. Unknowingly, they brought along the one thing that the Erie needed most and money couldn't buy—a priceless quality called Yankee ingenuity.

Instead of grubbing out underbrush, some forgotten genius attached a horizontal cutting blade to a plowshare so he could dig and shear at the same time. Another man attached one end of a cable high on a tree and the other end to a roller turned by a crank and an endless screw. This arrangement provided such tremendous leverage that he could topple over a tree of almost any size single-handed. John Brainard, of Rome, even invented a new wheelbarrow. Unlike the long-popular, squaresided box that Leonardo da Vinci first dreamed up centuries before, his had bottom and sides made from a single board bent to a semicircular shape, which made it lighter and far easier to handle. Farmers near Syracuse tinkered with a device called a stumppuller—two huge wheels connected by a 30-foot-long axle with a third wheel spoked into the axle's middle. They firmly braced the big wheels, wrapped a rope around the middle one to produce an eight-fold gain in power, and hooked the stump to it with a heavy chain. A team of husky horses tugged at the rope and "yanked the stump out as neatly as a dentist pulls a tooth." Seven men and two horses could grub up 30 to 40 stumps with it a day.

All but five miles of the Long Level were ready for water when the ground froze in December. Fifty-seven miles had been dug in two years. Shortly before closing for the year, Wright let in water to test a short stretch of the canal. It leaked. Four feet of water pressure was simply too much for the dirt berms no matter how well-packed and tramped. Fortunately, Canvass White had returned from England that fall after hiking 2,000 miles of British towpaths. British engineers prevented seepage by lining berms with clay, he reported, and there was plenty of clay along the Erie, especially a variety called "the blue mud of the meadows." Doubting workmen slapped some of the muck over the gaping holes, wiped their sticky hands on their breeches, stepped back—and blinked in amazement. Word quickly went up and down the line. Layer the inner sides of the crumbling embankment with blue mud. It made a perfect seepage-stopper.

"But what about the locks?" Wright asked. If built of wood, they would rot away in a few years. Canvass White agreed. The English, he said, used stone blocks sealed with hydraulic cement, which is the ordinary Portland cement from which we make most of our concrete today. Wright's staff blanched at the suggestion. There was no such cement in America. All of it came from England, an expense beyond the Erie's budget. They reluctantly decided to construct the locks of stone, putting the blocks together with common quicklime mortar and merely "pointing up" the joints with the costly imported cement.

Canvass shuddered at holding water under pressure with mortar. Maybe, he said, he might find a deposit of trass—a volcanic pumice that was the principal ingredient of hydraulic cement—somewhere in New York State. He scoured the countryside that winter poking here and digging there. No luck. Nothing but ice, dirt and more dirt. He was about to quit when he fingered a gray substance near Chittenango, a village on the canal line. He roasted a handful of it that night, pulverized it, mixed it with sand, formed it into a ball, and put it in a bucket of water. It was solid as a rock the next morning. The "genius of the Erie Canal," as historians later pegged him, had just made the first hydraulic cement in America.

Good fortune turned sour in 1819 when Irish workers tackled the Montezuma swamp west of Syracuse. Its smell was enough to turn a man's stomach, but the workmen shucked their pants and, "wearing naught but a flannel shirt and a slouch hat" as shields against the boiling summer sun, plodded into the knee-deep muck. They scooped it out, drove long spikes down through the mire to firm ground, nailed planks alongside the stakes to make a sort of retaining wall, and built up berms with heavy dirt carted from Syracuse. A jiggerman waded by every hour with a tot of whiskey to keep them going—and to ease the pain of ungluing the leeches that sucked at their swelling legs. The nicknames they gave the worst stretches said it all—Digger's Misery, Breakback Bog, Bottomless Pit, Mud-turtles' Delight. Still, Wright believed they would cross the 11-mile-wide swamp by fall.

The Cayuga Indians knew better. "When the black moschetto stands so upon the wall," a Cayuga warned Canvass, bunching his fingers to make his palm stand like a mosquito on long legs, "men will shake and burn and die." No one paid much attention to the prediction until July when the grubbers abruptly dropped their tools and lurched back to the bunkhouses, retching and swatting "clouds of mosquitoes as thick as maggots on a cow's carcass" as they went. A great many feverish laborers died of malaria in August. Ads soon filled the newspapers: "MEN WANTED at once for the Cayuga marshes. Top pay, no wet feet, no disease." And no takers. "Whiskey every night if you get the shakes," an Albany contractor promised prospective diggers. "And a pine box in the morning," a hollow voice replied.

Critics jeered that the "Governor's Gutter" was sunk forever in the ooze and slime of Montezuma. But in late September, as suddenly as it began, the sickness ended. Bleary-eyed workers picked up their shovels again. Little did they realize that cold weather froze out the malaria-carrying Anopheles mosquito. They were just thankful to be alive in the wake of the "Montezuma shakes." In spite of all the common-sense evidence, it was nearly a century before mosquitoes were recognized as the carriers of the disease.

Clinton resorted to a bit of showmanship to dispel rumors that the Erie had suffered a serious setback. On October 22, 1819, sluice gates opened and water poured into the channel between Rome and Utica. A gaily decorated boat, aptly named *Chief Engineer of Rome* in Wright's honor and towed by a single horse "sailed" down to Utica that afternoon in four hours and back up to Rome the next—without once scraping bottom. The Erie was becoming a reality after all.

Laborers finishing the swamp-crossing in 1820 before the mosquitoes swarmed. Work then started on both the eastern and western sections. Nothing seemed too daring now. At Little Falls, slabs of solid rock blocked the route. Wright figured chiseling would take three years, but the cream of the work force blew out a channel in less than three months using a new explosive called DuPont's Blasting Powder. It was only a crude forerunner of dynamite, perfected by Alfred Nobel more than 40 years later, but it served. "We went through that rock like mice through a cheese," a proud blaster announced. In its lowest 30 miles, between Schenectady and Albany, the canal made its most precipitous plunge, a dive of 218 feet. Masons threw up 27 locks in the cramped Mohawk gorge, lacing the gates with Canvass White's home-grown cement. Where needed, they built aqueducts supporting a towpath and a water-filled flume of timber which was, in fact, the canal itself. The Crescent Aqueduct, which by-passed Cohoes Falls a dozen miles from Albany, crossed from the south to the north side of the meandering Mohawk River on 26 stone piers and carried barge traffic 25 feet above the river's high-water level. It was an incredible 1,188 feet long.

Workmen bridged the turbulent Genesee River at Rochester with an aqueduct bolted and bound with iron that stretched 802 feet and had 11 masonry arches, nine of them 50 feet across. It was the longest arched bridge in America. Not far east of Rochester they grappled with the deep valley of Irondequoit Creek by throwing up an earthen, stone-faced embankment that was 70 feet high and a quarter-mile long. The canal and townpath ran on top and the creek ran through a culvert beneath it.

"There was a great deal more to the canal than met the eye," writes historian Ralph Andrist. "It was laid out so that there were streams or lakes to supply water for operating locks and to replace evaporation and leakage. The feeders bringing in this water required an elaborate system of gates and sluices, and formed a great network of small branch canals on which farmers could bring their butter and bacon by skiff to the Erie. There were waste weirs to discharge excess water in times of flood; there were more than 300 bridges that had to be built where the canal cut farmers' lands in two; and there were weigh-locks at principal points to determine toll charges."

They saved the worst for last.

Nathan Roberts, a self-taught "engineer" in charge of the western section, cringed when he stuck a metal-tipped surveyor's rod down into the thin soil at the summit of the Niagara Escarpmen. "Well, there it is," he recalled telling the fidgety contractors. "Seven miles of limestone and flint, 30 feet thick and harder than a tax collector's heart. There is no way around it. We can't carry the water over the top. We've got to go through it. What do you propose?" A man from Batavia threw down his rod. "I propose to go home and dig my potatoes."

Roberts ordered $500 worth of blasting powder from the DuPonts instead. Experienced Irish blasters from Little Falls taught the workers how to use the black stuff, but bandaged heads were a common sight. Over-zealous blowers often didn't "hug dirt" until all the flying pieces of stone whined past. They kept at the job just the same, cutting a deep, straight trough through the ridge with explosions that "sounded like Independence Day, Muster Day and the thunders of Doomsday all in one."

Everywhere else on the canal there were only single locks. At the eastern extremity of the Niagara obstacle, Roberts built the famous stair-stepped Lockport Five—double sets of five locks with 12-foot lifts —that simultaneously allowed boats to ascend and descend the canal's 60-foot rise, passing side by side to avoid traffic tie-ups. The long staircase of the lock gates created the impression of a five-tiered waterfall. When viewed from the bottom locks, one man said, two horses standing at the top of the cataract looked "like statues in the sky." Engineers marvel even today at how Roberts conjured up such a homespun masterpiece, much less built it with the tools at hand.

It took two years to burrow through the seven miles of cruel rock and to raise the awesome "Fives." But when the canal came out of its man-made gorge on the far side in 1825, jubilant Irishmen and strutting Yankees had every right to be proud. In less than ten years, just as predicted, the Great Western Canal sparkled with water from end to end. Few men have ever accomplished so much with so little in so short a time. The actual cost, including interest on the bonds, was a little over $7 million.

Wednesday, October 26, 1825, was a glorious day in Buffalo. It was eight years, six months and 11 days since the legislature had approved the project. More than 1,000 pushing and shoving spectators lined the breezy waterfront, anxious to see the ribboncutting ceremony that put the first practical transportation link between East and West in business, so that you could float a cargo from Chicago to New York. The noise was deafening. Drummers thumped, fifes whistled, hawkers screamed their wares. The most popular souvenirs were saucers and silk handkerchiefs stamped with replicas of Clinton and the Lockport locks. The local militia fired so many musket volleys "that even Perry might wonder if the War of 1812 had been re-declared."

Precisely at ten o'clock, Clinton clambered up a ladder to the cabin roof of the elegant red cedar packet *Seneca Chief* moored at dockside and raised his hands for silence. "The Erie Canal is declared open to navigation for its entire course, from Buffalo to Albany," he bellowed like a proud father. "May it serve the noble purpose for which the citizens of this State have built it." The packet cast off its lines and four silver-harnessed horses guided by two 16-year-old drivers slowly towed it past the cheering throngs to the canal entrance where a shivering choir sang a dedicatory anthem set to the tune of "Hail Columbia."

Most people were gaping at the two paintings draped over the packet's sides—one picturing Buffalo's soon-to-be bustling harbor, the other depicting Clinton as Hercules resting from his labors.

Aboard the flagship were beaver-hatted legislators and Wright and his staff, plus a cargo of pot ashes from Detroit, flour and butter from Ohio, and two gilded maple kegs filled with Lake Erie water. Behind it came other craft. The *Young Lion of the West* was as good as a circus. Its deckside cargo included a pair of eagles, several wolves, a fox, a faun, and four raccoons. *Noah's Ark* swung into line with a black bear and two Seneca Indian lads at the railing, followed by the *Commodore Perry*, *Superior* and *Buffalo*—all top-heavy with dignitaries making the first trip down to salt water.

There was no telegraph in those days. But a row of cannon spaced within earshot of each other stretched all the way to New York City. Buffalo artillerymen began the "Grand Salute" when the little flotilla entered the canal. Gunners ten miles away pulled their lanyards. A salvo answered in the east and passed the word along. The booms traveled the width of the state in 81 minutes flat. New York City returned the salute in 80 minutes. It was possibly the fastest transmission of long-distance news that the world had ever known.

Celebrating crowds greeted the cavalcade at every town and village along the canal. A 24-gun salute welcomed the hoarse speechmakers when they finally reached the Hudson at Albany on November 2nd. Two days later steamboats towed the *Seneca Chief* out to Sandy Hook at the entrance to New York harbor for the historic "wedding of the waters."

Two visiting British men-of-war and nearly every boat in New York harbor formed "a great circle three miles in circumference," a newsman reported, as Clinton opened his kegs of Lake Erie water and poured the contents overboard "to indicate and commemorate," in his words, "the navigable communication which has been established between our Mediterranean Sea and the Atlantic Ocean." Dr. Samuel Mitchell, the nation's foremost geographer, blessed the marriage by emptying vials of water gathered from the world's great rivers—the Nile, Ganges, Mississippi, Thames, Rhine and Danube among others—to symbolize the opening of commerce from the interior of America with nations in every part of the globe. The Britishers gave three cheers and played "Yankee Doodle." Bandsmen from West Point responded with "God Save the King." One listener remarked that both melodies sounded somewhat "off-key since neither was familiar with the other's hymns," but most on-lookers were too giddy from the heady experience to argue.

The best was yet to come.

Grain, foodstuffs, timber and furs funneled into Albany, lured by the shortcut and freight rates of $7.50 a ton from Buffalo in eight days instead of the former $100 a ton by wagon in 20 days. Towns with nautical names sprouted like mustard seed in a wet summer all along the canal—Gasport, Brockport, Port Gibson, Middleport. A Buffalo man sold two lots along the Niagara River for $20,000. He'd paid $200 for them in 1815. Rochester mushroomed into the nation's flour-milling center, its population jumping from 33 in 1817 to 13,000 by the time the Big Ditch was three years old. There was even talk of moving the capital to bustling Syracuse, which only two decades before had been such a desolate spot that "it would make an owl weep to fly over it." Toll collections in just nine years amounted to $8,500,-000—more than enough to pay off the canal's construction and interest charges of $7,143,789 by 1833.

Westward-looking Americans who wouldn't risk overland travel pulled up stakes, canaled up to Buffalo, and boarded steamers for the Great Lakes region and "God's country" beyond. Out there, they heard, land sold for $1.25 an acre, "corn grew 15 feet tall, and more peaches and apples rotted on the ground than would sink the British fleet." The Erie's magnetism all but emptied entire New England hill towns. "America Fever" spread overseas and swarms of immigrants joined the exodus. "Those who reside upon the Erie Canal," a bemused Lockport editor wrote, "must have thought that Europe was moving to this country, or at least the German states." Some 50,000 settlers were making the trip annually by 1830. "Probably no other single achievement in transportation had such decisive effects upon American history," says historian Don Fehrenbacher.

Horsedrawn packet boats traveled day and night. By changing animals every 12 miles or so they made it from Schenectady (where most passengers boarded) to Buffalo in four to six days, averaging 80 to 100 miles daily. The fare was four cents a mile with meals, three cents without. Immigrants riding freight boats paid only a penny a mile and furnished their own food. At first they streaked along at five miles an hour. But wakes washed the berms so badly that the state soon posted a speed limit—four miles an hour.

Most boats measured 80 by 14 feet, just long and wide enough to navigate the locks. Their height was limited by bridges along the way. A low-ceiling "saloon" extended the length of a passenger boat's deck and was the dining room by day. After supper, bench beds folded out from the walls and above them two tiers of frames suspended from the ceiling passed for hammocks. A drop-screen curtain separated the men from the women. Some companies wedged in as many as 150 sleepers per haul, "packed away like dead pigs in a Cincinnati porkhouse." Ventilation was nonexistent and "all night long there was a perfect storm of snoring and a tempest of spitting," one man said. Worse yet, sometimes a hammock broke. "A stout heavy man was too much for the well-worn canvas above me," an unfortunate lower-bunker recalled. "It gave way under the weightiest part of his form, which descended till it found support on my chest. Only the thrust of my cravat breastpin pressed with a firm hand in the mass above gave me the opportunity of making my escape."

Life was easier during the day. Men frequently dealt poker or strummed guitars to while away the time and "ladies danced on the deck." That is, until the bowsman yelled "Low bridge! Everybody down!" People might complain about the overcrowded boats and poor food, but it beat losing a wagon in a mudhole on the long haul over the rutted Appalachians or getting the "road pukes" from swaying in a stagecoach rumbling along narrow trails.

It took a crew of 25,000 men and boys to run the Erie once she hit her stride. There were steersmen and captains and lock-keepers. Towpath walkers patrolled ten-mile stretches of the canal daily looking for leaks and washouts. Countless teamsters rode two six-hour shifts a day, guiding six horses or mules pulling at a dead gallop on a boat's 90-foot towrope. One such lad was James Garfield, later President of the United States. Another was Michael Moran who, in the best Horatio Alger tradition, saved enough from his 50¢ a day wage to become captain of his own boat. By 1860, he owned a whole fleet and founded the Moran Towing Co. Today, the firm's tugs still dominate New York harbor—each decorated with a big block "M" on its stack.

Canal mania swept the country like wildfire as envious states watched the Erie's success. Between 1825 and 1850, some 4,500 miles of canal

were dug at a cost of $210 million. The Pennsylvania Canal connected
Philadelphia to Pittsburgh. The Ohio and Erie Canal linked Cleve-
land with Portsmouth, and the Miami and Erie Canal joined Cincinnati to Toledo. The Delaware and Raritan Canal crossed New Jersey
to provide an inland water route between Philadelphia and New York
City. The Chesapeake and Ohio from tidewater to the Ohio River
never reached its goal. Virginians gave up the ghost when they faced
the reality of the towering Alleghenies—after spending $14 million and
32 years to span 184 miles up to Cumberland, Md. Hoosiers built the
Wabash and Erie Canal from Evansville to Toledo, at 458 miles the
longest canal ever dug in the United States. The Illinois and Michigan
Canal tied Chicago with LaSalle on the upper Mississippi. Many of
these thrived for a while, but few ever paid back their cost. The Canal
Era, like the clipper ship, was doomed from the day it began.

The first railroad in America—a 13-mile stretch of track in Maryland—barely made the back pages of newspapers in 1830. By 1850, lo-
comotives chugged over a 9,021-mile network of tracks that crisscrossed
the country east of the Mississippi. A freight shipment from Cincinnati to New York by train now took six days; by canals, it took 18.

One traveling man from Albion, N.Y., never forgot his sleepless
nights on the Erie Canal. He revised the sleeping accommodations and
patented the result. His name was George Pullman and his invention
was the Pullman sleeping car.

But the railroads didn't entirely kill the canals, for where speed was
no object flotation remained practical for bulk cargoes, such as grain.
The Erie, if we include its successor (the New York State Barge Canal), is among the survivors. In 1918, New York spent $155 million
on its Barge Canal System. A hundred and one years after the original
authorization, most of the Erie was abandoned for brand new routing
that made more use of rivers and lakes, and a main canal 150 feet wide
was built. Some of the old aqueducts still remain in crumbling form, as
does some of the abandoned ditch, now overgrown and weed-choked.
Yet from Rochester west, the route is still the Erie's. Remodeled and
twice widened, the cut through the Niagara Escarpment is still used.
Lockport's five locks are now two.

The Barge Canal includes a network of many other routes lacing
New York State. Some of the heaviest freight traffic now travels a
north-south route connecting Albany with ports on Lake Champlain,

chiefly Plattsburg, N.Y., and Burlington, Vt. Pleasure boats can continue north through smaller waterways to the St. Lawrence.

Long after WW2, the Barge Canal still carried most of the grain from the West to New York City, but today it carries none. The St. Lawrence Seaway now permits ocean vessels to go all the way to Duluth, via Canada's Welland Canal around the Niagara Escarpment. Even so, the Barge Canal system carried 2½ million tons of freight last year, and, remarkably, perhaps more passengers than when the water route West was opened. This is chiefly local recreational traffic, mainly in the Finger Lakes area of central New York. In 1973, there were about 100,000 passages of passenger-carrying craft in the whole system, or nearly 300 a day. But of horses, there were none.

The West and the American Age of Exploration

WILLIAM H. GOETZMANN

• During the past decade one American in every five moved to a new home every year, a statistic often used to document the high degree of residential mobility in contemporary American society. But the United States has seemed always to be a nation on the move. In the 1830's the celebrated French visitor Alexis de Tocqueville wrote:

It is tempting to speak of this obsession with change and impatience with delay as the result of the geographical vastness of the United States. In the following essay, however, Professor William H. Goetzmann of the University of Texas studies several aspects of our culture to present a different perspective on the age of exploration. He argues that "westering" was part of a larger world-wide impulse, and he suggests that the American West had a powerful influence upon the East as well as the frontier.

Of all the major events in American history, none has been so central as the experience of the westward movement. The story of the confrontation and eventual domination of the vast empty continent by successive waves of pioneer Americans has become our national epic. This epic was most clearly articulated by the historian Frederick Jack-

From *Arizona and the West*, 2 (1960), 265–78. Reprinted by permission of *Arizona and the West*.

son Turner in his celebrated hypothesis on the significance of the frontier in American history. "Stand at Cumberland Gap," he declared, "and watch the procession of civilization marching single file —the buffalo following the trail to the salt springs, the Indian, the fur trader and hunter, the pioneer farmer—and the frontier has passed by. Stand at South Pass in the Rockies a century later and see the same procession with wider intervals between." For Turner, and for those who have followed after him in the celebration of his American myth, it was the frontier which focused American energies; and it was the West as the place—wild, isolated, and infinitely challenging—which formed that peculiarly adventurous democrat, the American. Turner asserted:

> This perennial rebirth, this fluidity of American life, this expansion westward with its new opportunities, its continuous touch with the simplicity of primitive society, furnish the forces dominating American character. The true point of view in the history of this nation is not the Atlantic Coast, it is the Great West.

Historians and poets of the West, taking their cue from Turner, have turned their backs upon the Atlantic Coast, and have looked at the great national experience as something Western—peculiarly Western. Indeed the very opposition between the Atlantic Coast and the Great West—between the rimland and the heartland, the old and wicked and the new and hopeful, as it were—has become a part of this national story. The westward movement of the American people has always been considered peculiarly "Western," and to suggest that it was anything else has been to taint somehow the pristine Americanness of the whole fable. The study of the westward movement is the study of what happened in the West and nothing else; unless, of course, one were to suggest that experiences in the West had great impact upon the rest of the country.

It has always been permissible, of course, for the Western historian to say with Turner, that "to the frontier the American intellect owes its striking characteristics." But perhaps in celebrating and studying the great story of the westward movement the Western historian has taken too narrow a view. Perhaps he has really been guilty of underestimating the extent of this impulse to move into the unknown and uncharted wildernesses of the world. Might it not be possible that this experience in the American West was an experience that was characteristic of the whole of America rather than just a part of it? Indeed, there is reason to suspect that the impulse for expansion over the globe might even be as characteristic of European civilization as a whole as it was for those hardy pioneers way out West. It might even be that one of the reasons for the enthusiastic acceptance of the myth of the American West was its very centrality to the whole of American experience at that particular time and place in the nineteenth century, and perhaps even today.

The recent interest in cultural history, and the corresponding use of new source materials, has begun to afford the historian new points of view toward all aspects of American history. Increasing importance has been attached to the cultural settings of well-known political events, and the historian has become more conscious of American behavioral patterns as they exist within the whole context of modern European experience. A recent example of this is Walter Prescott Webb's *The Great Frontier*, which takes a long view of the American frontier experience and designates to it a relatively small place in the course of the great 400-year boom which he declares has characterized European development since 1500. Inaccurate though his work might be in detail and in some of the conclusions he draws, nevertheless Professor Webb's thesis must stand as a significant attempt to break free of traditional approaches to the American West which have been dominated too much by nationalism and emphasis upon internal political events. If it does nothing else, Professor Webb's thesis at least has the advantage of suggesting a new dimension for the expansion impulse and a new set of kinship relationships which extend to all parts of our common culture.

The purpose here is a similar one. Let us abandon for the moment the traditional narrow view of the expansion impulse and take up another point of view. Let us focus upon the history of exploration in the American West as part of the general history of American and European culture between the years 1800 and 1860, a quite arbitrary time span but one that is central to the course of American westward expansion. In this period public enthusiasm for the discovery and exploration of exotic places reached a culmination due to the impetus of the romantic imagination and the rapid development of scientific techniques. So widespread was such enthusiasm that one might almost be justified in calling this sixty-year period "The American Age of Exploration." The keynote of this public enthusiasm was struck on Columbus Day, 1855, in the Washington *National Intelligencer*:

> The present is emphatically the age of discovery. At no period since the days of Columbus and Cortez has the thirst for exploration been more active and universal than now. One by one the outposts of barbarism are stormed and carried, advanced parallels are thrown up, and the besieging lines of knowledge, which when once established can never be retaken, are gradually closing around the yet unconquered mysteries of the globe. Modern exploration is intelligent, and its results are therefore positive and permanent. The traveller no longer wanders bewildered in a cloud of fables prepared to see marvels, and but too ready to create them. He tests every step of his way by the sure light of science and his pioneer trail becomes a plain and easy path to those who follow. The pencil, the compass, the barometer, and the sextant are his aids; and by these helps his single brain achieves results now which it would once have required an armed force to win.

The *Intelligencer* was not referring solely to American exploration but to activity by Americans and Europeans all over the globe. Stimulated by the eighteenth-century voyages of Captain Cook, the daring adventures of Alexander McKenzie, and the exotic excursions of Alexander von Humboldt into the green world of the Amazon Basin, Europeans and Americans alike increasingly began to undertake important expeditions—with the result that by about 1900 virtually all the interiors of the great continents had been explored, the sea lanes charted, and the Arctic and Antarctic discovered and to some extent explored.

Humboldt was a key figure of the period not only because of his work in South and Central America, but because somehow he combined the cosmopolitan rationalism of the eighteenth century with the newer romantic feeling for the grandeur and exoticism of nature into a scientific approach that could be understood and imitated by those who came after him. His purpose was a clear as any in that time of romantic strivings. From his field headquarters in the heart of the Andes he wrote:

The ultimate aim of physical geography is . . . to recognize
unity in the vast diversity of phenomena. . . . I have conceived
the mad notion of presenting, in a graphic and attractive manner, the whole of the physical aspect of the universe in one work,
which is to include all that is at present known of celestial and
terrestrial phenomena, from the nature of the nebula down to
the geography of the mosses clinging to a granite rock. . . .

Throughout the period he remained a kind of spiritual godfather and
grand advisor to great numbers of American and European scientists
and explorers. His influence on American explorers of the early West,
for example, is clearly indicated by the fact that his name even today
is attached to such prominent geographical features as the Humboldt
Range and the Humboldt River.

At the outset certain geographical areas and problems were of special interest to various nations. Since Napoleon's campaigns in Egypt,
French, British, and German explorers roamed over the continent of
Africa in increasing numbers, searching for everything from gorillas
to the source of the Nile. Men like Speke, Burton, du Chaillu, Krapf,
and Livingstone were heroes of the hour as they searched out the secrets of the dark continent. In North America the central focus was for
a long time upon the discovery of a Northwest Passage, or at least a
satisfactory trade route to India. McKenzie's great Canadian explorations had not entirely solved this problem, and it was not until Lewis
and Clark marched down the Columbia to the Pacific, that any satisfactory answer was forthcoming. National rivalries over the priority of
discoveries developed a particular intensity, not only in North America
and Africa, but even in such remote areas as the Antarctic where Europeans and Americans hotly contested the honor of discovering the new
continent—even to the extent of warping the viewpoints of old and
established learned societies. And all the while they remained virtually
ignorant of its prior discovery by commercial sealers from Stonington,
Connecticut, some twenty years before.

Although these various expeditions throughout the world were based
to a large extent upon the exigencies of national economic and political considerations, they were motivated also by an insatiable scientific curiosity. Most of the explorers seemed bent on collecting, examining, and classifying all of the various phenomena of nature which,

in and of itself, seemed a vast and infinitely mysterious thing. Darwin's voyage on the *Beagle* (1832–36), inspired by the work of Humboldt, is an outstanding example of such intellectual activity.

In all of this furious activity the young republic of the United States played an important part. Under the guidance of Thomas Jefferson, Americans turned after 1800 to the task of exploring the Great West. Official expeditions were sent out under Lewis and Clark, Dunbar and Hunter, Dunbar and Freeman, Pike, and Stephen H. Long. Private John Colter of the United States Army, on detached duty from the Lewis and Clark Expedition, became the first American to see the marvels of Yellowstone Park. It was Jefferson who played the key role not only in the planning of the expeditions but in devising a proper way to present the projects to an economy-minded Congress little interested at the time in the possible contributions of "pure science." Invariably these expeditions were presented to Congress as economic and political necessities, with their scientific objectives appearing to be an afterthought.

In considering the total picture of American achievement in exploration it would, of course, be a serious mistake to overlook the private interests that accomplished so much between 1806 and 1842. The mountain men, in particular, formed one of the most spectacular groups of explorers in all history as they roamed free and unrestrained (except by the Indians) all over the western half of North America. Jim Bridger, Jedediah Smith, and James Pattie were among the first Americans to see such geographical landmarks as the South Pass, the Great Basin, the Great Salt Lake, and the Grand Canyon. Fur magnates like John Jacob Astor, Pierre Chouteau, William H. Ashley, and Charles Bent, sponsored expeditions of their own which searched out the hitherto secret places of the West. On numerous occasions they afforded opportunities for savants, like the botanist Thomas Nuttall, or the geographer Joseph Nicollet, to extend their researches into the West.

By 1842, however, the day of the mountain man was about at an end, and in that year Jim Bridger settled down to the life of a trader in his fort at the South Pass in the Rockies. Then a new era began, one that was dominated by the United States Army's Topographical Engineers, of which the most representative figure was the boyish hero

John C. Fremont. Fremont's expeditions to the Far West in 1842, '43, '44, and '45 are all well known, but less well known are the exploits of his colleagues in the Corps of Topographical Engineers. Unlike the mountain men, these new explorers were interested in mapping the West and making its resources known to the generations of pioneers that would follow them. For the most part the Topographical Engineers considered themselves men of science, and they rarely failed to utilize the opportunities afforded them by their Western expeditions to record and publish their scientific data to the world.

During the Mexican War Lieutenants William H. Emory and James W. Abert explored and mapped the Southwest, calling the attention of scholars to the importance of the pueblos and other evidences of vanished Indian civilizations. Later Captain Lorenzo Sitgreaves and Lieutenant James Hervey Simpson explored the pueblo country of Arizona and New Mexico more closely, and together with Emory and Abert they were instrumental in launching the study of archaeology in the Southwest with reports on such important sites as the Chaco and Chelly Canyons and the Casa Grande on the Gila River. Captain Howard Stansbury and his assistant, Lieutenant John W. Gunnison, made the first scientific map of the Great Salt Lake in 1850, and Stansbury explored the western edge of the Lake for the first time. Captain John N. Macomb picked his way through the incredibly difficult country along the San Juan River to the junction of the Green and Grand Rivers, and thus became the first American to thoroughly understand the broad outlines of the Colorado River system. Lieutenant Joseph Christmas Ives chugged up the Colorado River in a homemade steamboat and led a party on foot to the floor of the Grand Canyon for the first time. This was a sublime moment in the history of Western exploration. Captain Randolph Barnes Marcy discovered the long elusive sources of the Red River in the Palo Duro Canyon of the Staked Plains of West Texas. Other Army explorers mapped the Great Basin and the Upper Missouri-Yellowstone River Country.

When these Army officers returned to make their findings known, they were assisted by the leading scientific men in the country—men like John Torrey, Asa Gray, James Hall, John Strong Newberry, and Louis Agassiz. F. V. Hayden's work with Lieutenant G. K. Warren

in the Dakotas helped to launch the serious study of vertebrate pale-
ontology in the United States. Some of the scientists who accompanied
the expeditions were so enthusiastic in the pursuit of knowledge that
they even attempted to pickle some of the Indians and bring them
back to the Smithsonian in a jar!

The outstanding publications of this period of military exploration
in the West were the Mexican Boundary Survey report and the report on the surveys for the Pacific Railroad. The Boundary Survey
report, in three massive volumes, constituted a matchless compendium
of information on the Southwest, particularly in the fields of geology,
botany and zoology. The Pacific Railroad reports were published in
thirteen volumes between 1853 and 1859, and these also included
monumental data on bird, fishes, mammals, plants and geology. The
most important contribution of the Pacific Railroad reports, however,
was Lieutenant G. K. Warren's master map of the whole trans-
Mississippi West published in 1857. It presented for the first time a
reasonably accurate and scientific outline of the whole country west
of the Mississippi, and it was a climactic event in the history of Western exploration.

The maps, the reports, the illustrations, the scientific data, and
most of all the accounts of the expeditions themselves all added up
to a picture of the American West as a vast and exotic place—a land
of gigantic sunless canyons, towering mountains, burning lakes and
fountains, mud-daubed Indians who lived in sky-high palaces, locust-
eaters scarcely out of the Stone Age, immense herds of buffalo stretch-
ing for miles over the limitless horizon—all virtually untouched by
the hand of civilization. And though these reports were intended as
scientific documents, they helped to set the tone of an age devoted
to exploration and the romantic desire to see ever outward from the
immediate circle of one's own existence to the remote frontiers of
the universe, just as Humboldt had dreamed of being the single genius
who would capture all knowledge of the cosmos in one massive compendium. This compulsion, as much as the often-stressed desire for
free land, drove the spearhead of American civilization into the West
during the so-called period of Manifest Destiny.

This aspect of Manifest Destiny, however, was not confined solely
to the desire to explore the Western land frontier. While most of the

agrarian states were urging Federal sponsorship of Western surveys, maritime interests on the Eastern seaboard and professional scientists in Washington saw to the launching of naval expeditions to all parts of the world, some of them with the admitted purpose of maintaining the national prestige in competition with the other nations bent on exploring and subduing the globe. The first of these expeditions was conceived by John Quincy Adams, the most scientifically-inclined of American presidents. He had proposed, during his presidency, a naval expedition to the Northwest Coast that would not only collect scientific data but would also be of direct assistance to American maritime interests in whaling and trading. His plan would complete the much desired passage to India. The plan, however, languished during the administration of Andrew Jackson. Finally in 1838 the United States Exploring Expedition, commanded by Lieutenant Charles Wilkes, set sail for the Pacific by way of South America and Cape Horn. This expedition, the most spectacular of its day, was gone for four years during which time it made scientific surveys and collections in South America, re-discovered the Antarctic Continent, charted its coast, made extensive explorations in the South Seas and Polynesian Islands, and cruised along the Northwest Coast of North America where a short party mapped much of what is now Washington and Oregon. Although the expedition included only one first-rate scientist, James Dwight Dana, it still contributed a great deal to science in the form of maps and collections.

South America proved irresistible to Navy explorers. Like the Portuguese adventurers of the fifteenth century they sailed southward in a series of expeditions designed partially to secure scientific information, but primarily to open up a vast new continent to commercial exploitation. The most sincerely scientific American expedition was Lieutenant James Melville Gilliss's astronomical expedition to Chili in 1849–50. Gilliss's chief objective was to measure the distance of the sun from the earth by making an observation of the planet Venus at a time when it was being observed by astronomers at the Naval Observatory in Washington. This part of his plan was frustrated, however, when officials at the Naval Observatory failed to carry out their part of the operation. Other expeditions sent to South America by the Navy included Lieutenant Page's expedition to the Rio De La

Plata in 1853–56, Lieutenant Michler's Atrato expedition, a joint Army-Navy venture to reconnoiter for an isthmian canal, and the spectacular exploration of the Amazon and Orinoco rivers by Lieutenant William L. Herndon and Midshipman Lardner Gibbon. This latter expedition was sent out purposely to survey the possibilities of the Amazon Basin for the establishment of a future slave empire when the South might be forced to give up its slaves due to Northern pressure. It was inspired by an arch-Southerner, Lieutenant Matthew Fontaine Maury, commander of the Naval Observatory in Washington and unofficial "Prince Henry the Navigator" to the American maritime expeditions of the whole period.

The Herndon and Gibbon expedition inflamed the imagination of the whole country. Upon reading of it in 1853, young Sam Clemens quit his newspaper job and started down the Mississippi, determined to be a coffee planter in Brazil. It was only a lack of funds that prevented him from reaching the Amazon, and turned him instead to the profession of Mississippi riverboat pilot. A few years later Frederick Church, a young Connecticut painter, also inspired by his reading of Humboldt and Herndon, actually made the journey to South America, where he recorded on canvas the grandeur and sublimity so often felt by the explorers.

Maury, as head of the Naval Observatory, served the cause of exploration in still another important way. He devised a system of logbooks to be carried by every merchant and whaling ship. These logbooks were forwarded to Washington and used by Maury to complete his important *Wind and Current Charts*, which amounted to a unique and accurate geography of the ocean. This project, along with his significant volume of *Sailing Directions*, has caused Maury to be regarded as a pioneer of the modern science of oceanography. His work also had the immense practical consequence of cutting the sailing time from New York to San Francisco by forty-seven days at a time when eager gold seekers had every reason to be eternally grateful.

Other naval expeditions of the period included Matthew Perry's voyage to Japan, Ringgold and Rodgers' North Pacific Exploring Expedition, and Elisha Kent Kane's voyage to the Arctic in search of the lost British explorer, Sir John Franklin. At the same time, too, Lieutenant Lynch was sent on a special mission to explore the Dead

Sea and parts of the West Coast of Africa. Thus, taken as a while, there was a considerable amount of official maritime exploration during the entire period. The official exploration was matched on sea as it was on land by the numerous private expeditions of whalers, sealers, and merchant adventurers. Any account of maritime exploration in this period can no more afford to ignore these than can the historian of the West afford to leave out the mountain men.

One further form of exploration during this period was the semi-private expedition in which a man received a governmental post which sent him to the place where he could do the exploring that he desired. The most notable examples of this were John Lloyd Stephens and Ephraim George Squier, who were sent to Central America on diplomatic missions so that they might explore the jungle regions. Stephens produced the monumental *Incidents of Travel in Central America, Chiapas, and Yucatan* which, with its magnificent illustrations executed by Frederick Catherwood, gave the first clear picture of the lost civilization of the Mayas. Squier also produced some highly important archaeological works on Central America.

Most of these men belonged to a curious literary group, interested in travel books, which met at Bartlett and Welford's bookstore in New York's Astor Hotel. The patriarch of the group was the aged Albert Gallatin; it also included such figures as Dr. F. S. Hawks, William Kennedy, George Folsom, and Brantz Mayer, author of *Mexico As It Is and As It Was*. On occasion, Edgar Allan Poe dropped in for meetings and gathered material for his own fictionalized versions of the travel book. The guiding spirit of the group was John Russell Bartlett, who got himself made United States-Mexican Boundary Commissioner in 1852 so that he could go to the Southwest and write a sequel to Stephens' enormously successful work on the Mayas. Bartlett proved to be a colossal failure as Boundary Commissioner; but he produced still another interesting travel book, his *Personal Narrative of Exploration in Texas, New Mexico, California, Sonora, and Chihuahua*, which is one of the most delightful books in the entire literature of the American West.

In general these men produced works on the borderline between serious science and romantic travel literature in which the strange and the exotic were the most important objectives. As it was for Humboldt himself, it was quite difficult for them to separate the two because the main impetus for scientific investigation seems to have been generated by the romantic interest in the unique and the marvelous—in the minutiae of nature as well as in the extremities of the cosmos—that hung over and dominated the entire period.

Much of the literature of the day contributed to and drew inspiration from this spirit, suggesting that it was all part of an imaginative whole. Books like Francis Parkman's *Oregon Trail* or Washington Irving's *Astoria & the Adventures of Captain Bonneville* were romanticized chronicles that nevertheless also contributed factual information about the West at a time when such information was sorely needed. *The Adventures of James Ohio Pattie,* Lewis H. Garrard's *Wah-to-Yah and the Taos Trail,* and Josiah Gregg's *Commerce of the Prairies* all belong in this category. They conveyed much useful data about the West; but their chief significance was that they presented a picture of the West as an exotic unknown, a place of adventure for the man of spirit and daring to go and make his mark. In the 1840's and '50's the West was our Africa, or Polynesia, or the Road to Xanadu. Yet the majority of serious economic and political historians tend to take this for granted—if they do not scorn it entirely as a motive for moving West. The color and spirit of the West have been left to Hollywood, as if it never really did matter as an operative force which spurred people westward. But surely such a spirit played its part in the settlement of Western America and should not be overlooked. It was an integral part of the age.

It is relatively easy, for example, to trace the impact of the whole age of exploration upon imaginative and popular literature. Cooper used Sir John Franklin's expedition as source material for the *Sea Lions,* the Wilkes Expedition for the *Crater,* and the Long Expedition for the *Prairie.* Poe, always a devotee of romantic science, used the theory of Semmes Hole as the basis for his *MS. Found in a Bottle* and the *Narrative of A. Gordon Pym.* His work, usually regarded as science fiction, was actually more closely attuned to the age of exploration than it was to pure science. Indeed every major writer of the period was touched to some extent in plot, character, and imagery by the spirit of exploration. Melville was, of course, in *Typee,* so carefully researched, and in *Moby Dick* and *Mardi* and virtually all the rest of his work. Hawthorne had a fling at the travel book in his *Marble Faun*, and he too was swayed by the exotic. Emerson was devoted to Humboldt; and Thoreau, his friend, always traveled West in spirit from Walden Pond. Walt Whitman epitomizes the entire complex of travel, and the romantic exploration of the open road, with his endless catalogues celebrating everything in nature. He was likewise enamored with the idea of the West and the passage to India.

If we put all of these aspects of American culture together—the scientific, the literary, the impact of the frontier, the rational techniques and the romantic enthusiasms—we get a somewhat different perspective on this period of American history. What was happening on the trans-Mississippi frontier was akin to the activities on the Eastern seaboard. The drive for maritime expansion, as Professor Norman Graebner has recently pointed out, had as much to do with the course of Manifest Destiny as the desire for free land. All aspects of American expansionism were to some extent part of a larger impulse which was world-wide and extremely competitive. Intellectually, this might be explained by the fact that at this moment the scientific and rational mind of the eighteenth century was exposed to a true world horizon—and, as that mind went to work in the effort of comprehension, it became romantic. Whatever was but dimly known became irresistibly attractive, and it was this attraction itself that had much to do with stimulating the impulse of Manifest Destiny on a global basis.

Viewed in this way, the experience in the American West seems somewhat less than unique. Rather it appears as a part of a much larger whole—a great synthesis which extends all the way from the picturesque trappers' rendezvous in Cache Valley to the dimly lit study of Humboldt in Potsdam. When we have worked long enough and hard enough at studying this whole complex of ideas and emotions, we may perhaps arrive at a different view of our national and international history in which the old concepts will have been given a new and richer dimension. With particular regard to our own American West, we will have broken away from the old Turnerean tyranny which has failed to satisfy us for a number of years but which is still too valuable emotionally to part with completely. We will then be closer to understanding what the old Westerner meant when he said:

It wasn't Indians that were important, nor adventures, nor even getting out here. It was a whole bunch of people made into one big crawling beast. . . . It was westering and westering. Every man wanted something for himself, but the big beast that was all of us wanted only westering. . . . It wasn't getting out here that mattered, it was movement and westering.

The Cult of True Womanhood: 1820–1860

BARBARA WELTER

• The nineteenth century cult of the lady so well described in the following article by Barbara Welter insisted that every woman—meaning, however, only white, middle class ones—was a lady and should follow a prescribed code of behavior. Earlier, in colonial times, women were not required to be ladies. There was little opportunity for women to be relegated to such frivolous roles; all hands were needed in the earliest days of the country. Women were valued for their much-needed economic contributions to their families and were engaged in providing such necessities of daily life as food and clothing through the back-breaking labor that was the norm in those pre-labor-saving-devices times. Even the southern lady, described always as a carefree belle forever waltzing among magnolia blossoms, was engaged in the continual and arduous task of planning and managing plantation life.

As Welter points out, the emergence in the nineteenth century of the lady as the model of what every woman should be came at a significant time in American history. During a period when men were busily expanding geographic and economic frontiers, intent on materialistic concerns, it gave them a sense of security to believe that the spiritual and moral side of life was being taken care of by their women, safe at home. Thus the cult of the lady had a very important function to society at large; it provided assurance that at home and with the women was peace and stability, two qualities so lacking in the outside world of a nation on the move. Welter's article underscores the value of the current explorations into women's history; it is not only to recapture the

From *American Quarterly*, Vol. XVIII, No. 2, Part 1, pp. 151–74 (Summer 1966). Copyright © 1966, Trustees of the University of Pennsylvania. Reprinted by permission of the journal, the author, and University of Pennsylvania, publisher.

female past but also to point up new insights into the nature of the whole society at various periods of time.

The nineteenth-century American man was a busy builder of bridges and railroads, at work long hours in a materialistic society. The religious values of his forebears were neglected in practice if not in intent, and he occasionally felt some guilt that he had turned this new land, this temple of the chosen people, into one vast countinghouse. But he could salve his conscience by reflecting that he had left behind a hostage, not only to fortune, but to all the values which he held so dear and treated so lightly. Woman, in the cult of True Womanhood presented by the women's magazines, gift annuals and religious literature of the nineteenth century, was the hostage in the home. In a society where the values changed frequently, where fortunes rose and fell with frightening rapidity, where social and economic mobility provided instability as well as hope, one thing at least remained the same—a true woman was a true woman, wherever she was found. If anyone, male or female, dared to tamper with the complex of virtues which made up True Womanhood, he was damned immediately as an enemy of God, of civilization and of the Republic. It was a fearful obligation, a solemn responsibility, which the nineteenth-century American woman had—to uphold the pillars of the temple with her frail white hand.

The attributes of True Womanhood, by which a woman judged herself and was judged by her husband, her neighbors and society could be divided into four cardinal virtues—piety, purity, submissiveness and domesticity. Put them all together and they spelled mother, daughter, sister, wife—woman. Without them, no matter whether there was fame, achievement or wealth, all was ashes. With them she was promised happiness and power.

Religion or piety was the core of woman's virtue, the source of her strength. Young men looking for a mate were cautioned to search first for piety, for if that were there, all else would follow. Religion belonged to woman by divine right, a gift of God and nature. This "peculiar susceptibility" to religion was given her for a reason: "the vestal flame of piety, lighted up by Heaven in the breast of woman" would throw its beams into the naughty world of men. So far would its candle power reach that the "Universe might be Enlightened, Improved, and Harmonized by WOMAN!!" She would be another, better Eve, working in cooperation with the Redeemer, bringing the world back "from its revolt and sin." The world would be reclaimed for God through her suffering, for "God increased the cares and sorrows of woman, that she might be sooner constrained to accept the terms of salvation." A popular poem by Mrs. Frances Osgood, "The Triumph of the Spiritual Over the Sensual" expressed just this sentiment, woman's purifying passionless love bringing an erring man back to Christ.

Dr. Charles Meigs, explaining to a graduating class of medical students why women were naturally religious, said that "hers is a pious mind. Her confiding nature leads her more readily than men to accept the proffered grace of the Gospel." Caleb Atwater, Esq., writing in *The Ladies' Repository*, saw the hand of the Lord in female piety: "Religion is exactly what a woman needs, for it gives her that dignity that best suits her dependence." And Mrs. John Sandford, who had no very high opinion of her sex, agreed thoroughly: "Religion is just what woman needs. Without it she is ever restless or unhappy. . . ." Mrs. Sandford and the others did not speak only of that restlessness of the human heart, which St. Augustine notes, that can only find its peace in God. They spoke rather of religion as a kind of tranquilizer for the many undefined longings which swept even the most pious young girl, and about which it was better to pray than to think.

One reason religion was valued was that it did not take a woman away from her "proper sphere," her home. Unlike participation in other societies or movements, church work would not make her less domestic or submissive, less a True Woman. In religious vineyards, said the *Young Ladies' Literary and Missionary Report*, "you may labor without the apprehension of detracting from the charms of feminine delicacy." Mrs. S. L. Dagg, writing from her chapter of the Society in Tuscaloosa, Alabama, was equally reassuring: "As no sensible woman will suffer her intellectual pursuits to clash with her domestic duties" she should concentrate on religious work "which promotes these very duties."

The women's seminaries aimed at aiding women to be religious, as well as accomplished. Mt. Holyoke's catalogue promised to make female education "a handmaid to the Gospel and an efficient auxiliary in the great task of renovating the world." The Young Ladies' Seminary at Bordentown, New Jersey, declared its most important function to be "the forming of a sound and virtuous character." In Keene, New Hampshire, the Seminary tried to instill a "consistent and useful character" in its students, to enable them in this life to be "a good friend, wife and mother" but more important, to qualify them for "the enjoyment of Celestial Happiness in the life to come." And Joseph M' D. Mathews, Principal of Oakland Female Seminary in Hillsborough, Ohio, believed that "female education should be preeminently religious."

If religion was so vital to a woman, irreligion was almost too awful to contemplate. Women were warned not to let their literary or intellectual pursuits take them away from God. Sarah Josepha Hale spoke darkly of those who, like Margaret Fuller, threw away the "One True Book" for others, open to error. Mrs. Hale used the unfortunate Miss Fuller as fateful proof that "the greater the intellectual force, the greater and more fatal the errors into which women fall who wander from the Rock of Salvation, Christ the Saviour. . . ."

One gentleman, writing on "Female Irreligion" reminded his readers that "Man may make himself a brute, and does so very often, but can woman brutify herself to his level—the lowest level of human nature—without exerting special wonder?" Fanny Wright, because she was godless, "was no woman, mother though she be." A few years ago, he recalls, such women would have been whipped. In any case, "woman never looks lovelier than in her reverence for religion" and, conversely, "female irreligion is the most revolting feature in human character."

Purity was as essential as piety to a young woman, its absence as unnatural and unfeminine. Without it she was, in fact, no woman at all, but a member of some lower order. A "fallen woman" was a "fallen angel," unworthy of the celestial company of her sex. To contemplate the loss of purity brought tears; to be guilty of such a crime, in the women's magazines at least, brought madness or death. Even the language of the flowers had bitter words for it: a dried white rose symbolized "Death Preferable to Loss of Innocence." The marriage night was the single great event of a woman's life, when she bestowed her greatest treasure upon her husband, and from that time on was completely dependent upon him, an empty vessel, without legal or emotional existence of her own.

Therefore all True Women were urged, in the strongest possible terms, to maintain their virtue, although men, being by nature more sensual than they, would try to assault it. Thomas Branagan admitted in *The Excellency of the Female Character Vindicated* that his sex would sin and sin again, they could not help it, but woman, stronger and purer, must not give in and let man "take liberties incompatible with her delicacy." "If you do," Branagan addressed his gentle reader, "You will be left in silent sadness to bewail your credulity, imbecility, duplicity, and premature prostitution."

Mrs. Eliza Farrar, in *The Young Lady's Friend*, gave practical logistics to avoid trouble: "Sit not with another in a place that is too narrow; read not out of the same book; let not your eagerness to see anything induce you to place your head close to another person's."

If such good advice was ignored the consequences were terrible and inexorable. In *Girlhood and Womanhood: Or Sketches of My Schoolmates*, by Mrs. A. J. Graves (a kind of mid-nineteenth-century *The Group*), the bad ends of a boarding school class of girls are scrupulously recorded. The worst end of all is reserved for "Amelia Dorrington: The Lost One." Amelia died in the almshouse "the wretched victim of depravity and intemperance" and all because her mother had let her be "high-spirited not prudent." These girlish high spirits had been misinterpreted by a young man, with disastrous results. Amelia's "thoughtless levity" was "followed by a total loss of virtuous principle" and Mrs. Graves editorializes that "the coldest reserve is more admirable in a woman a man wishes to make his wife, than the least approach to undue familiarity."

A popular and often-reprinted story by Fanny Forester told the sad tale of "Lucy Dutton." Lucy "with the seal of innocence upon her heart, and a rose-leaf on her cheek" came out of her vine-covered cottage and ran into a city slicker. "And Lucy was beautiful and trusting, and thoughtless: and he was gay, selfish and profligate. Needs the story to be told? . . . Nay, censor, Lucy was a child—consider how young, how very untaught—oh! her innocence was no match for the sophistry of a gay, city youth! Spring came and shame was stamped upon the cottage at the foot of the hill." The baby died; Lucy went mad at the funeral and finally died herself. "Poor, poor Lucy Dutton! The grave is a blessed couch and pillow to the wretched. Rest thee there, poor Lucy!" The frequency with which derangement follows loss of virtue suggests the exquisite sensibility of woman, and the possibility that, in the women's magazines at least, her intellect was geared to her hymen, not her brain.

If, however, a woman managed to withstand man's assaults on her virtue, she demonstrated her superiority and her power over him. Eliza Farnham, trying to prove this female superiority, concluded smugly that "the purity of women is the everlasting barrier against which the tides of man's sensual nature surge."

A story in *The Lady's Amaranth* illustrates this dominance. It is set, improbably, in Sicily, where two lovers, Bianca and Tebaldo, have been separated because her family insisted she marry a rich old man. By some strange circumstance the two are in a shipwreck and cast on a desert island, the only survivors. Even here, however, the rigid standards of True Womanhood prevail. Tebaldo unfortunately forgets himself slightly, so that Bianca must warn him: "We may not indeed gratify our fondness by caresses, but it is still something to bestow our kindest language, and looks and prayers, and all lawful and honest attentions on each other." Something, perhaps, but not enough, and Bianca must further remonstrate: "It is true that another man is my husband, but you are my guardian angel." When even that does not work she says in a voice of sweet reason, passive and proper to the end, that she wishes he wouldn't but "still, if you insist, I will become what you wish; but I beseech you to consider, ere that decision, that debasement which I must suffer in your esteem." This appeal to his own double standards holds the beast in him at bay. They are rescued, discover that the old husband is dead, and after "mourning a decent season" Bianca finally gives in, legally.

Men could be counted on to be grateful when women thus saved them from themselves. William Alcott, guiding young men in their relations with the opposite sex, told them that "Nothing is better calculated to preserve a young man from contamination of low pleasures and pursuits than frequent intercourse with the more refined and virtuous of the other sex." And he added, one assumes in equal innocence, that youths should "observe and learn to admire, that purity and ignorance of evil which is the characteristic of well-educated young ladies, and which, when we are near them, raises us above those sordid and sensual considerations which hold such sway over men in their intercourse with each other."

The Rev. Jonathan F. Stearns was also impressed by female chastity in the face of male passion, and warned woman never to compromise the source of her power: "Let her lay aside delicacy, and her influence over our sex is gone."

Women themselves accepted, with pride but suitable modesty, this priceless virtue. *The Ladies' Wreath*, in "Woman the Creature of God and the Manufacturer of Society" saw purity as her greatest gift and chief means of discharging her duty to save the world: "Purity is the highest beauty—the true pole-star which is to guide humanity aright in its long, varied, and perilous voyage."

Sometimes, however, a woman did not see the dangers to her treasure. In that case, they must be pointed out to her, usually by a male. In the nineteenth century any form of social change was tantamount to an attack on woman's virtue, if only it was correctly understood. For example, dress reform seemed innocuous enough and the bloomers worn by the lady of that name and her followers were certainly modest attire. Such was the reasoning only of the ignorant. In another issue of *The Ladies' Wreath* a young lady is represented in dialogue with her "Professor." The girl expresses admiration for the bloomer costume—it gives freedom of motion, is healthful and attractive. The "Professor" sets her straight. Trousers, he explains, are "only one of the many manifestations of that wild spirit of socialism and agrarian radicalism which is at present so rife in our land." The young lady recants immediately: "If this dress has any connexion with Fourierism or Socialism, or fanaticism in any shape whatever, I have no disposition to wear it at all . . . no true woman would so far compromise her delicacy as to espouse, however unwittingly, such a cause."

America could boast that her daughters were particularly innocent. In a poem on "The American Girl" the author wrote proudly:

> Her eye of light is the diamond bright,
> Her innocence the pearl,
> And these are ever the bridal gems
> That are worn by the American girl.

Lydia Maria Child, giving advice to mothers, aimed at preserving that spirit of innocence. She regretted that "want of confidence between mothers and daughters on delicate subjects" and suggested a woman tell her daughter a few facts when she reached the age of twelve to "set her mind at rest." Then Mrs. Child confidently hoped that a young lady's "instinctive modesty" would "prevent her from dwelling on the information until she was called upon to use it." In the same vein, a book of advice to the newly-married was titled *Whisper to a Bride*. As far as intimate information was concerned, there was no need to whisper, since the book contained none at all.

A masculine summary of this virtue was expressed in a poem "Female Charms":

> I would have her as pure as the snow on the mount—
>   As true as the smile that to infamy's given—
> As pure as the wave of the crystalline fount,
>   Yet as warm in the heart as the sunlight of heaven.
> With a mind cultivated, not boastingly wise,
>   I could gaze on such beauty, with exquisite bliss;
> With her heart on her lips and her soul in her eyes—
>   What more could I wish in dear woman than this.

Man might, in fact, ask no more than this in woman, but she was beginning to ask more of herself, and in the asking was threatening the third powerful and necessary virtue, submission. Purity, considered as a moral imperative, set up a dilemma which was hard to resolve. Woman must preserve her virtue until marriage and marriage was necessary for her happiness. Yet marriage was, literally, an end to innocence. She was told not to question this dilemma, but simply to accept it.

Submission was perhaps the most feminine virtue expected of women. Men were supposed to be religious, although they rarely had time for it, and supposed to be pure, although it came awfully hard to them, but men were the movers, the doers, the actors. Women were the passive, submissive responders. The order of dialogue was, of course, fixed in Heaven. Man was "woman's superior by God's appointment, if not in intellectual dowry, at least by official decree." Therefore, as Charles Elliott argued in *The Ladies' Repository*, she should submit to him "for the sake of good order at least." In *The Ladies Companion* a young wife was quoted approvingly as saying that she did not think woman should "feel and act for herself" because "When, next to God, her husband is not the tribunal to which her heart and intellect appeals—the golden bowl of affection is broken." Women were warned that if they tampered with this quality they tampered with the order of the Universe.

The Young Lady's Book summarized the necessity of the passive virtues in its readers' lives: "It is, however, certain, that in whatever situation of life a woman is placed from her cradle to her grave, a spirit of obedience and submission, pliability of temper, and humility of mind, are required from her."

Woman understood her position if she was the right kind of woman, a true woman. "She feels herself weak and timid. She needs a protector," declared George Burnap, in his lectures on *The Sphere and Duties of Woman*. "She is in a measure dependent. She asks for wisdom, constancy, firmness, perseverance, and she is willing to repay it all by the surrender of the full treasure of her affections. Woman despises in man every thing like herself except a tender heart. It is enough that she is effeminate and weak; she does not want another like herself." Or put even more strongly by Mrs. Sandford: "A really sensible woman feels her dependence. She does what she can, but she is conscious of inferiority, and therefore grateful for support."

Mrs. Sigourney, however, assured young ladies that although they were separate, they were equal. This difference of the sexes did not imply inferiority, for it was part of that same order of Nature established by Him "who bids the oak brave the fury of the tempest, and the alpine flower lean its cheek on the bosom of eternal snows." Dr. Meigs had a different analogy to make the same point, contrasting the anatomy of the Apollo of the Belvedere (illustrating the male principle) with the Venus de Medici (illustrating the female principle). "Woman," said the physician, with a kind of clinical gallantry, "has a head almost too small for intellect but just big enough for love."

This love itself was to be passive and responsive. "Love, in the heart of a woman," wrote Mrs. Farrar, "should partake largely of the nature of gratitude. She should love, because she is already loved by one deserving her regard."

Woman was to work in silence, unseen, like Wordsworth's Lucy. Yet, "working like nature, in secret" her love goes forth to the world "to regulate its pulsation, and send forth from its heart, in pure and temperate flow, the life-giving current." She was to work only for pure affection, without thought of money or ambition. A poem, "Woman and Fame," by Felicia Hemans, widely quoted in many of the gift books, concludes with a spirited renunciation of the gift of fame:

> Away! to me, a woman, bring
> Sweet flowers from affection's spring.

"True feminine genius," said Grace Greenwood (Sara Jane Clarke) "is ever timid, doubtful, and clingingly dependent; a perpetual childhood." And she advised literary ladies in an essay on "The Intellectual Woman"—"Don't trample on the flowers while longing for the stars." A wife who submerged her own talents to work for her husband was extolled as an example of a true woman. In *Women of Worth: A Book for Girls*, Mrs. Ann Flaxman, an artist of promise herself, was praised because she "devoted herself to sustain her husband's genius and aid him in his arduous career."

Caroline Gilman's advice to the bride aimed at establishing this proper order from the beginning of marriage: "Oh, young and lovely bride, watch well the first moments when your will conflicts with his to whom God and society have given the control. Reverence his *wishes* even when you do not his *opinions*."

Mrs. Gilman's perfect wife in *Recollections of a Southern Matron* realizes that "the three golden threads with which domestic happiness is woven" are "to repress a harsh answer, to confess a fault, and to stop (right or wrong) in the midst of self-defense, in gentle submission." Woman could do this, hard though it was, because in her heart she knew she was right and so could afford to be forgiving, even a trifle condescending. "Men are not unreasonable," averred Mrs. Gilman. "Their difficulties lie in not understanding the moral and physical nature of our sex. They often wound through ignorance, and are surprised at having offended." Wives were advised to do their best to reform men, but if they couldn't, to give up gracefully. "If any habit of his annoyed me, I spoke of it once or twice, calmly, then bore it quietly."

A wife should occupy herself "only with domestic affairs—wait till your husband confides to you those of a high importance—and do not give your advice until he asks for it," advised the *Lady's Token*. At all times she should behave in a manner becoming a woman, who had "no arms other than gentleness." Thus "if he is abusive, never retort." A *Young Lady's Guide to the Harmonious Development of a Christian Character* suggested that females should "become as little children" and "avoid a controversial spirit." *The Mother's Assistant and Young Lady's Friend* listed "Always Conciliate" as its first commandment in "Rules for Conjugal and Domestic Happiness." Small wonder that these same rules ended with the succinct maxim: "Do not expect too much."

As mother, as well as wife, woman was required to submit to fortune. In *Letters to Mothers* Mrs. Sigourney sighed: "To bear the evils and sorrows which may be appointed us, with a patient mind, should be the continual effort of our sex. . . . It seems, indeed, to be expected of us; since the passive and enduring virtues are more immediately within our province." Of these trials "the hardest was to bear the loss of children with submission" but the indomitable Mrs. Sigourney found strength to murmur to the bereaved mother: "The Lord loveth a cheerful giver." *The Ladies' Parlor Companion* agreed thoroughly in "A Submissive Mother," in which a mother who had already buried two children and was nursing a dying baby saw her sole remaining child "probably scalded to death. Handing over the infant to die in the arms of a friend, she bowed in sweet submission to the double stroke." But the child "through the goodness of God survived, and the mother learned to say 'Thy will be done.'"

Woman then, in all her roles, accepted submission as her lot. It was a lot she had not chosen or deserved. As *Godey's* said, "the lesson of submission is forced upon woman." Without comment or criticism the writer affirms that "To suffer and to be silent under suffering seems the great command she has to obey." George Burnap referred to a woman's life as "a series of suppressed emotions." She was, as Emerson said, "more vulnerable, more infirm, more mortal than man." The death of a beautiful woman, cherished in fiction, represented woman as the innocent victim, suffering without sin, too pure and good for this world but too weak and passive to resist its evil forces.

The best refuge for such a delicate creature was the warmth and safety of her home.

The true woman's place was unquestionably by her own fireside—as daughter, sister, but most of all as wife and mother. Therefore domesticity was among the virtues most prized by the women's magazines. "As society is constituted," wrote Mrs. S. E. Farley, on the "Domestic and Social Claims on Woman," "the true dignity and beauty of the female character seem to consist in a right understanding and faithful and cheerful performance of social and family duties." Sacred Scripture re-enforced social pressure: "St. Paul knew what was best for women when he advised them to be domestic," said Mrs. Sandford. "There is composure at home; there is something sedative in the duties which home involves. It affords security not only from the world, but from delusions and errors of every kind."

From her home woman performed her great task of bringing men back to God. *The Young Ladies' Class Book* was sure that "the domestic fireside is the great guardian of society against the excesses of human passions." *The Lady at Home* expressed its convictions in its very title and concluded that "even if we cannot reform the world in a moment, we can begin the work by reforming ourselves and our households—It is woman's mission. Let her not look away from her own little family circle for the means of producing moral and social reforms, but begin at home."

Home was supposed to be a cheerful place, so that brothers, husbands and sons would not go elsewhere in search of a good time. Woman was expected to dispense comfort and cheer. In writing the biography of Margaret Mercer (every inch a true woman) her biographer (male) notes: "She never forgot that it is the peculiar province of woman to minister to the comfort, and promote the happiness, first, of those most nearly allied to her, and then of those, who by the Province of God are placed in a state of dependence upon her." Many other essays in the women's journals showed woman as comforter: "Woman, Man's Best Friend," "Woman, the Greatest Social Benefit," "Woman, A Being to Come Home To," "The Wife: Source of Comfort and the Spring of Joy."

One of the most important functions of woman as comforter was her role as nurse. Her own health was probably, although regrettably, delicate. Many homes had "little sufferers," those pale children who wasted away to saintly deaths. And there were enough other illnesses of youth and age, major and minor, to give the nineteenth-century American woman nursing experience. The sickroom called for the exercise of her higher qualities of patience, mercy and gentleness as well as for her housewifely arts. She could thus fulfill her dual feminine function—beauty and usefulness.

The cookbooks of the period offer formulas for gout cordials, oint ment for sore nipples, hiccough and cough remedies, opening pills and refreshing drinks for fever, along with recipes for pound cake, jumbles, stewed calves head and currant wine. *The Ladies' New Book of Cookery* believed that "food prepared by the kind hand of a wife, mother, sister, friend" tasted better and had a "restorative power which money cannot purchase."

A chapter of *The Young Lady's Friend* was devoted to woman's privilege as "ministering spirit at the couch of the sick." Mrs. Farrar advised a soft voice, gentle and clean hands, and a cheerful smile. She also cautioned against an excess of female delicacy. That was all right for a young lady in the parlor, but not for bedside manners. Leeches, for example, were to be regarded as "a curious piece of mechanism . . . their ornamental stripes should recommend them even to the eye, and their valuable services to our feelings." And she went on calmly to discuss their use. Nor were women to shrink from medical terminology, since "If you cultivate right views of the wonderful structure of the body, you will be as willing to speak to a physician of the bowels as the brains of your patient."

Nursing the sick, particularly sick males, not only made a woman feel useful and accomplished, but increased her influence. In a piece of heavy-handed humor in *Godey's* a man confessed that some women were only happy when their husbands were ailing that they might have the joy of nursing him to recovery "thus gratifying their medical vanity and their love of power by making him more dependent upon them." In a similar vein a husband sometimes suspected his wife "almost wishes me dead—for the pleasure of being utterly inconsolable."

In the home women were not only the highest adornment of civilization, but they were supposed to keep busy at morally uplifting tasks. Fortunately most of housework, if looked at in true womanly fashion, could be regarded as uplifting. Mrs. Sigourney extolled its virtues: "The science of housekeeping affords exercise for the judgment and energy, ready recollection, and patient self-possession, that are the characteristics of a superior mind." According to Mrs. Farrar, making beds was good exercise, the repetitiveness of routine tasks inculcated patience and perseverance, and proper management of the home was a surprisingly complex art: "There is more to be learned about pouring out tea and coffee, than most young ladies are willing to believe." *Godey's* went so far as to suggest coyly, in "Learning vs. Housewifery" that the two were complementary, not opposed: chemistry could be utilized in cooking, geometry in dividing cloth, and phrenology in discovering talent in children.

Women were to master every variety of needlework, for, as Mrs. Sigourney pointed out, "Needle-work, in all its forms of use, elegance, and ornament, has ever been the appropriate occupation of woman." Embroidery improved taste; knitting promoted serenity and economy. Other forms of artsy-craftsy activity for her leisure moments included painting on glass or velvet, Poonah work, tussy-mussy frames for her own needlepoint or water colors, stands for hyacinths, hair bracelets or baskets of feathers.

She was expected to have a special affinity for flowers. To the editors of *The Lady's Token* "A Woman never appears more truly in her sphere, than when she divides her time between her domestic avocations and the culture of flowers." She could write letters, an activity particularly feminine since it had to do with the outpourings of the heart, or practice her drawingroom skills of singing and playing an instrument. She might even read.

Here she faced a bewildering array of advice. The female was dangerously addicted to novels, according to the literature of the period. She should avoid them, since they interfered with "serious piety." If she simply couldn't help herself and read them anyway, she should choose edifying ones from lists of morally acceptable authors. She should study history since it "showed the depravity of the human heart and the evil nature of sin." On the whole, "religious biography was best."

The women's magazines themselves could be read without any loss of concern for the home. *Godey's* promised the husband that he would find his wife "no less assiduous for his reception, or less sincere in welcoming his return" as a result of reading their magazine. *The Lily of the Valley* won its right to be admitted to the boudoir by confessing that it was "like its namesake humble and unostentatious, but it is yet pure, and, we trust, free from moral imperfections."

No matter what later authorities claimed, the nineteenth century knew that girls *could* be ruined by a book. The seduction stories regard "exciting and dangerous books" as contributory causes of disaster. The man without honorable intentions always provides the innocent maiden with such books as a prelude to his assault on her virtue. Books which attacked or seemed to attack woman's accepted place in society were regarded as equally dangerous. A reviewer of Harriet Martineau's *Society in America* wanted it kept out of the hands of American women. They were so susceptible to persuasion, with their "gentle yielding natures" that they might listen to "the bold ravings of the hard-featured of their own sex." The frightening result: "such reading will unsettle them for their true station and pursuits, and they will throw the world back again into confusion."

The debate over women's education posed the question of whether a "finished" education detracted from the practice of housewifely arts. Again it proved to be a case of semantics, for a true woman's education was never "finished" until she was instructed in the gentle science of homemaking. Helen Irving, writing on "Literary Women," made it very clear that if women invoked the muse, it was as a genie of the household lamp. "If the necessities of her position require these duties at her hands, she will perform them nonetheless cheerfully, that she knows herself capable of higher things." The literary woman must conform to the same standards as any other woman: "That her home shall be made a loving place of rest and joy and comfort for those who are dear to her will be the first wish of every true woman's heart." Mrs. Ann Stephens told women who wrote to make sure they did not sacrifice one domestic duty. "As for genius, make it a domestic plant. Let its roots strike deep in your house. . . ."

The fear of "blue stockings" (the eighteenth-century male's term of derision for educated or literary women) need not persist for nine-teenth-century American men. The magazines presented spurious dialogues in which bachelors were convinced of their fallacy in fearing educated wives. One such dialogue took place between a young man and his female cousin. Ernest deprecates learned ladies ("A *Woman* is far more lovable than a *philosopher*") but Alice refutes him with the beautiful example of their Aunt Barbara who "although she *has* perpetrated the heinous crime of writing some half dozen folios" is still a model of "the spirit of feminine gentleness." His memory prodded, Ernest concedes that, by George, there was a woman: "When I last had a cold she not only made me a bottle of cough syrup, but when I complained of nothing new to read, set to work and wrote some twenty stanzas on consumption."

The magazines were filled with domestic tragedies in which spoiled young girls learned that when there was a hungry man to feed French and china painting were not helpful. According to these stories many a marriage is jeopardized because the wife has not learned to keep house. Harriet Beecher Stowe wrote a sprightly piece of personal experience for *Godey's*, ridiculing her own bad housekeeping as a bride. She used the same theme in a story "The Only Daughter," in which the pampered beauty learns the facts of domestic life from a rather difficult source, her mother-in-law. Mrs. Hamilton tells Caroline in the sweetest way possible to shape up in the kitchen, reserving her rebuke for her son: "You are her husband—her guide—her protector—now see what you can do," she admonishes him. "Give her credit for every effort: treat her faults with tenderness; encourage and praise whenever you can, and depend upon it, you will see another woman in her." He is properly masterful, she properly domestic and in a few months Caroline is making lumpless gravy and keeping up with the darning. Domestic tranquillity has been restored and the young wife moralizes: "Bring up a girl to feel that she has a responsible part to bear in promoting the happiness of the family, and you make a reflecting being of her at once, and remove that lightness and frivolity of character which makes her shrink from graver studies." These stories end with the heroine drying her hands on her apron and vowing that *her* daughter will be properly educated, in piecrust as well as Poonah work.

The female seminaries were quick to defend themselves against any suspicion of interfering with the role which nature's God had assigned to women. They hoped to enlarge and deepen that role, but not to change its setting. At the Young Ladies' Seminary and Collegiate Institute in Monroe City, Michigan, the catalogue admitted few of its graduates would be likely "to fill the learned professions." Still, they were called to "other scenes of usefulness and honor." The average woman is to be "the presiding genius of love" in the home, where she is to "give a correct and elevated literary taste to her children, and to assume that influential station that she ought to possess as the companion of an educated man."

At Miss Pierce's famous school in Litchfield, the students were taught that they had "attained the perfection of their characters when they could combine their elegant accomplishments with a turn for solid domestic virtues." Mt. Holyoke paid pious tribute to domestic skills: "Let a young lady despise this branch of the duties of woman, and she despises the appointments of her existence." God, nature and the Bible "enjoin these duties on the sex, and she cannot violate them with impunity." Thus warned, the young lady would have to seek knowledge of these duties elsewhere, since it was not in the curriculum at Mt. Holyoke. "We would not take this privilege from the mother."

One reason for knowing her way around a kitchen was that America was "a land of precarious fortunes," as Lydia Maria Child pointed out in her book *The Frugal Housewife: Dedicated to Those Who Are Not Ashamed of Economy.* Mrs. Child's chapter "How To Endure Poverty" prescribed a combination of piety and knowledge—the kind of knowledge found in a true woman's education, "a thorough religious *useful* education." The woman who had servants today, might tomorrow, because of a depression or panic, be forced to do her own work. If that happened she knew how to act, for she was to be the same cheerful consoler of her husband in their cottage as in their mansion.

An essay by Washington Irving, much quoted in the gift annuals, discussed the value of a wife in case of business reverses: "I have observed that a married man falling into misfortune is more apt to achieve his situation in the world than a single one . . . it is beautifully ordained by Providence that woman, who is the ornament of man in his happier hours, should be his stay and solace when smitten with sudden calamity."

A story titled simply but eloquently "The Wife" dealt with the quiet heroism of Ellen Graham during her husband's plunge from fortune to poverty. Ned Graham said of her: "Words are too poor to tell you what I owe to that noble woman. In our darkest seasons of adversity, she has been an angel of consolation—utterly forgetful of self and anxious only to comfort and sustain me." Of course she had a little help from "faithful Dinah who absolutely refused to leave her beloved mistress," but even so Ellen did no more than would be expected of any true woman.

Most of this advice was directed to woman as wife. Marriage was the proper state for the exercise of the domestic virtues. "True Love and a Happy Home," an essay in *The Young Ladies' Oasis*, might have been carved on every girl's hope chest. But although marriage was best, it was not absolutely necessary. The women's magazines tried to remove the stigma from being an "Old Maid." They advised no marriage at all rather than an unhappy one contracted out of selfish motives. Their stories showed maiden ladies as unselfish ministers to the sick, teachers of the young, or moral preceptors with their pens, beloved of the entire village. Usually the life of single blessedness resulted from the premature death of a fiancé, or was chosen through fidelity to some high mission. For example, in "Two Sisters," Mary devotes herself to Ellen and her abandoned children, giving up her own chance for marriage. "Her devotion to her sister's happiness has met its reward in the consciousness of having fulfilled a sacred duty." Very rarely, a "woman of genius" was absolved from the necessity of marriage, being so extraordinary that she did not need the security or status of being a wife. Most often, however, if girls proved "difficult," marriage and a family were regarded as a cure. The "sedative quality" of a home could be counted on to subdue even the most restless spirits.

George Burnap saw marriage as "that sphere for which woman was originally intended, and to which she is so exactly fitted to adorn and bless, as the wife, the mistress of a home, the solace, the aid, and the counsellor of that ONE, for whose sake alone the world is of any consequence to her." Samuel Miller preached a sermon on women: "How interesting and important are the duties devolved on females as WIVES . . . the counsellor and friend of the husband; who makes it her daily study to lighten his cares, to soothe his sorrows, and to augment his joys; who, like a guardian angel, watches over his interests, warns him against dangers, comforts him under trials; and by her pious, assiduous, and attractive deportment, constantly endeavors to render him more virtuous, more useful, more honourable, and more happy." A woman's whole interest should be focused on her husband, paying him "those numberless attentions to which the French give the title of *petits soins* and which the woman who loves knows so well how to pay . . . she should consider nothing as trivial which could win a smile of approbation from him."

Marriage was seen not only in terms of service but as an increase in authority for woman. Burnap concluded that marriage improves the female character "not only because it puts her under the best possible tuition, that of the affections, and affords scope to her active energies, but because it gives her higher aims, and a more dignified position." *The Lady's Amaranth* saw it as a balance of power: "The man bears rule over his wife's person and conduct. She bears rule over his inclinations: he governs by law; she by persuasion. . . . The empire of the woman is an empire of softness . . . her commands are caresses, her menaces are tears."

Woman should marry, but not for money. She should choose only the high road of true love and not truckle to the values of a materialistic society. A story "Marrying for Money" (subtlety was not the strong point of the ladies' magazines) depicts Gertrude, the heroine, rueing the day she made her crass choice: "It is a terrible thing to live without love. . . . A woman who dares marry for aught but the purest affection, calls down the just judgments of heaven upon her head."

The corollary to marriage, with or without true love, was motherhood, which added another dimension to her usefulness and her prestige. It also anchored her even more firmly to the home. "My Friend," wrote Mrs. Sigourney, "If in becoming a mother, you have reached the climax of your happiness, you have also taken a higher place in the scale of being . . . you have gained an increase of power." The Rev.

J. N. Danforth pleaded in *The Ladies' Casket*, "Oh, mother, acquit thyself well in thy humble sphere, for thou mayest affect the world." A true woman naturally loved her children; to suggest otherwise was monstrous.

America depended upon her mothers to raise up a whole generation of Christian statesmen who could say "all that I am I owe to my angel mother." The mothers must do the inculcating of virtue since the fathers, alas, were too busy chasing the dollar. Or as *The Ladies' Companion* put it more effusively, the father "weary with the heat and burden of life's summer day, or trampling with unwilling foot the decaying leaves of life's autumn, has forgotten the sympathies of life's joyous springtime. . . . The acquisition of wealth, the advancement of his children in worldly honor—these are his self-imposed tasks." It was his wife who formed "the infant mind as yet untainted by contact with evil . . . like wax beneath the plastic hand of the mother."

The Ladies' Wreath offered a fifty-dollar prize to the woman who submitted the most convincing essay on "How May An American Woman Best Show Her Patriotism." The winner was Miss Elizabeth Wetherell who provided herself with a husband in her answer. The wife in the essay of course asked her husband's opinion. He tried a few jokes first—"Call her eldest son George Washington," "Don't speak French, speak American"—but then got down to telling her in sober prize-winning truth what women could do for their country. Voting was no asset, since that would result only in "a vast increase of confusion and expense without in the smallest degree affecting the result." Besides, continued this oracle, "looking down at their child," if "we were to go a step further and let the children vote, their first act would be to vote their mothers at home." There is no comment on this devastating male logic and he continues: "Most women would follow the lead of their fathers and husbands," and the few who would "fly off on a tangent from the circle of home influence would cancel each other out."

The wife responds dutifully: "I see all that. I never understood so well before." Encouraged by her quick womanly perception, the master of the house resolves the question—an American woman best shows her patriotism by staying at home, where she brings her influence to bear "upon the right side for the country's weal." That woman will instinctively choose the side of right he has no doubt. Besides her "natural refinement and closeness to God" she has the "blessed advantage of a quiet life" while man is exposed to conflict and evil. She stays home with "her Bible and a well-balanced mind" and raises her sons to be good Americans. The judges rejoiced in this conclusion and paid the prize money cheerfully, remarking "they deemed it cheap at the price."

If any woman asked for greater scope for her gifts the magazines were sharply critical. Such women were tampering with society, undermining civilization. Mary Wollstonecraft, Frances Wright and Harriet Martineau were condemned in the strongest possible language—they were read out of the sex. "They are only semi-women, mental hermaphrodites." The Rev. Harrington knew the women of America could not possibly approve of such perversions and went to some wives and mothers to ask if they did want a "wider sphere of interest" as these nonwomen claimed. The answer was reassuring. " 'NO!' they cried simultaneously, 'Let the men take care of politics, *we will take care of the children!* ' " Again female discontent resulted only from a lack of understanding: women were not subservient, they were rather "chosen vessels." Looked at in this light the conclusion was inescapable: "Noble, sublime is the task of the American mother."

"Women's Rights" meant one thing to reformers, but quite another to the True Woman. She knew her rights,

> The right to love whom others scorn,
> The right to comfort and to mourn,
> The right to shed new joy on earth,
> The right to feel the soul's high worth . . .
> Such women's rights, and God will bless
> And crown their champions with success.

The American woman had her choice—she could define her rights in the way of the women's magazines and insure them by the practice of the requisite virtues, or she could go outside the home, seeking other rewards than love. It was a decision on which, she was told, everything in her world depended. "Yours it is to determine," the Rev. Mr. Stearns solemnly warned from the pulpit, "whether the beautiful order of society . . . shall continue as it has been" or whether "society shall break up and become a chaos of disjointed and unsightly elements." If she chose to listen to other voices than those of her proper mentors, sought other rooms than those of her home, she lost both her happiness and her power—"that almost magic power, which, in her proper sphere, she now wields over the destinies of the world."

But even while the women's magazines and related literature encouraged this ideal of the perfect woman, forces were at work in the nineteenth century which impelled woman herself to change, to play a more creative role in society. The movements for social reform, westward migration, missionary activity, utopian communities, industrialism, the Civil War—all called forth responses from woman which differed from those she was trained to believe were hers by nature and divine decree. The very perfection of True Womanhood, moreover, carried within itself the seeds of its own destruction. For if woman was so very little less than the angels, she should surely take a more active part in running the world, especially since men were making such a hash of things.

Real women often felt they did not live up to the ideal of True Womanhood: some of them blamed themselves, some challenged the standard, some tried to keep the virtues and enlarge the scope of womanhood. Somehow through this mixture of challenge and acceptance, of change and continuity, the True Woman evolved into the New Woman—a transformation as startling in its way as the abolition of slavery or the coming of the machine age. And yet the stereotype, the "mystique" if you will, of what woman was and ought to be persisted, bringing guilt and confusion in the midst of opportunity.

The women's magazines and related literature had feared this very dislocation of values and blurring of roles. By careful manipulation and interpretation they sought to convince woman that she had the best of both worlds—power and virtue—and that a stable order of society depended upon her maintaining her traditional place in it. To that end she was identified with everything that was beautiful and holy.

"Who Can Find a Valiant Woman?" was asked frequently from

the pulpit and the editorial pages. There was only one place to look for her—at home. Clearly and confidently these authorities proclaimed the True Woman of the nineteenth century to be the Valiant Woman of the Bible, in whom the heart of her husband rejoiced and whose price was above rubies.

The Female Animal: Medical and Biological Views of Woman and Her Role in Nineteenth-Century America

CARROLL SMITH-ROSENBERG AND

CHARLES ROSENBERG

• *The idea that woman's sphere is the home has been a constant throughout American history and has been highly resistant to change. Even today when women make up 44 per cent of the working force the idea, actually a myth, that women are defined primarily by their domestic activities, remains strong. Attempts to change sex role definitions are viewed by many as an attack on the very social fabric of American life. Hence we see in recent times derogation and abuse heaped on active participants in the women's liberation movement.*

In the nineteenth century, as the Rosenbergs point out, new attempts by women to enlarge their sphere by venturing into higher and better education and by controlling family size and thus family responsibility met with the same dismay and resistance evident in the reactions to modern-day feminist thrusts for more equal rights. Nineteenth-century attempts by women to expand their activities encountered a scientific and medical defense which proclaimed that woman's role was circumscribed by her frail and emotionally directed constitution. At a time when science was achieving a new respectability and acceptance, so-called scientific rationalizations on woman's place served to bolster up the commonly held assumption that woman flourished best when she remained at home, where so many nineteenth-century males, doctors included, liked her to be.

From *Journal of American History*, Vol. LX (Sept. 1973), 332–56.

Since at least the time of Hippocrates and Aristotle, the roles assigned women have attracted an elaborate body of medical and biological justification. This was especially true in the nineteenth century as the intellectual and emotional centrality of science increased steadily. Would-be scientific arguments were used in the rationalization and legitimization of almost every aspect of Victorian life, and with particular vehemence in those areas in which social change implied stress in existing social arrangements.

This essay is an attempt to outline some of the shapes assumed by the nineteenth-century debate over the ultimate bases for woman's domestic and child-bearing role. In form it resembles an exercise in the history of ideas; in intent it represents a hybrid with social and psychological history. Biological and medical views serve as a sampling device suggesting and illuminating patterns of social continuity, change, and tension.

The relationships between social change and social stress are dismayingly complex and recalcitrant to both psychological theorists and to the historian's normal modes of analysis. In an attempt to gain insight into these relationships the authors have chosen an analytic approach based on the study of normative descriptions of the female role at a time of widespread social change; not surprisingly emotion-laden attempts to reassert and redefine this role constitute one response to the stress induced by such social change.

This approach was selected for a variety of reasons. Role definitions exist on a level of prescription beyond their embodiment in the individuality and behavior of particular historical persons. They exist rather as a formally agreed upon set of characteristics understood by and acceptable to a significant proportion of the population. As formally agreed upon social values they are, moreover, retrievable from historical materials and thus subject to analysis. Such social role definitions, however, have a more than platonic reality; for they exist as parameters with which and against which individuals must either conform or define their deviance. When inappropriate to social, psychological, or biological reality such definitions can themselves engender anxiety, conflict, and demands for change.

During the nineteenth century, economic and social forces at work within Western Europe and the United States began to compromise traditional social roles. Some women at least began to question—and a few to challenge overtly—their constricted place in society. Naturally enough, men hopeful of preserving existing social relationships, and in some cases threatened themselves both as individuals and as members of particular social groups, employed medical and biological arguments to rationalize traditional sex roles as rooted inevitably and irreversibly in the prescriptions of anatomy and physiology. This essay examines the ideological attack mounted by prestigious and traditionally minded men against two of the ways in which women expressed their dissatisfaction and desire for change: women's demands for improved educational opportunities and their decision to resort to birth control and abortion. That much of this often emotionally charged debate was oblique and couched in would-be scientific and medical language and metaphor makes it even more significant; for few spokesmen could explicitly and consciously confront those changes which impinged upon the bases of their particular emotional adjustment.

The Victorian woman's ideal social characteristics—nurturance, intuitive morality, domesticity, passivity, and affection—were all assumed to have a deeply rooted biological basis. These medical and scientific arguments formed an ideological system rigid in its support of tradition, yet infinitely flexible in the particular mechanisms which could be made to explain and legitimate woman's role.

Woman, nineteenth-century medical orthodoxy insisted, was starkly different from the male of the species. Physically, she was frailer, her skull smaller, her muscles more delicate. Even more striking was the difference between the nervous system of the two sexes. The female nervous system was finer, "more irritable," prone to overstimulation and resulting exhaustion. "The female sex," as one physician explained in 1827,

> is far more sensitive and susceptible than the male, and extremely liable to those distressing affections which for want of some better term, have been denominated nervous, and which consist chiefly in painful affections of the head, heart, side, and indeed, of almost every part of the system.

"The nerves themselves," another physician concurred a generation later, "are smaller, and of a more delicate structure. They are endowed with greater sensibility, and, of course, are liable to more frequent and stronger impressions from external agents or mental influences." Few if any questioned the assumption that in males the intellectual propensities of the brain dominated, while the female's nervous system and emotions prevailed over her conscious and rational faculties. Thus it was only natural, indeed inevitable, that women should be expected and permitted to display more affect than men; it was inherent in their very being.

Physicians saw woman as the product and prisoner of her reproductive system. It was the ineluctable basis of her social role and behavioral characteristics, the cause of her most common ailments; woman's uterus and ovaries controlled her body and behavior from puberty through menopause. The male reproductive system, male physicians assured, exerted no parallel degree of control over man's body. Charles D. Meigs, a prominent Philadelphia gynecologist, stated with assurance in 1847 that a woman is "a moral, a sexual, a germiferous, gestative and parturient creature." It was, another physician explained in 1870, "as if the Almighty, in creating the female sex, had taken the uterus and built up a woman around it." A wise deity had designed woman as keeper of the hearth, as breeder and rearer of children.

Medical wisdom easily supplied hypothetical mechanisms to explain the interconnection between the female's organs of generation and the functioning of her other organs. The uterus, it was assumed, was connected to the central nervous system; shocks to the nervous system might alter the reproductive cycle—might even mark the gestating fetus—while changes in the reproductive cycle shaped emotional states. This intimate and hypothetical link between ovaries, uterus, and nervous system was the logical basis for the "reflex irritation" model of disease causation so popular in middle and late nineteenth-century medical texts and monographs on psychiatry and gynecology. Any imbalance, exhaustion, infection, or other disorders of the reproductive organs could cause pathological reactions in parts of the body seemingly remote. Doctors connected not only the paralyses and headaches of the hysteric to uterine disease but also ailments in virtually every part of the body. "These diseases," one physician explained, "will be found, on due investigation, to be in reality, no disease at all, but merely the sympathetic reaction or the symptoms of one disease, namely, a disease of the womb."

Yet despite the commonsensical view that many such ailments resulted from childbearing, physicians often contended that far greater difficulties could be expected in childless women. Motherhood was woman's normal destiny, and those females who thwarted the promise immanent in their body's design must expect to suffer. The maiden lady, many physicians argued, was fated to a greater incidence of both physical and emotional disease than her married sisters and to a shorter life-span. Her nervous system was placed under constant pressure, and her unfulfilled reproductive organs—especially at menopause—were prone to cancer and other degenerative ills.

Woman was thus peculiarly the creature of her internal organs, of tidal forces she could not consciously control. Ovulation, the physical and emotional changes of pregnancy, even sexual desire itself were determined by internal physiological processes beyond the control or even the awareness of her conscious volition. All women were prisoners of the cyclical aspects of their bodies, of the great reproductive cycle bounded by puberty and menopause, and by the shorter but recurrent cycles of childbearing and menstruation. All shaped her personality, her social role, her intellectual abilities and limitations; all presented as well possibly "critical" moments in her development, possible turning points in the establishment—or deterioration—of future physical and mental health. As the president of the American Gynecological Society stated in 1900: "Many a young life is battered and forever crippled in the breakers of puberty; if it crosses these unharmed and is not dashed to pieces on the rock of childbirth, it may still ground on the ever-recurring shallows of menstruation, and lastly, upon the final bar of the menopause ere protection is found in the unruffled waters of the harbor beyond the reach of sexual storms."

Woman's physiology and anatomy, physicians habitually argued, oriented her toward an "inner" view of herself and her worldly sphere. (Logically enough, nineteenth-century views of heredity often assumed that the father was responsible for a child's external musculature and skeletal development, the mother for the internal viscera, the father for analytical abilities, the mother for emotions and piety.) Their secret internal organs, women were told, determined their behavior; their concerns lay inevitably within the home. In a passage strikingly reminiscent of some mid-twentieth-century writings, a physician in 1869 depicted an idealized female world, rooted in the female reproductive system, sharply limited socially and intellectually, yet offering women covert and manipulative modes of exercising power:

> Mentally, socially, spiritually, she is more interior than man. She herself is an interior part of man, and her love and life are always something interior and incomprehensible to him. . . . Woman is to deal with domestic affections and uses, not with philosophies and sciences. . . . She is priest, not king. The house, the chamber, the closet, are the centres of her social life and power, as surely as the sun is the centre of the solar system. . . . Another proof of the interiority of woman, is the wonderful secretiveness and power of dissimulation which she possesses. . . . Woman's secrecy is not cunning; her dissimulation is not fraud. They are intuitions or spiritual perceptions, full of tact and wisdom, leading her to conceal or reveal, to speak or be silent, to do or not to do, exactly at the right time and in the right place.

The image granted women in these hypothetical designs was remarkably consistent with the social role traditionally allotted them. The instincts connected with ovulation made her by nature gentle, affectionate, and nurturant. Weaker in body, confined by menstruation and pregnancy, she was both physically and economically dependent upon the stronger, more forceful male, to whom she necessarily looked up to with admiration and devotion.

Such stylized formulae embodied, however, a characteristic yet entirely functional ambiguity. The Victorian woman was more spiritual than man, yet less intellectual, closer to the divine, yet prisoner of her most animal characteristics, more moral than man, yet less in control of her very morality. While the sentimental poets placed woman among the angels and doctors praised the transcendent calling of her reproductive system, social taboos made woman ashamed of menstruation, embarrassed and withdrawn during pregnancy, self-conscious and purposeless during and after menopause. Her body, which so inexorably defined her personality and limited her role, appeared to woman often degrading and confining. The very romantic rhetoric which tended to suffocate nineteenth-century discussions of femininity only underlined with irony the distance between behavioral reality and the forms of conventional ideology.

The nature of the formalistic scheme implied as well a relationship between the fulfilling of its true calling and ultimate social health. A woman who lived "unphysiologically"—and she could do so by reading or studying in excess, by wearing improper clothing, by long hours of factory work, or by a sedentary, luxurious life—could produce only weak and degenerate offspring. Until the twentieth century, it was almost universally assumed that acquired characteristics in the form of damage from disease and improper life-styles in parents would be transmitted through heredity; a nervous and debilitated mother could have only nervous, dyspeptic, and undersized children. Thus appropriate female behavior was sanctioned not only by traditional injunctions against the avoidance of individual sin in the form of inappropriate and thus unnatural modes of life but also by the higher duty of protecting the transcendent good of social health, which could be maintained only through the continued production of healthy children. Such arguments were to be invoked with increasing frequency as the nnieteenth century progressed.

In mid-nineteenth-century America it was apparent that women—or at least some of them—were growing dissatisfied with traditional roles. American society in mid-nineteenth century was committed—at least formally—to egalitarian democracy and evangelical piety. It was thus a society which presumably valued individualism, social and economic mobility, and free will. At the same time it was a society experiencing rapid economic growth, one in which an increasing number of families could think of themselves as middle class and could seek a life-style appropriate to that station. At least some middle-class women, freed economically from the day-to-day struggle for subsistence, found in these values a motivation and rationale for expanding their roles into areas outside the home. In the Jacksonian crusades for piety, for temperance, for abolition, and in pioneering efforts to aid the urban poor, women played a prominent role, a role clearly outside the confines of the home. Women began as well to demand improved educational opportunities—even admission to colleges and medical schools. A far greater number began, though more covertly, to see family limitation as a necessity if they would preserve health, status, economic security, and individual autonomy.

Only a handful of nineteenth-century American women made a commitment to overt feminism and to the insecurity and hostility such a commitment implied. But humanitarian reform, education, and birth control were all issues which presented themselves as real alternatives to every respectable churchgoing American woman. Contemporary medical and biological arguments identified, reflected, and helped to eliminate two of these threats to traditional role definitions: demands by women for higher education and family limitation.

Since the beginnings of the nineteenth century, American physicians and social commentators generally had feared that American women were physically inferior to their English and Continental sisters. The young women of the urban middle and upper classes seemed in particular less vigorous, more nervous than either their own grandmothers or European contemporaries. Concern among physicians, educators, and publicists over the physical deterioration of American womanhood grew steadily during the nineteenth century and reached a high point in its last third.

Many physicians were convinced that education was a major factor in bringing about this deterioration, especially education during puberty and adolescence. It was during these years that the female reproductive system matured, and it was this process of maturation that determined the quality of the children which American women would ultimately bear. During puberty, orthodox medical doctrine insisted, a girl's vital energies must be devoted to development of the reproductive organs. Physicians saw the body as a closed system possessing only a limited amount of vital force; energy expended in one area was necessarily removed from another. The girl who curtailed brain work during puberty could devote her body's full energy to the optimum development of its reproductive capacities. A young woman, however, who consumed her vital force in intellectual activities was necessarily diverting these energies from the achievement of true womanhood. She would become weak and nervous, perhaps sterile, or more commonly, and in a sense more dangerously for society, capable of bearing only sickly and neurotic children—children able to produce only feebler and more degenerate versions of themselves. The brain and ovary could not develop at the same time. Society, mid-century physicians warned, must protect the higher good of racial health by avoiding situations in which adolescent girls taxed their intellectual faculties in academic competition. "Why," as one physician pointedly asked, "spoil a good mother by making an ordinary grammarian?"

Yet where did America's daughters spend these years of puberty and adolescence, doctors asked, especially the daughters of the nation's most virtuous and successful middle-class families? They spent these years in schools; they sat for long hours each day bending over desks, reading thick books, competing with boys for honors. Their health and that of their future children would be inevitably marked by the consequences of such unnatural modes of life. If such evils resulted from secondary education, even more dramatically unwholesome was the influence of higher education upon the health of those few women intrepid enough to undertake it. Yet their numbers increased steadily, especially after a few women's colleges were established in the East and state universities in the Midwest and Pacific Coast began cautiously to accept coeducation. Women could now, critics agonized, spend the entire period between the beginning of menstruation and the maturation of their ovarian systems in nerve-draining study. Their adolescence, as one doctor pointed out, contrasted sadly with those experienced by healthier, more fruitful forebears: "Our great-grandmothers got their schooling during the winter months and let their brains lie fallow for the rest of the year. They knew less about Euclid and the classics than they did about housekeeping and housework. But they made good wives and mothers, and bore and nursed sturdy sons and buxom daughters and plenty of them at that."

Constant competition among themselves and with the physically stronger males disarranged the coed's nervous system, leaving her anxious, prey to hysteria and neurasthenia. One gynecologist complained as late as 1901:

> the nervous force, so necessary at puberty for the establishment of the menstrual function, is wasted on what may be compared as trifles to perfect health, for what use are they without health? The poor sufferer only adds another to the great army of neurasthenia and sexual incompetents, which furnish neurologists and gynecologists with so much of their material . . . bright eyes have been dulled by the brain-fag and sweet temper transformed into irritability, crossness and hysteria, while the womanhood of the land is deteriorating physically.
>
> She may be highly cultured and accomplished and shine in society, but her future husband will discover too late that he has married a large outfit of headaches, backaches and spine aches, instead of a woman fitted to take up the duties of life.

Such speculations exerted a strong influence upon educators, even those connected with institutions which admitted women. The state universities, for example, often prescribed a lighter course load for females or refused to permit women admission to regular degree programs. "Every physiologist is well aware," the Regents of the University of Wisconsin explained in 1877, "that at stated times, nature makes a great demand upon the energies of early womanhood and that at these times great caution must be exercised lest injury be done. . . . Education is greatly to be desired," the Regents concluded:

> but it is better that the future matrons of the state should be without a University training than that it should be produced at the fearful expense of ruined health; better that the future mothers of the state should be robust, hearty, healthy women, than that, by over study, they entail upon their descendants the germs of disease.

This fear for succeeding generations born of educated women was widespread. "We want to have body as well as mind," one commentator noted, "otherwise the degeneration of the race is inevitable." Such transcendent responsibilities made the individual woman's personal ambitions seem trivial indeed.

One of the remedies suggested by both educators and physicians lay in tempering the intensely intellectualistic quality of American education with a restorative emphasis on physical education. Significantly, health reformers' demands for women's physical education were ordinarily justified not in terms of freeing the middle-class woman from traditional restrictions on bodily movement, but rather as upgrading her ultimate maternal capacities. Several would-be physiological reformers called indeed for active participation in house-cleaning as an ideal mode of physical culture for the servant-coddled American girl. Bed-making, clothes scrubbing, sweeping, and scouring provided a varied and highly appropriate regimen.

Late nineteenth-century women physicians, as might have been expected, failed ordinarily to share the alarm of their male colleagues when contemplating the dangers of coeducation. No one, a female physician commented sardonically, worked harder or in unhealthier conditions than the washer-woman; yet, would-be saviors of American womanhood did not inveigh against this abuse—washing, after all, was appropriate work for women. Women doctors often did agree with the general observation that their sisters were too frequently weak and unhealthy; however, they blamed not education or social activism but artificialities of dress and slavery to fashion, aspects of the middle-class woman's life-style which they found particularly demeaning. "The fact is that girls and women can bear study," Alice Stockham explained, "but they cannot bear compressed viscera, tortured stomachs and displaced uterus," the results of fashionable clothing and an equally fashionable sedentary life. Another woman physician, Sarah Stevenson, wrote in a similar vein: " 'How do I look?' is the everlasting story from the beginning to the end of woman's life. Looks, not books, are the murderers of American women."

Even more significant than this controversy over woman's education was a parallel debate focusing on the questions of birth control and abortion. These issues affected not simply a small percentage of middle- and upper-middle-class women, but all men and women. It is one of the great and still largely unstudied realities of nineteenth-century social history. Every married woman was immediately affected by the realities of childbearing and child rearing. Though birth control and abortion had been practiced, discussed—and reprobated—for centuries, the mid-nineteenth century saw a dramatic increase in concern among spokesmen for the ministry and medical profession.

Particularly alarming was the casualness, doctors charged, with which seemingly respectable wives and mothers contemplated and undertook abortions, and how routinely they practiced birth control. One prominent New York gynecologist complained in 1874 that well-dressed women walked into his consultation room and asked for abortions as casually as they would for a cut of beefsteak at their butcher. In 1857, the American Medical Association nominated a special committee to report on the problem; then appointed another in the 1870s; between these dates and especially in the late 1860s, medical societies throughout the country passed resolutions attacking the prevalence of abortion and birth control and condemning physicians who performed and condoned such illicit practices. Nevertheless, abortions could in the 1870s be obtained in Boston and New York for as little as ten dollars, while abortifacients could be purchased more cheaply or through the mail. Even the smallest villages and rural areas provided a market for the abortionist's services; women often aborted any pregnancy which occurred in the first few years of marriage. The Michigan Board of Health estimated in 1898 that one third of all the state's pregnancies ended in abortion. From 70 to 80 percent of these were secured, the board contended, by prosperous and otherwise respectable married women who could not offer even the unmarried mother's "excuse of shame." By the 1880s, English medical moralists could refer to birth control as the "American sin" and warn against England's women following in the path of America's faithless wives.

So general a phenomenon demands explanation. The only serious attempts to explain the prevalence of birth control in this period have emphasized the economic motivations of those practicing it—the need in an increasingly urban, industrial, and bureaucratized society to limit numbers of children so as to provide security, education, and inheritance for those already brought into the world. As the nineteenth century progressed, it has been argued, definitions of appropriate middle-class life-styles dictated a more and more expansive pattern of consumption, a pattern—especially in an era of recurring economic instability—particularly threatening to those large numbers of Americans only precariously members of the secure economic classes. The need to limit offspring was a necessity if family status was to be maintained.

Other aspects of nineteenth-century birth control have received much less historical attention. One of these needs only to be mentioned for it poses no interpretative complexities; this was the frequency with which childbirth meant for women pain and often lingering incapacity. Death from childbirth, torn cervixes, fistulae, prolapsed uteri were widespread "female complaints" in a period when gynecological practice was still relatively primitive and pregnancy every few years common indeed. John Humphrey Noyes, perhaps the best-known advocate of family planning in nineteenth-century America, explained poignantly why he and his wife had decided to practice birth control in the 1840s:

> The [decision] was occasioned and even forced upon me by very sorrowful experiences. In the course of six years my wife went through the agonies of five births. Four of them were premature. Only one child lived. . . . After our last disappointment, I pledged my word to my wife that I would never again expose her to such fruitless suffering. . . .

The Noyeses' experience was duplicated in many homes. Young women were simply terrified of having children.

Such fears, of course, were not peculiar to nineteenth-century America. The dangers of disability and death consequent upon childbirth extended back to the beginning of time, as did the anxiety and depression so frequently associated with pregnancy. What might be suggested, however, was that economic and technological changes in society added new parameters to the age-old experience. Family limitation for economic and social reasons now appeared more desirable to a growing number of husbands; it was, perhaps, also, more technically feasible. Consequently married women could begin to consider, probably for the first time, alternative life-styles to that of multiple pregnancies extending over a third of their lives. Women could begin to view the pain and bodily injury which resulted from such pregnancies not simply as a condition to be borne with fatalism and passivity, but as a situation that could be avoided. It is quite probable, therefore, that, in this new social context, increased anxiety and depression would result once a woman, in part at least voluntarily, became pregnant. Certainly, it could be argued, such fears must have altered women's attitudes toward sexual relations generally. Indeed the decision to practice birth control must necessarily have held more than economic and status implications for the family; it must have become an element in the fabric of every marriage's particular psycho-sexual reality.

A third and even more ambiguous aspect of the birth control controversy in nineteenth-century America relates to the way in which attitudes toward contraception and abortion reflected role conflict within the family. Again and again, from the 1840s on, defenders of family planning—including individuals as varied and idealistic as Noyes and Stockham, on the one hand, and assorted quack doctors and peddlers of abortifacients, on the other—justified their activities not in economic terms, but under the rubric of providing women with liberty and autonomy. Woman, they argued with remarkable unanimity, must control her own body; without this she was a slave not only to the sexual impulses of her husband but also to endless childbearing and rearing. "Woman's equality in all the relations of life," a New York physician wrote in 1866, "implies her absolute supremacy in the sexual relation. . . . it is her absolute and indefeasible right to determine when she will and when she will not be exposed to pregnancy." "God and Nature," another physician urged, "have given to the female the complete cnotrol of her own person, so far as sexual congress and reproduction are concerned." The assumption of all these writers was clear and unqualified: women, if free to do so, would choose to have sexual relations less frequently, and to have far fewer pregnancies.

Implied in these arguments as well were differences as to the nature and function of sexual intercourse. Was its principal and exclusively justifiable function, as conservative physicians and clergymen argued, the procreation of children, or could it be justified as an act of love, of tenderness between individuals? Noyes argued that the sexual organs had a social, amative function separable from their reproductive function. Sex was justifiable as an essential and irreplaceable form of human affection; no man could demand this act unless it was freely given. Nor could it be freely given in many cases unless effective modes of birth control were available to assuage the woman's anxieties. A man's wife was not his chattel, her individuality to be violated at will, and forced—ultimately—to bear unwanted and thus almost certainly unhealthy children.

Significantly, defenders of women's right to limit childbearing employed many of the same arguments used by conservatives to attack women's activities outside the home; all those baleful hereditary consequences threatened by over-education were seen by birth control advocates as resulting from the bearing of children by women unwilling and unfit for the task, their vital energies depleted by excessive childbearing. A child, they argued, carried to term by a woman who desired only its death could not develop normally; such children proved inevitably a source of physical and emotional degeneracy. Were women relieved from such accustomed pressures, they could produce fewer but better offspring.

Many concerned mid-nineteenth-century physicians, clergymen, and journalists failed to accept such arguments. They emphasized instead the unnatural and thus necessarily deleterious character of any and all methods of birth control and abortion. Even coitus interruptus, obviously the most common mode of birth control in this period, was attacked routinely as a source of mental illness, nervous tension, and even cancer. This was easily demonstrated. Sex, like all aspects of human bodily activity, involved an exchange of nervous energy; without the discharge of such accumulated energies in the male orgasm and the soothing presence of the male semen "bathing the female reproductive organs," the female partner could never, the reassuring logic ran, find true fulfillment. The nervous force accumulated and concentrated in sexual excitement would build up dangerous levels of undischarged energy, leading ultimately to a progressive decay in the unfortunate woman's physical and mental health. Physicians warned repeatedly that condoms and diaphragms—when the latter became available after mid-century—could cause an even more startlingly varied assortment of ills. In addition to the mechanical irritation they promoted, artificial methods of birth control increased the lustful impulse in both partners, leading inevitably to sexual excess. The resultant nervous exhaustion induced gynecological lesions, and then through "reflex irritation" caused such ills as loss of memory, insanity, heart disease, and even "the most repulsive nymphomania."

Conservative physicians similarly denounced the widespread practice of inserting sponges impregnated with supposedly spermicidal chemicals into the vagina immediately before or after intercourse. Such practices, they warned, guaranteed pelvic injury, perhaps sterility. Even if a woman seemed in good health despite a history of practicing birth control, a Delaware physician explained in 1873 that ". . . as soon as this vigor commences to decline . . . about the fortieth year, the disease [cancer] grows as the energies fail—the cancerous fangs penetrating deeper and deeper until, after excruciating suffering, the writhing victim is yielded up to its terrible embrace." Most importantly, this argument followed, habitual attempts at contraception meant—even if successful—a mother permanently injured and unable to bear healthy children. If unsuccessful, the children resulting from such unnatural matings would be inevitably weakened. And if such grave ills resulted from the practice of birth control, the physical consequences of abortion were even more dramatic and immediate.

Physicians often felt little hesitation in expressing what seems to the historian a suspiciously disproportionate resentment toward such unnatural females. Unnatural was of course the operational word; for woman's presumed maternal instinct made her primarily responsible for decisions in regard to childbearing. So frequent was this habitual accusation that some medical authors had to caution against placing the entire weight of blame for birth control and abortion upon the woman; men, they reminded, played an important role in most such decisions. In 1871, for example, the American Medical Association Committee on Criminal Abortion described women who patronized abortionists in terms which conjured up fantasies of violence and punishment:

She becomes unmindful of the course marked out for her by Providence, she overlooks the duties imposed on her by the marriage contract. She yields to the pleasures—but shrinks from the pains and responsibilities of maternity; and, destitute of all delicacy and refinement, resigns herself, body and soul, into the hands of unscrupulous and wicked men. Let not the husband of such a wife flatter himself that he possesses her affection. Nor can she in turn ever merit even the respect of a virtuous husband. She sinks into old age like a withered tree, stripped of its foliage; with the stain of blood upon her soul, she dies without the hand of affection to smooth her pillow.

The frequency with which attacks on family limitation in mid-nineteenth-century America were accompanied by polemics against expanded roles for the middle-class woman indicates with unmistakable clarity something of one of the motives structuring such jeremiads. Family limitation necessarily added a significant variable within conjugal relationships generally; its successful practice implied potential access for women to new roles and a new autonomy.

Nowhere is this hostility toward women and the desire to inculcate guilt over women's desire to avoid pregnancy more strikingly illustrated than in the warnings of "race suicide" so increasingly fashionable in the late-nineteenth century. A woman's willingness and capacity to bear children was a duty she owed not only to God and husband but to her "race" as well. In the second half of the nineteenth century, articulate Americans forced to evaluate and come to emotional terms with social change became, like many of their European contemporaries, attracted to a world view which saw racial identity and racial conflict as fundamental. And within these categories, birthrates became all-important indices to national vigor and thus social health.

In 1860 and again in 1870, Massachusetts census returns began to indicate that the foreign born had a considerably higher birthrate than that of native Americans. Indeed, the more affluent and educated a family, the fewer children it seemed to produce. Such statistics indicated that native Americans in the Bay State were not even reproducing themselves. The social consequences seemed ominous indeed.

The Irish, though barely one quarter of the Massachusetts population, produced more than half of the state's children. "It is perfectly clear," a Boston clergyman contended in 1884, "that without a radical change in the religious ideas, education, habits, and customs of the natives, the present population and their descendants will not rule that state a single generation." A few years earlier a well-known New England physician, pointing to America's still largely unsettled western territories, had asked: "Shall they be filled by our own children or by those of aliens? This is a question that our own women must answer; upon their loins depends the future destiny of the nation." Native-born American women had failed themselves as individuals and society as mothers of the Anglo-Saxon race. If matters continued for another half century in the same manner, "the wives who are to be mothers in our republic must be drawn from trans-Atlantic homes. The Sons of the New World will have to re-act, on a magnificent scale, the old story of unwived Rome and the Sabines."

Such arguments have received a goodly amount of historical attention, especially as they figured in the late-nineteenth and early twentieth centuries as part of the contemporary rationale for immigration restriction. Historians have interpreted the race suicide argument in several fashions. As an incident in a general Western acceptance of racism, it has been seen as product of a growing alienation of the older middle and upper classes in the face of industrialization, urbanization, and bureaucratization of society. More specifically, some American historians have seen these race suicide arguments as rooted in the fears and insecurities of a traditionally dominant middle class as it perceived new and threatening social realities.

Whether or not historians care to accept some version of this interpretation—and certainly such motivational elements seem to be suggested in the rhetorical formulae employed by many of those bemoaning the failure of American Protestants to reproduce in adequate numbers—it ignores another element crucial to the logical and emotional fabric of these arguments. This is the explicit charge of female sexual failure. To a significant extent, contemporaries saw the problem as in large measure woman's responsibility; it was America's potential mothers, not its fathers, who were primarily responsible for the impending social cataclysm. Race suicide seemed a problem in social gynecology.

Though fathers played a necessary role in procreation, medical opinion emphasized that it was the mother's constitution and reproductive capacity which most directly shaped her offspring's physical, mental, and emotional attributes. And any unhealthy mode of life—anything in short which seemed undesirable to contemporary medical moralists, including both education and birth control—might result in a woman becoming sterile or capable of bearing only stunted offspring. Men, it was conceded, were subject to vices even more debilitating, but the effects of male sin and imprudence were, physicians felt, "to a greater extent confined to adult life; and consequently do not, to the same extent, impair the vitality of our race or threaten its physical destruction." Women's violation of physiological laws implied disaster to "the unborn of both sexes."

Though such social critics tended to agree that woman was at fault, they expressed some difference of opinion as to the nature of her guilt. A few felt that lower birthrates could be attributed simply to the conscious and culpable decision of American women to curtail family size. Other physicians and social commentators, while admitting that many women felt little desire for children, saw the roots of the problem in somewhat different—and perhaps even more apocalyptic—terms. It was not, they feared, simply the conscious practice of family limitation which resulted in small families; rather the increasingly unnatural lifestyle of the "modern American woman" had undermined her reproductive capacities so that even when she would, she could not bear adequate numbers of healthy children. Only if American women returned to the simpler life-styles of the eighteenth and early nineteenth centuries could the race hope to regain its former vitality; women must from childhood see their role as that of robust and self-sacrificing mothers. If not, their own degeneration and that of the race was inevitable.

Why the persistence and intensity of this masculine hostility, or its recurring echoes of conflict, rancor, and moral outrage? There are at least several possible, though by no means exclusive, explanations. One centers on the hostility implied and engendered by the sexual deprivation—especially for the male—implicit in many of the modes of birth control employed at this time. One might, for example, speculate —as Oscar Handlin did some years ago—that such repressed middle-class sexual energies were channeled into a xenophobic hostility toward the immigrant and the black and projected into fantasies incorporating the enviable and fully expressed sexuality of these alien groups. A similar model could be applied to men's attitudes toward women as well; social, economic, and sexual tensions which beset late nineteenth-century American men might well have caused them to express their anxieties and frustrations in terms of hostility toward the middle-class female.

Such interpretations are, however, as treacherous as they are inviting. Obviously, the would-be scientific formulations outlined here mirror something of post-bellum social and psychic reality. Certainly some middle-class men in the late-nineteenth century had personality needs —sexual inadequacies or problems of status identification—which made traditional definitions of gender roles functional to them. The hostility, even the violent imagery expressed toward women who chose to limit the number of children they bore indicates a significant personal and emotional involvement on the part of the male author. Some women, moreover, obviously used the mechanisms of birth control and, not infrequently sexual rejection, as role-sanctioned building blocks in the fashioning of their particular adjustment. Their real and psychic gains were numerous: surcease from fear and pain, greater leisure, a socially acceptable way of expressing hostility, and a means of maintaining some autonomy and privacy in a life which society demanded be devoted wholeheartedly to the care and nurturance of husband and children. Beyond such statements, however, matters become quite conjectural. At this moment in the development of both historical methodology and psychological theory great caution must be exercised in the development of such hypotheses—especially since the historians of gender and sexual behavior have at their disposal data which from a psychodynamic point of view is at best fragmentary and suggestive.

What the nineteenth-century social historian can hope to study with a greater degree of certainty, however, is the way in which social change both caused and reflected tensions surrounding formal definitions of gender roles. Obviously, individuals as individuals at all times and in all cultures have experienced varying degrees of difficulty in assimilating the prescriptions of expected role behavior. When such discontinuities begin to affect comparatively large numbers and become sufficiently overt as to evoke a marked ideological response one can then speak with assurance of having located fundamental cultural tension.

Students of nineteenth-century American and Western European society have long been aware of the desire of a growing number of women for a choice among roles different from the traditional one of mother and housekeeper. It was a theme of Henry James, Henrik Ibsen, and a host of other, perhaps more representative if less talented, writers. Women's demands ranged from that of equal pay for equal work and equal education for equal intelligence to more covert demands for abortion, birth control information, and sexual autonomy within the marriage relationship. Their demands paralleled and were in large part dependent upon fundamental social and economic developments. Technological innovation and economic growth, changed patterns of income distribution, population concentrations, demographic changes in terms of life expectancy and fertility all affected woman's behavior and needs. Fewer women married; many were numbered among the urban poor. Such women had to become self-supporting and at the same time deal with the changed self-image that self-support necessitated. Those women who married generally did so later, had fewer children, and lived far beyond the birth of their youngest child. At the same time ideological developments began to encourage both men and women to aspire to increased independence and self-fulfillment. All these factors interacted to create new ambitions and new options for American women. In a universe of varying personalities and changing economic realities, it was inevitable that some women at least would—overtly or covertly—be attracted by such options and that a goodly number of men would find such choices unacceptable. Certainly for the women who did so the normative role of home-bound nurturant and passive woman was no longer appropriate or functional, but became a source of conflict and anxiety.

It was inevitable as well that many men, similarly faced with a rapidly changing society, would seek in domestic peace and constancy a sense of the continuity and security so difficult to find elsewhere in their society. They would—at the very least—expect their wives, their daughters, and their family relationships generally to remain unaltered. When their female dependents seemed ill-disposed to do so, such men responded with a harshness sanctioned increasingly by the new gods of science.

Search for an Ancestor

ALEX HALEY

• Many years ago the black poet, Langston Hughes, asked,
"What is Africa to me?" The significance of Africa to black
Americans has not been constant. Africa is the homeland, the
point of origin. Yet throughout the eighteenth and nineteenth centuries Africa was considered by white America an
unknown and barbaric continent. It was difficult, therefore,
for American blacks to feel proud of their ancient homeland.
True, there were some blacks who looked to Africa as a place
of refuge and possible resettlement, but most plans to send
blacks back to Africa in the nineteenth century originated
with whites eager to eliminate the black population and avoid
the problems of how the two races could live together. In the
twentieth century two notable blacks, W. E. B. DuBois, an
intellectual of outstanding caliber, and Marcus Garvey, a
charismatic, popular leader of the 1920s, encouraged their fellow blacks to be proud of the historical connection with
Africa. Later on in the century, members of the black power
movement of the 1960s, inspired by the all-black leadership
in the newly independent African states, donned dashikis and
wore Afros and, at a deeper level, looked with new interest
at the historical connection of their lives to the African past.

Alex Haley shows in this article how one man embarked on
a personal quest for his origins in the remote African past of
his ancestors. Reading more like an adventure story than historical research, Haley's article describes how a few African
words passed down through generations in his family led him
to the very African village where his forebears lived before he
was sold into slavery. Haley's effort is heartening, not only as
one man's search for his historical roots but also because it
offers both inspiration and method for further research into
the history of American blacks which for too long has been
cut off from the richness of its African past.

From *The Listener* (January 10, 1974), pp. 43-47.

I grew up in a little town called Henning, Tennessee, about fifty miles
west of Memphis, and I lived there in the home of my grandmother,
my mother's mother. Every summer my grandmother would have vis-
itors come to our home. They would be older women of the family,
her nieces, aunts and cousins, and every single evening that I can remember, they would sit out on the front porch in rocking-chairs, and
I would sit behind my grandmother's rocking-chair and listen to them
talking. They would tell about things that had happened to the family
when they had been slaves, and they went back and back and back.
The furthest-back person they would ever talk about was someone
they described as "the African," and they would tell how this African
had been brought on a ship to a place they pronounced as "Napalis."
They told how he had been bought off that ship by a man whose name
was John Waller, who had a plantation in a place called Spotsylvania
County, Virginia, and they told how the African had kept trying to
escape. The first three times he escaped he was caught, brought back,
given a worse beating each time, and then, the fourth time he escaped,
he had the misfortune to be caught by a professional slave-catcher. I
have since done some peripheral research on the profession of slave-
catching and I think there's never been a more bestial one in the
United States. This particular man brought the African back, and it
was decided on the spot that he would be given a punishment at the
decision of the slave-catcher. I grew up hearing how the slave was
offered the punishment either of being castrated or of having a foot
cut off. He chose the foot, and it was cut off with an axe against a tree
stump. It was a very hideous act and as it turned out it was to play a
major role in keeping the African's story alive in a black family. In the
middle of the 1700s, slaves, particularly male slaves, were sold back and
forth so frequently that there was very little sense of family continuity among them. In that part of Virginia they were sold at auction and,
on the average, each would bring around eight dollars. At the end of
every slave auction there would be what they called a "scrap sale":
slaves who were ill, or otherwise incapacitated, would bring in smaller
amounts, generally one dollar or less. When this particular slave managed to survive and then to convalesce, he posed an economic question
to his master: slavery, after all, was an economic matter. Although he
was crippled and hobbled around, he could do limited work around
the house and yard-area of the plantation, so the master decided he

would be worth more kept to do this limited work than he would be just sold away for less than one dollar in cash. And so he was kept on one plantation for what turned out to be quite a long period of time.

On that plantation, this slave met and mated with another slave. My grandmother and the others said that she was named Belle, the Big House cook, and of that union was born a little girl, who was given the name Kissy. When Kissy got to be four or five, and could begin to understand things, this African, whenever he got a chance, would take her by the hand (he knew her to be his daughter, she knew him to be her father—an unusual thing in slavery at that point) and lead her round the plantation. He would point out to her various natural objects and tell her the names for them in his native tongue: some sounds for *tree, rock, cow*. In the slave-cabin area, he would point out a banjo or a guitar and he would say one syllable, *ko*, and in time the little girl came to associate the sound *ko* with a banjo or a guitar. On the outer edges of the plantation there was a small river, and when they were out in that area, he would say to her something like *Kamby-Bolongo*, and the little girl came to know that this sound meant river.

All the Africans who were brought to the United States as slaves gradually learned a word here, a phrase there, of the new language, English. As this began to happen with this particular African, he would tell his daughter more involved things, little anecdotes about himself. He seemed to have a passion for trying to communicate to her a sense of his past. For instance, he would tell her how he had been captured. He told her he had not been far away from his village, chopping wood, when he had been set upon by four men, kidnapped and taken into slavery. The first thing that happened to slaves when they got to a plantation was that they were given an Anglicised name: that was the first step in the psychic dehumanisation of an individual—the removal from that individual of the name he had carried all his life, with which went, as it goes for us today, the sense of who we are. The master had given this African the name of "Toby" but, whenever any of the other slaves used the word "Toby," he would strenuously reject it and tell them his name was Kin-Tay.

Kissy stayed directly exposed to her father from Africa until she was 16 years old. She had quite a considerable repertoire of knowledge about him, when she herself was sold away to a man named Tom Lea who had a much smaller plantation in North Carolina. It was on that plantation that Tom Lea became the father of Kissy's first child, a boy who was given the name of George. When George got to be about four or five, Kissy began to tell him the things she had learned from her father. Among the other slave children, his peers, he began to run into the common phenomenon that slave children rarely knew who their fathers were. He had something that made him singular: he had direct knowledge of a grandfather. The boy grew up and, when he got into his teens, became a gamecock fighter: that was a great sport in the Ante-Bellum South. When he was about seventeen, he gained the nickname that he would take to his grave—"Chicken George."

When he was about eighteen, Chicken George took a mate, another slave, whose name was Matilda, and in time Matilda gave birth to seven children. On another plantation, a generation later, in another section of North Carolina, Chicken George would tell his children the story which had come down from his mother Kissy. Those children grew up, took mates and had children. One of them was named Tom. He became an apprentice blacksmith and was sold to a man named Murray who had a tobacco plantation in Alamance County, North Carolina. He met and mated with a slave whose name was Irene, the weaver on the plantation, and she bore him seven children. Tom the blacksmith would tell his seven children about something virtually unique among the slaves: direct knowledge of a great-great-grandfather. The youngest of his seven children was a little girl whose name was Cynthia, and Cynthia was to become my maternal grandmother. That was how it happened that I grew up in my grandmother's home in Tennessee, hearing from her that story which had passed down the family about all the rest of the family going back to that African who said his name was Kin-Tay, who called the river *Kamby-Bolongo*, and the guitar *ko*, and who said he had been chopping wood when he was captured. By the time I was in my mid-teens, I knew this story pretty well, having heard it for fully a decade.

I went to school briefly at small Black Land grant colleges around the South where my father was teaching, and when World War Two came along I went into the US Coastguards. It was the time when if you were black and you went into one of the Naval Services in the United States, you went into the Stewards' Department. You were mess-boy, you cleaned up the state rooms, waited on tables, washed the dishes, and, if you did well, advanced to cook. I became cook on a ship in the southwest Pacific during the war. It was boring. We would be put to sea for two or three months at a time before we could get ashore in Australia or New Zealand. My most precious possession was a portable typewriter. I had learned to type when I was in high school, and I would write letters to everybody I could think of: I would get thirty or forty letters at a time, simply because I wrote so much. Then I began trying to write marine dramas, sea stories. They didn't sell for a long time, but I kept writing for eight years, until finally a small magazine began to buy some of my stories. I stayed on in the Service, began to write for somewhat larger magazines, and finally, when I was 37, I retired from the Coastguards with 20 years service. At that time, something happened that seems to me to have been the first of a series of miracles that were to make it possible to pull together a document, a book of which I am now at the finishing stages, having to do in an unusual way with black history, black culture, black pride, relating to the whole area of blackness in Africa and the United States and the continuities.

The first thing that happened could scarcely have seemed to have less to do with blackness. *Playboy* asked me if I would fly over to London to do an interview with a film actress, Julie Christie. There were long gaps when I couldn't get to see her. One morning I was in the British Museum, and I came upon the Rosetta Stone. I had read how the French scholar, Champollion, had matched the unknown characters on the stone with the Greek, and had finally been able to prove that the demotic and the hieroglyphics had the same text as the Greek. That fascinated me: I would go round in London doing other things, but I would find my mind going back to that Rosetta Stone.

I was on a plane going back to the United States when an idea hit me. What Jean Champollion really did was to match the unknown with the known, and so find the meaning of what hitherto had been unknown. In that story always told in our family there had been a language: the sounds that this African always said when he pointed to different objects. Obviously, many sounds would have been lost in the transmission down the generations, but I could see that the sounds which had survived tended to be hard, angular sounds of the sort that would survive: like *ko*, Kin-Tay, *Kamby-Bolongo*. They had to be fragments of some native tongue. Could I possibly find out where these sounds had come from? My research assistant George Simms, came up with a list of people who were very knowledgeable in the field of African linguistics. One of them was at the University of Wisconsin. His name was Doctor Jan Vansina. He had been trained in his native Belgium, and then at the University of London's Oriental and African Studies department. He had worked in Africa, living in African villages, and had written a book called *The Oral Tradition*. In the Vansinas' living-room that evening I told Dr Vansina everything I could remember from the time I was a little boy: every bit of the stories, the sounds, the names of the people, the chronology of the family. As an oral historian, he was particularly interested in the physical transmission of the story from one generation to another. The following morning, Dr Vansina came down with a very serious expression on his face. I learned that he had already been on the phone to knowledgeable colleagues of his. He said that they felt that the greatest possibility was that the sounds represented the Mandinka dialect. I had never heard of such a thing as Mandinka. From his knowledge of it, he began to guess-translate what those sounds had meant. There was a sound that probably meant the *beobab tree*, generic in West Africa: there was a sound that probably meant *cow*. I heard about something that could be said to look like a banjo, an instrument called the *kora*, well-known where Mandinka was spoken. Finally, we came to *Kamby-Bolongo*: I heard that in Mandinka *bolongo* would mean *river* or *stream*. Preceded by *Kamby*, very probably it would mean *Gambia River*. I tend to be, if something hits me just right, very impulsive. It was Thursday morning when I heard the words *Gambia River*. On Monday morning I was in Africa.

On the Friday morning, I had looked among the names of African students in the United States. From that small country, the Gambia, the one I found who was physically closest to where I was was a fellow called Ebon Manga, attending Hamilton College at Clinton, New York. I hit that campus around 3.30, Friday afternoon, and practically snatched Ebon Manga out of an economics class. We got onto a Pan-American that night and flew to Dakar. From there we got a light plane and flew over to Yanda, near Bathurst. We took a van into Bathurst. Ebon and his father helped to assemble a group of about eight members of the Gambian Government, mature men who met me in the patio of the Hotel Atlantic in Bathurst. There I sat with them, telling them the stories that had been passed down. It gives me the quivers sometimes when I reflect how tissue-thin have been the hinges upon which this whole adventure has swung at one time or another. What these men in the Gambia reacted to most was a sound which I had no idea had any particular meaning. They said: "There may be great significance in the fact that your forefather said his name was Kin-Tay. In our country, our older villages are often named from the families which founded those villages centuries ago." And they showed me a little map, with names of villages like Kinte-Kundah Janneh-Ya. They also told me about men of whom I had never heard called *griots*, who were like walking, living archives. A line of *griots* would know the history of one village, they told me, or of one large family clan. They told me that they would look about to see what *griot* might be able to help me.

I went back to the United States. About six weeks later, a letter came to me from the Gambia saying that when I was able it might be worth-while for me to return—as casually as that. In about a week I was back in Bathurst. The same men with whom I had talked at the Atlantic Hotel told me that the word had been put out in the back-country, and a *griot* knowledgeable about the history of the Kinte clan had been found. "Where is he?" I asked. I would have figured, from my experience as an American magazine writer, that the Government should have had him there with a public relations man for me to talk to. They said: "He's in his village." In order to see this man, I had to get together a total of 14 people, three of which were interpreters, and four musicians—they told me that, in the back-country, the *griots* wouldn't talk without music in the background.

Mud walls, conical-roofed huts, thatched roofs: there were only about seventy people in the village. As soon as I saw a man, I knew somehow that he was the man we had come to see. Small of build with a pill-box hat and off-white robe: I was later to learn that his name was Kebba Kanga Fofana. The interpreter with me went straight to him. Meanwhile I had stepped into a succession of events that were almost traumatic in their emotional effect upon me. First, the people, about seventy of them, crowded very closely around me. I began to notice how they were staring at me. Their brows were forward and the intensity of the eyes was just raking. It was as if they wanted to know me in corpuscular detail. I dropped my eyes: I had this sensation of looking at my own hands, my own complexion, and I had a

tremendous feeling within me, like a gale-force wind. I was looking
at a crowd of people and, for the first time in my life, everybody in
the crowd was jet-black in colour. That just hit me like a sledge-
hammer. And then, I had this second sledgehammer-type feeling: a
kind of guilt, a feeling of being hybrid, of being impure among pure.
Then the old man, Kebba Kanga Fofana, began to tell me, through
the interpreters, the history of the Kinte clan.

Griots can talk for hours on end, telling the stories they have
learned. Every now and then when the griot was spilling out lineage
details of who married whom, who had what children and in what
order, a couple of centuries ago, he would stop: a translation would
come of some little detail about an individual—for example, that in
the year of the Big Water he slew a water buffalo. Kebba Kanga
Fofana said that the Kinte clan had begun in the country called Old
Mali, and a branch of the clan had moved into Mauretania. In Old
Mali, the clan had been characterised by the men being blacksmiths as
a rule; the women were habitually potters and weavers. There had
come out of Mauretania a son of the clan whose name was Kairaba
Kunta Kinte. He came from Mauretania to the country of the Gambia.
He stopped first in a village called Pakali N'Ding. He went next to a
village called Jiffarong, and then to a village called Juffure. It was in
Juffure that he took his first wife, a Mandinka maiden whose name
was Sireng. By her he begot two sons whose names were Janneh and
Saloum. Then he took (Moslem men, plural marriages) a second wife.
Her name was Yaisa, and by Yaisa he begot a son whose name was
Omoro.

The three sons grew up in the village of Juffure, and when they
came of age the older two, Janneh and Saloum, went away and founded
a new village called to this day Kinte-Kundah Janneh-Ya. The youngest son, Omoro, stayed there until he had 39 rains; and at the age of
30 rains he took a wife whose name was Binta Kebba. Between 1750
and 1760, there were born four sons to Omoro and Binta Kebba: Kunta,
Lamin, Suwadu and Madi. When he named those four brothers, the
old man stopped and the interpreter said: "about the time the King's
soldiers came." That was one of the time-fixing references which griots
use. Later, in London, I found the British Parliamentary records, because I had to know the date. He was talking about a group called
Colonel O'Hare's Forces, which had been sent from London to the

Gambia River to guard the then British-held fort, James Slave Fort, and the date was right on.

Then Kebba Kanga Fofana said: "About the time the King's soldiers came, the eldest of these four sons, Kunta, went away from this village to chop wood, and he was never seen again." I sat there with goose-pimples the size of lemons popping over me. He had no way of know-ing that what he had told me meshed with what I had heard as a little boy on the front porch of my grandmother's home in Tennessee.

I suddenly became aware that the people of the village had formed a circle and were moving counter-clockwise around me. They were chanting: up, down, loud, soft. I had been sitting on a chair, and I popped up as if I had been full of helium. All I could do was stand up. Then there came the music that was always in the background. I remember my ears slowly becoming aware that I was hearing sounds I had to recognise from a *kora* player, who was singing. I was hearing in a way I could understand. I could distinguish the words "Alex Haley." I could understand Kinte. I didn't know then that, in the way of *griots*, my having come to that village, my having been found to be a descendant of that village, was there and then being recorded as part of the village's history. They carried me into the mosque, and there was a prayer. It was translated as: "Praise be to Allah for one lost long from us whom God has returned."

We finally had to go back. I had to return to America and, on the road going out, I was full of the emotion of it. We got to the first village, and I saw people lined up on either side of the road. The peo-ple in this village already knew what had happened in the village of Juffure. As we came close with the Land-Rover, the driver slowed down, and I was looking down at these people standing on either side waving, a great cacophony of sound coming out of them, from wizened elders to little naked youngsters. I though it was nothing but caprice: they were there, never having left Africa, and I, symbolising to them all of us in America, happened to be standing up in there simply be-cause of the caprice—which of our forefathers had been taken out. That was the only thing which had made the difference. Then I grad-ually became aware what the sound was they were crying out: "Mr Kin-Tay, Mr Kin-Tay." I'm a man, but a sob rolled up from foot-level, and I just flung up my hands and cried as I never had in my life. It seemed to me that if you knew the story of how the black people in

America had come there, taken as slaves from all those countries, and you knew the continuity of us as a people, then, whatever else you might do, you really needed to start by weeping, because there were no words and no actions which could ever assuage what had happened in that terrible time in the history of both countries.

That's the saga of the black people in America, and I had to write it. I had to know everything I could to put into this book. I wanted to find, if I could, the symbolic boat that, it is said, brought 1,500,000 of our forefathers to the USA. To be the proper ship, it had to be the one that brought Kunta-Kinte out of the Gambia River. I knew now about the time "the King's soldiers had come," and I had found that Colonel O'Hare's Forces were his reference. I knew that it had happened in mid-1767. I went to Lloyds of London and I got help from them with the marine records of the 1700s. I searched for seven weeks. One afternoon in the Public Records Office, I was on the 123rd set of slaveship records when I found a sheet with 30 ships' movements on it. Number 18 was moving out of Gambia River, James Fort. Number 18 was a ship that had stated her destination as Annapolis, Maryland. I knew that Kunta-Kinte had been taken to Annapolis.

In the next ten days I crossed the Atlantic Ocean three times, patching together little things I had to find out about that ship. I found she was called the *Lord Ligonier*, named after a British field-marshal. She had been built in 1765 in the New England Colonies. She set sail in 1766, with a cargo of rum, as a new slave-ship to Gravesend. There she sold the rum. The profits were used to buy a cargo, the slaving hardware—the chains, the shackles, the other restraining objects to put on the extra crew—and the extra foodstuffs she would need, and she started sailing to Africa, to the source of what was called the "black gold" of Africa. I was able to follow the ship from the records along the Channel, and it became almost like running along the Channel, watching her. I knew her timbers, I knew her planking was loblolly pine and hackmatack cedar. I knew she had red oak timbers. I knew that the flax in her sails was out of New Jersey. I knew the kind of nails that held her together, how the black lopes were held together with a wedge of oak. I could almost read the captain's mind as he was driving to get to the African coast.

She went southerly across the Bay of Biscay, down past the Canaries, the Cape Virgins, into the mouth of the Gambia River. She was to spend the next ten months in the Gambia River, slaving. In the course of that ten months she got a cargo of 3,265 elephant tusks, 3,700 pounds of beeswax, 800 pounds of rough raw Gambian cotton, 32 ounces of Gambian gold and 140 slaves. She set sail on Sunday, 5 July 1767, headed directly for Annapolis. Her crossing voyage of about 5,000 miles took two months, three weeks and two days. She arrived in Annapolis, Maryland, on the morning of 29 September 1767.

29 September 1967: I was standing on a pier in Annapolis looking seaward, drenched in tears. It was two hundred years to the day since my forebear had come to that city, and there in Annapolis I went into the tax records to find out what she had come in with. I found she came in with a cargo. She declared the same cargo she had leaving James Fort, Gambia River, except that her original 140 slaves had become 98. Forty-two had died on the crossing, which was about average for the ships making that trip in that period. I knew that when slaves were brought in they were always advertised, and I went down to the microfilm records of the Annapolis media of the time, the *Maryland Gazette*, and in the issue of 1 October 1967, on page three, was the ad of the agents of the ship, saying that the *Lord Ligonier* had just arrived under Captain Davies from the River Gambia, with a cargo of fresh, choice, healthy slaves for sale, to be sold the following Wednesday at Meg's Wharf. Among them was Kunta-Kinte, who had come from the village of Juffure.

One thing remained to complete it. I knew that my grandmother and the others had always said that he had been named Toby by his master, and I knew that every kind of deal involving slaves was a matter of legal records. I went to Richmond, Virginia, and went into the legal deeds of the transactions of the 1760s. I found a deed dated 5 September 1768 between two brothers, John and William Waller, transferring goods between them: on the second page were the words "and also one Negro man slave named Toby."

Slavery Through the Prism
of Black Folklore

STERLING STUCKEY

• *The institution of slavery started on the North American
continent as an attempt to cope with severe labor shortages.
The first boatload of Africans arrived in 1619, and for the
next forty years blacks were sometimes treated as indentured
servants—workers who toiled for a fixed period of time and
were then free to pursue their own lives—and sometimes kept
forever in bondage. Not until the 1660s did the custom develop to keep all Afro-Americans in permanent servitude.
Thereafter the African slaves provided the bulk of the labor-
ing force in the southern colonies. Slavery existed in the
North also during this period, but the institution was generally curbed and the bondsmen released before the Civil War.
In the South, by contrast, the invention of the cotton gin in
1793 created an enormous need for slaves to support an essentially agricultural economy.*

*In recent years, historians have done valuable work on the
nature of racist thought, on the conditions of plantation
life, on the effect of bondage upon personality, and on the
profitability of slavery. What is lacking is printed evidence
from the slaves themselves, a gap caused in large part by the
fact that most slaves were not permitted to learn to read and
write. In the following essay, Professor Sterling Stuckey suggests that folklore provides important clues about the meaning of the black experience.*

Originally appeared as "Through the Prism of Folklore: The Black Ethos
in Slavery" in *The Massachusetts Review*. Copyright © 1968. The Massachusetts Review, Inc.

It is not excessive to advance the view that some historians, because they have been so preoccupied with demonstrating the absence of significant slave revolts, conspiracies, and "day to day" resistance among slaves, have presented information on slave behavior and thought which is incomplete indeed. They have, in short, devoted very little attention to trying to get "inside" slaves to discover what bondsmen thought about their condition. Small wonder we have been saddled with so many stereotypical treatments of slave thought and behavior.

Though we do not know enough about the institution of slavery or the slave experience to state with great precision how slaves felt about their condition, it is reasonably clear that slavery, however draconic and well supervised, was not the hermetically sealed monolith —destructive to the majority of slave personalities—that some historians would have us believe. The works of Herbert Aptheker, Kenneth Stampp, Richard Wade, and the Bauers, allowing for differences in approach and purpose, indicate that slavery, despite its brutality, was not so "closed" that it robbed most of the slaves of their humanity.

It should, nevertheless, be asserted at the outset that blacks could not have survived the grim experience of slavery unscathed. Those historians who, for example, point to the dependency complex which slavery engendered in many Afro-Americans, offer us an important insight into one of the most harmful effects of that institution upon its victims. That slavery caused not a few bondsmen to question their worth as human beings—this much, I believe, we can posit with certitude. We can also safely assume that such self-doubt would rend one's sense of humanity, establishing an uneasy balance between affirming and negating aspects of one's being. What is at issue is not whether American slavery was harmful to slaves but whether, in their struggle to control self-lacerating tendencies, the scales were tipped toward a despair so consuming that most slaves, in time, became reduced to the level of "Sambos."

My thesis, which rests on an examination of folk songs and tales, is that slaves were able to fashion a life style and set of values—an ethos— which prevented them from being imprisoned altogether by the definitions which the larger society sought to impose. This ethos was an amalgam of Africanisms and New World elements which helped slaves, in Guy Johnson's words, "feel their way along the course of American slavery, enabling them to endure. . . ." As Sterling Brown, that wise student of Afro-American culture, has remarked, the values expressed in folklore acted as a "wellspring to which slaves" trapped in the wasteland of American slavery "could return in times of doubt to be refreshed." In short, I shall contend that the process of dehumanization was not nearly as pervasive as Stanley Elkins would have us believe; that a very large number of slaves, guided by this ethos, were able to maintain their essential humanity. I make this contention because folklore, in its natural setting, is of, by and for those who create and respond to it, depending for its survival upon the accuracy with which it speaks to needs and reflects sentiments. I therefore consider it safe to assume that the attitudes of a very large number of slaves are represented by the themes of folklore.

Frederick Douglass, commenting on slave songs, remarked his utter astonishment, on coming to the North, "to find persons who could speak of the singing among slaves as evidence of their contentment and happiness." The young DuBois, among the first knowledgeable critics of the spirituals, found white Americans as late as 1903 still telling Afro-Americans that "life was joyous to the black slave, careless and happy." "I can easily believe this of some," he wrote, "of many. But not all the past South, though it rose from the dead, can gainsay the heart-touching witness of these songs."

> They are the music of an unhappy people, of the children of disappointment; they tell of death and suffering and unvoiced longing toward a truer world, of misty wanderings and hidden ways.

Though historians have been interested in such wanderings and ways, Frederick Douglass, probably referring to the spirituals, said the songs of slaves represented the sorrows of the slave's heart, serving to relieve the slave "only as an aching heart is relieved by its tears." "I have often sung," he continued, "to drown my sorrow, but seldom to express my happiness. Crying for joy, and singing for joy, were alike uncommon to me while in the jaws of slavery."

Sterling Brown, who has much to tell us about the poetry and meaning of these songs, has observed: "As the best expression of the slave's deepest thoughts and yearnings, they (the spirituals) speak with convincing finality against the legend of contented slavery." Rejecting the formulation that the spirituals are mainly otherworldly,

Brown states that though the creators of the spirituals looked toward heaven and "found their triumphs there, they did not blink their eyes to trouble here." The spirituals, in his view, "never tell of joy in the 'good old days'. . . . The only joy in the spirituals is in dreams of escape."

Rather than being essentially otherworldly, these songs, in Brown's opinion, "tell of his life, of 'rollin' through an unfriendly world!" To substantiate this view, he points to numerous lines from spirituals: "Oh, bye and bye, bye and bye, I'm going to lay down this heavy load"; "My way is cloudy"; "Oh, stand the storm, it won't be long, we'll anchor by and by"; "Lord help me from sinking down"; and "Don't know what my mother wants to stay here fuh, Dis ole world ain't been no friend to huh." To those scholars who "would have us believe that when the Negro sang of freedom, he meant only what the whites meant, namely freedom from sin," Brown rejoins:

> Free individualistic whites on the make in a prospering civiliza-tion, nursing the American dream, could well have felt their only bondage to be that of sin, and freedom to be religious salvation. But with the drudgery, the hardships, the auction block, the slave-mart, the shackles, and the lash so literally present in the Negro's experience, it is hard to imagine why for the Negro they would remain figurative. The scholars certainly did not make this clear, but rather take refuge in such dicta as: "the slave never contemplated his low condition."

"Are we to believe," asks Brown, "that the slave singing 'I been rebuked, I been scorned, done had a hard time sho's you bawn,' re-ferred to his being outside the true religion?" A reading of additional spirituals indicates that they contained distinctions in meaning which placed them outside the confines of the "true religion." Sometimes, in these songs, we hear slaves relating to divinities on terms more West African than American. The easy intimacy and argumentation, which come out of a West African frame of reference, can be heard in "Hold the Wind."

> When I get to heaven, gwine be at ease,
> Me and my God *gonna do as we please.*

> Gonna chatter with the Father, argue with the Son,
> *Tell um 'bout the world I just come from.* (Italics added.)

If there is a tie with heaven in those lines from "Hold the Wind," there is also a clear indication of dislike for the restrictions imposed by slavery. And at least one high heavenly authority might have a few questions to answer. *Tell um 'bout the world I just come from* makes it abundantly clear that some slaves—even when released from the burdens of the world—would keep alive painful memories of their oppression.

If slaves could argue with the son of God, then surely, when on their knees in prayer, they would not hesitate to speak to God of the treatment being received at the hands of their oppressors.

> Talk about me much as you please, (2)
> Chillun, talk about me much as you please,
> Gonna talk about you when I get on my knees.

That slaves could spend time complaining about treatment received from other slaves is conceivable, but that this was their only complaint, or even the principal one, is hardly conceivable. To be sure, there is a certain ambiguity in the use of the word "chillun" in this context. The reference appears to apply to slaveholders.

The spiritual, *Samson*, as Vincent Harding has pointed out, probably contained much more (for some slaves) than mere biblical implications. Some who sang these lines from *Samson*, Harding suggests, might well have meant tearing down the edifice of slavery. If so, it was the ante-bellum equivalent of today's "burn baby burn."

> He said, 'An' if I had-'n my way,'
> He said, 'An' if I had-'n my way,'
> He said, 'An' if I had-'n my way,
> I'd tear the build-in' down!'

> He said, 'And now I got my way, (3)
> And I'll tear this buildin' down.'

Both Harriet Tubman and Frederick Douglass have reported that some of the spirituals carried double meanings. Whether most of the slaves who sang those spirituals could decode them is another matter. Harold Courlander has made a persuasive case against widespread understanding of any given "loaded" song, but it seems to me that he fails to recognize sufficiently a further aspect of the subject: slaves, as their folktales make eminently clear, used irony repeatedly, especially with animal stories. Their symbolic world was rich. Indeed, the various masks which many put on were not unrelated to this symbolic process. It seems logical to infer that it would occur to more than a few to seize upon some songs, even though created originally for religious purposes, assign another meaning to certain words, and use these songs for a variety of purposes and situations.

At times slave bards created great poetry as well as great music. One genius among the slaves couched his (and their) desire for freedom in a magnificent line of verse. After God's powerful voice had "Rung through Heaven and down in Hell," he sang, "My dungeon shook and my chains, they fell."

In some spirituals, Alan Lomax has written, Afro-Americans turned sharp irony and "healing laughter" toward heaven, again like their West African ancestors, relating on terms of intimacy with God. In one, the slaves have God engaged in a dialogue with Adam:

> 'Stole my apples, I believe.'
> 'No, marse Lord, I spec it was Eve.'
> Of this tale there is no mo'
> Eve et the apple and Adam de co'.

Douglass informs us that slaves also sang ironic seculars about the institution of slavery. He reports having heard them sing: "We raise de wheat, dey gib us de corn; We sift de meal, dey gib us he huss; We peel de meat, dey gib us de skin; An dat's de way dey take us in." Slaves would often stand back and see the tragicomic aspects of their situation, sometimes admiring the swiftness of blacks:

> Run, nigger, run, de patrollers will ketch you,
> Run, nigger run, its almost day.
> Dat nigger run, dat nigger flew;
> Dat nigger tore his shirt in two.

And there is:

> My ole mistiss promise me
> W'en she died, she'd set me free,
> She lived so long dat 'er head got bal'
> An' she give out'n de notion a-dyin' at all.

In the ante-bellum days, work songs were of crucial import to slaves. As they cleared and cultivated land, piled levees along rivers, piled loads on steamboats, screwed cotton bales into the holds of ships, and cut roads and railroads through forest, mountain and flat, slaves sang while the white man, armed and standing in the shade, shouted his orders. Through the sense of timing and coordination which characterized work songs well sung, especially by the leaders, slaves sometimes quite literally created works of art. These songs not only militated against injuries but enabled the bondsmen to get difficult jobs done more easily by not having to concentrate on the dead level of their work. "In a very real sense the chants of Negro labor," writes Alan Lomax, "may be considered the most profoundly American of all our folk songs, for they were created by our people as they tore at American rock and earth and reshaped it with their bare hands, while rivers of sweat ran down and darkened the dust."

> Long summer day makes a white man lazy,
>   Long summer day.
> Long summer day makes a nigger run away, sir,
>   Long summer day.

Other slaves sang lines indicating their distaste for slave labor:

> Ol' massa an' ol' missis,
> Sittin' in the parlour,
> Jus' fig'in' an' a-plannin'
> How to work a nigger harder.

And there are these bitter lines, the meaning of which is clear:

> Missus in the big house,
> Mammy in the yard,
> Missus holdin' her white hands,
> Mammy workin' hard (3)
> Missus holdin' her white hands,
> Mammy workin' hard.

> Old Marse ridin' all time,
> Niggers workin' round,
> Marse sleepin' day time,
> Niggers diggin' in the ground, (3)
> Marse sleepin' day time,
> Niggers diggin' in the ground.

Courlander tells us that the substance of the work songs "ranges from the humorous to the sad, from the gentle to the biting, and from the tolerant to the unforgiving." The statement in a given song can be metaphoric, tangent or direct, the meaning personal or impersonal.

"As throughout Negro singing generally, there is an incidence of social criticism, ridicule, gossip, and protest." Pride in their strength rang with the downward thrust of axe—

> When I was young and in my prime, (hah!)
> Sunk my axe deep every time, (hah!)

Blacks later found their greatest symbol of manhood in John Henry, descendant of Trickster John of slave folk tales:

> A man ain't nothing but a man,
> But before I'll let that steam driver beat me down
> I'll die with my hammer in my hand.

Though Frances Kemble, an appreciative and sensitive listener to work songs, felt that "one or two barbaric chants would make the fortune of an opera," she was on one occasion, "displeased not a little" by a self-deprecating song, one which "embodied the opinion that 'twenty-six black girls not make mulatto yellow girl,' and as I told them I did not like it, they have since omitted it." What is pivotal here is not the presence of self-laceration in folklore, but its extent and meaning. While folklore contained some self-hatred, on balance it gives no indication whatever that blacks, as a group, liked or were indifferent to slavery, which is the issue.

To be sure, only the most fugitive of songs sung by slaves contained direct attacks upon the system. Two of these were associated with slave rebellions. The first, possibly written by ex-slave Denmark Vesey himself, was sung by slaves on at least one island off the coast of Charleston, S.C., and at meetings convened by Vesey in Charleston. Though obviously not a folksong, it was sung by the folk.

> Hail! all hail! ye Afric clan,
> Hail! ye oppressed, ye Afric band,
> Who toil and sweat in slavery bound
> And when your health and strength are gone
> Are left to hunger and to mourn,
> Let independence be your aim,
> Ever mindful what 'tis worth.
> Pledge your bodies for the prize,
> Pile them even to the skies!

The second, a popular song derived from a concrete reality, bears the marks of a conscious authority:

> You mought be rich as cream
> And drive you coach and four-horse team,
> But you can't keep de world from moverin' round
> Nor Nat Turner from gainin' ground.
>
> And your name it mought be Caesar sure,
> And got you cannon can shoot a mile or more,
> But you can't keep de world from moverin' round
> Nor Nat Turner from gainin' ground.

The introduction of Denmark Vesey, class leader in the A.M.E. Church, and Nat Turner, slave preacher, serves to remind us that some slaves and ex-slaves were violent as well as humble, impatient as well as patient.

It is also well to recall that the religious David Walker, who had lived close to slavery in North Carolina, and Henry Highland Garnett, ex-slave and Presbyterian minister, produced two of the most inflammatory, vitriolic and doom-bespeaking polemics America has yet seen. There was theological tension here, loudly proclaimed, a tension which emanated from and was perpetuated by American slavery and race prejudice. This dimension of ambiguity must be kept in mind, if for no other reason than to place in bolder relief the possibility that a great many slaves and free Afro-Americans could have interpreted Christianity in a way quite different from white Christians.

Even those songs which seemed most otherworldly, those which expressed profound weariness of spirit and even faith in death, through their unmistakable sadness, were accusatory, and God was not their object. If one accepts as a given that some of these appear to be almost wholly escapist, the indictment is no less real. Thomas Wentworth Higginson came across one—". . . a flower of poetry in that dark soil," he called it.

> I'll walk in de graveyard, I'll walk through de graveyard,
>   To lay dis body down.
> I'll lie in de grave and stretch out my arms,
>   Lay dis body down.

Reflecting on "I'll lie in de grave and stretch out my arms," Higginson said that "Never, it seems to me, since man first lived and suffered, was his infinite longing for peace uttered more plaintively than in that line."

There seems to be small doubt that Christianity contributed in large measure to a spirit of patience which militated against open rebellion among the bondsmen. Yet to overemphasize this point leads one to obscure a no less important reality: Christianity, after being reinterpreted and recast by slave bards, also contributed to that spirit of endurance which powered generations of bondsmen, bringing them to that decisive moment when for the first time a real choice was available to scores of thousands of them.

When that moment came, some slaves who were in a position to decide for themselves did so. W. E. B. DuBois re-created their mood and the atmosphere in which they lived.

> There came the slow looming of emancipation.
> Crowds and armies of the unknown, inscrutable,
> unfathomable Yankees; cruelty behind and before;
> rumors of a new slave trade, but slowly,
> continuously, the wild truth, the bitter truth,
> the magic truth, came surging through. There
> was to be a new freedom! And a black nation
> went tramping after the armies no matter what
> it suffered; no matter how it was treated, no
> matter how it died.

The gifted bards, by creating songs with an unmistakable freedom ring, songs which would have been met with swift, brutal repression in the ante-bellum days, probably voiced the sentiments of all but the most degraded and dehumanized. Perhaps not even the incredulous slavemaster could deny the intent of the new lyrics. "In the wake of the Union Army and in the contraband camps," remarked Sterling Brown, "spirituals of freedom sprang up suddenly. . . . Some celebrated the days of Jubilo: 'O Freedom; O Freedom!' and 'Before I'll be a slave, I'll be buried in my grave!, and 'Go home to my lord and be free.'" And there was: "'No more driver's lash for me. . . . Many thousand go.'"

DuBois brought together the insights of the poet and historian to get inside the slaves:

> There was joy in the South. It rose like perfume—like a prayer.
> Men stood quivering. Slim dark girls, wild and beautiful with
> wrinkled hair, wept silently; young women, black, tawny, white
> and golden, lifted shivering hands, and old and broken mothers,

black and gray, raised great voices and shouted to God across the
fields, and up to the rocks and the mountains.

Some sang:

> Slavery chain done broke at last, broke at last, broke at last,
> Slavery chain done broke at last,
> Going to praise God till I die.

> I did tell him how I suffer,
> In de dungeon and de chain,
> *And de days I went with head bowed down,*
> And my broken flesh and pain,
> Slavery chain done broke at last, broke at last, broke at last.

Whatever the nature of the shocks generated by the war, among
those vibrations felt were some that had come from Afro-American
singing ever since the first Africans were forcibly brought to these
shores. DuBois was correct when he said that the new freedom song
had not come from Africa, but that "the dark throb and beat of that
Ancient of Days was in and through it." Thus, the psyches of those
who gave rise to and provided widespread support for folk songs had
not been reduced to *tabula rasas* on which a slave-holding society could
at pleasure sketch out its wish fulfillment fantasies.

We have already seen the acute degree to which some slaves realized
they were being exploited. Their sense of the injustice of slavery made
it so much easier for them to act out their aggression against whites
(by engaging in various forms of "day to day" resistance) without being
overcome by a sense of guilt, or a feeling of being ill-mannered. To
call this nihilistic thrashing about would be as erroneous as to refer to
their use of folklore as esthetic thrashing about. For if they did not
regard themselves as the equals of whites in many ways, their folklore
indicates that the generality of slaves must have at least felt superior to
whites morally. And that, in the context of oppresssion, could make
the difference between a viable human spirit and one crippled by the
belief that the interests of the master are those of the slave.

When it is borne in mind that slaves created a large number of extraordinary songs and greatly improved a considerable proportion of
the songs of others, it is not at all difficult to believe that they were
conscious of the fact that they were leaders in the vital area of art—
giving protagonists rather than receiving pawns. And there is some evi-

dence that slaves were aware of the special talent which they brought to music. Higginson has described how reluctantly they sang from hymnals—"even on Sunday"—and how "gladly" they yielded "to the more potent excitement of their own 'spirituals.'" It is highly unlikely that the slaves' preference for their own music went unremarked among them, or that this preference did not affect their estimate of themselves. "They soon found," commented Alan Lomax, "that when they sang, the whites recognized their superiority as singers, and listened with respect." He might have added that those antebellum whites who listened probably seldom understood.

What is of pivotal import, however, is that the esthetic realm was the one area in which slaves knew they were not inferior to whites. Small wonder that they borrowed many songs from the larger community, then quickly invested them with their own economy of statement and power of imagery rather than yield to the temptation of merely repeating what they had heard. Since they were essentially group rather than solo performances, the values inherent in and given affirmation by the music served to strengthen bondsmen in a way that solo music could not have done. In a word, slave singing often provided a form of group therapy, a way in which a slave, in concert with others, could fend off some of the debilitating effects of slavery.

The field of inquiry would hardly be complete without some mention of slave tales. Rich in quantity and often subtle in conception, these tales further illumine the inner world of the bondsmen, disclosing moods and interests almost as various as those found in folksongs. That folk tales, like the songs, indicate an African presence, should not astonish; for the telling of tales, closely related to the African griot's vocation of providing oral histories of families and dynasties, was deeply rooted in West African tradition. Hughes and Bontemps have written that the slaves brought to America the "habit of storytelling as pastime, together with a rich bestiary." Moreover, they point out that the folk tales of slaves "were actually projections of personal experiences and hopes and defeats, in terms of symbols," and that this important dimension of the tales "appears to have gone unnoticed."

Possessing a repertoire which ranged over a great many areas, perhaps the most memorable tales are those of Brer Rabbit and John. Brer Rabbit, now trickster, ladies' man and braggart, now wit, joker and glutton, possessed the resourcefulness, despite his size and lack of strength, to outsmart stronger, larger animals. "To the slave in his condition," according to Hughes and Bontemps, "the theme of weakness overcoming strength through cunning proved endlessly fascinating." John, characterized by a spiritual resilience born of an ironic sense of life, was a secular high priest of mischief and guile who delighted in matching wits with Ole Marster, the "patterollers," Ole Missy, and the devil himself. He was clever enough to sense the absurdity of his predicament and that of white people, smart enough to know the limits of his powers and the boundaries of those of the master class. While not always victorious, even on the spacious plane of the imagination, he could hardly be described as a slave with an inferiority complex. And in this regard it is important to note that his varieties of triumphs, though they sometimes included winning freedom, often realistically cluster about ways of coping with everyday negatives of the system.

Slaves were adept in the art of storytelling, as at home in this area as they were in the field of music. But further discussion of the scope of folklore would be uneconomical, for we have already seen a depth and variety of thought among bondsmen which embarrasses stereotypical theories of slave personality. Moreover, it should be clear by now that there are no secure grounds on which to erect the old, painfully constricted "Sambo" structure. For the personalities which lay beneath the plastic exteriors which slaves turned on and off for white people were too manifold to be contained by cheerful, childlike images. When it is argued, then, that "too much of the Negro's own lore" has gone into the making of the Sambo picture "to entitle one in good conscience to condemn it as 'conspiracy',," one must rejoin: Only if you strip the masks from black faces while refusing to read the irony and ambiguity and cunning which called the masks into existence. Slave folklore, on balance, decisively repudiates the thesis that Negroes *as a group* had internalized "Sambo" traits, committing them, as it were, to psychological marriage.

It is one of the curiosities of American historiography that a people who were as productive esthetically as American slaves could be studied as if they had moved in a cultural cyclotron, continually bombarded by devastating, atomizing forces which denuded them of meaningful Africanisms while destroying any and all impulses toward creativity. One historian, for example, has been tempted to wonder how it was ever possible that "*all* this (West African) native resourcefulness and vitality have been brought to such a point of *utter* stultification in America." (Italics added.) This sadly misguided view is, of course, not grounded in any recognition or understanding of the Afro-American dimension of American culture. In any event, there is a great need for students of American slavery to attempt what Gilberto Freyre tried to do for Brazilian civilization—an effort at discovering the contributions of slaves toward the shaping of the Brazilian national character. When such a study has been made of the American slave we shall probably discover that, though he did not rival his Brazilian brother in staging bloody revolutions, the quality and place of art in his life compared favorably. Now this suggests that the humanity of people can be asserted through means other than open and widespread rebellion, a consideration that has not been appreciated in violence-prone America. We would do well to recall the words of F. S. C. Northrop who has observed:

> During the pre-Civil War period shipowners and southern landowners brought to the United States a considerable body of people with a color of skin and cultural values different from those of its other inhabitants. . . . Their values are more emotive, esthetic and intuitive . . . (These) characteristics can become an asset for our culture. For these are values with respect to which Anglo-American culture is weak.

These values were expressed on the highest level in the folklore of slaves. Through their folklore black slaves affirmed their humanity and left a lasting imprint on American culture. No study of the institutional aspects of American slavery can be complete, nor can the larger dimensions of slave personality and style be adequately explored, as long as historians continue to avoid that realm in which, as DuBois has said, "the soul of the black slave spoke to man."

In its nearly two and one half centuries of existence, the grim system of American slavery doubtless broke the spirits of uncounted numbers of slaves. Nevertheless, if we look through the prism of folklore, we can see others transcending their plight, appreciating the tragic irony of their condition, then seizing upon and putting to use those aspects of their experience which sustain in the present and renew in the future. We can see them opposing their own angle of vision to that of their oppressor, fashioning their own techniques of defense and aggression in accordance with their own reading of reality and doing those things well enough to avoid having their sense of humanity destroyed.

Slave folklore, then, affirms the existence of a large number of vital, tough-minded human beings who, though severely limited and abused by slavery, had found a way both to endure and preserve their humanity in the face of insuperable odds. What they learned about handling misfortune was not only a major factor in their survival as a people, but many of the lessons learned and esthetic standards established would be used by future generations of Afro-Americans in coping with a hostile world. What a splendid affirmation of the hopes and dreams of their slave ancestors that some of the songs being sung in antebellum days are the ones Afro-Americans are singing in the freedom movement today: "Michael, row the boat ashore"; "Just like a tree planted by the water, I shall not be moved."

Republican Ideology and the Coming of the Civil War

ERIC FONER

• The Civil War is the central event in the domestic history of the United States. Measured in terms of loss of life, property damage, or enduring bitterness it was the costliest of all American wars. One-fourth of all the able-bodied white males in the South died in the conflict, and conditions were only slightly better for the Northerners. Walt Whitman, who had left his home in Brooklyn, observed the reality of war first hand as a Union army nurse. After comforting many a dying soldier and closing his eyes in death, Whitman asserted that "the real war will never get in the books. Future years will never know the seething hell and the black infernal background of countless minor scenes and interiors of the Secession war; and it is best they should not. . . ."

Most of the men who died in the struggle probably had no clear commitment either to abolition or to slavery; General Robert E. Lee himself refused to defend either slavery or secession. Why then did war come? Was it the moral question posed by involuntary servitude? Or was it a constitutional question relating to the powers reserved for the federal government? Or was it the inevitable result of irresistible economic forces? The question has puzzled politicians and scholars for over a century. In the following essay, Professor Eric Foner emphasizes the importance to the Republican Party of the slogan: Free Soil, Free Labor, Free Men. In this young historian's view, the ideology of a political organization offers a penetrating insight into the causes of the American Civil War.

Originally appeared as "Slavery and the Republican Sociology" in *Free Soil, Free Labor, Free Men: The Ideology of the Republican Party Before the Civil War*. Copyright © 1970 by Eric Foner. Reprinted by permission of Oxford University Press, Inc.

"Of the American Civil War," James Ford Rhodes wrote over a half a century ago, "it may safely be asserted that there was a single cause, slavery." In this opinion, Rhodes was merely echoing a view which seemed self-evident to Abraham Lincoln and many other participants in the sectional conflict. Their interpretation implicitly assumes that the ante-bellum Republican party was primarily a vehicle for anti-slavery sentiment. Yet partly because historians are skeptical of explanations made by participants of their own behavior, Rhodes' view quickly fell under attack. Even before Rhodes wrote, John R. Commons had characterized the Republicans as primarily a homestead party, and Charles and Mary Beard later added the tariff as one of its fundamental concerns. More recently, historians have stressed aversion to the presence of blacks—free or slave—in the western territories as the Republicans' motive for opposing the extension of slavery. Because the Republicans disavowed the intention of attacking slavery in states where it already existed by direct federal action, their anti-slavery declarations have been dismissed by some historians as hypocritical. And recently, a political analyst, not a professional historian, revealed how commonplace a cynical attitude toward the early Republican party has become when he wrote: "The Republican Party succeeded by soft-pedalling the issue of slavery altogether and concentrating on economic issues which would attract Northern businessmen and Western farmers."

Controversy over the proper place of anti-slavery in the Republican ideology is hardly new. During the 1850's, considerable debate occurred within abolitionist circles on the proper attitude toward Republicanism. In part, this was simply an extension of the traditional schism between political and non-political abolitionists, and it is not surprising that William Lloyd Garrison and his followers should have wasted little enthusiasm on the Republicans. Yet many abolitionists who had no objection on principle to political involvements considered the anti-slavery commitment of the Republican party insufficient to merit their support. Gerrit Smith and William Goodell, for example, who had been instrumental in organizing the Liberty party in New York State, declared that they could not support a party which recognized the constitutionality of slavery anywhere in the Union. The Republican party, Smith charged, "refuses to oppose slavery where it is, and opposes it only where it is not," and he continuously urged radi-

cals like Chase and Giddings to take an abolitionist stance. Theodore
Parker made the same criticism. When Chase declared in the Senate
that the federal government would not interfere with slavery in the
states, Parker wrote that while he did not object to attacking slavery
one step at a time, he "would not promise *not to take other steps*."

Yet it is important to remember that despite their criticisms of the
Republican party, leading abolitionists maintained close personal relations with Republican leaders, particularly the radicals. The flow of
letters between Chase and Smith, cordial even while each criticized
the attitude of the other, is one example of this. Similarly, Parker kept
up a correspondence with Henry Wilson, Charles Sumner, and William Seward as well as Chase. And he and Wendell Phillips, both
experts at the art of political agitation, recognized the complex inter-
relationship between abolitionist attempts to create a public sentiment
hostile to slavery, and the political anti-slavery espoused by Republicans.
"Our agitation, you know, helps keep yours alive in the rank and file,"
was the way Wendell Phillips expressed it to Sumner. And Seward
agreed that the abolitionists played a vital role in awakening the public
conscience—"open[ing] the way where the masses can follow." For
their part, abolitionists like Theodore Parker were happy to borrow
statistics and arguments from the anti-slavery speeches of politicians.

The evidence strongly suggests that outside of Garrison's immediate
circle, most abolitionists voted with the Republican party despite their
wish that the party adopt a more aggressive anti-slavery position. Indeed, abolitionist societies experienced financial difficulties in the late
1850's, as former contributors began giving their money to the Republicans. Even Gerrit Smith, who insisted he could "never vote for
any person who recognizes a law for slavery," contributed five hundred
dollars to the Frémont campaign. The attitude of many abolitionists
was summed up by Elizur Wright, a proponent of Smith and Goodell's
brand of political anti-slavery who nonetheless voted for Lincoln in
1860. While Wright criticized the Republicans for their shortcomings
on slavery, he acknowledged that "the greatest recommendation of the
Republican Party is, that its enemies do not quite believe its disclaim-
ers, while they do believe that [it is] sincerely opposed to slavery as far
as it goes." Prophetically, he added: "Woe to the slave power under
a Republican President if it strikes the first blow."

The fact that so many abolitionists, not to mention radical Republicans, supported the Republican party, is an indication that anti-slavery formed no small part of the Republican ideology. Recent historians have concluded, moreover, that writers like Beard greatly overestimated the importance of economic issues in the elections of 1856, 1858, and 1860. We have already seen how tentative was the Republican commitment to the tariff. As for the homestead issue, Don E. Fehrenbacher has pointed out that the Republicans carried most of the Northwest in 1856 when free land was not a political issue, and that in 1860, Douglas Democrats supported the measure as ardently as Republicans. More important, it would have been suicidal for the Republicans to have put their emphasis on economic policies, particularly the neo-Whiggism described by Beard. If one thing is evident after analyzing the various elements which made up the party, it is that anti-slavery was one of the few policies which united all Republican factions. For political reasons, if for no other, the Republicans were virtually obliged to make anti-slavery the main focus of their political appeal. Such questions as the tariff, nativism, and race were too divisive to be stressed, while the homestead issue could be advanced precisely because it was so non-controversial in the North.

Conservative Republicans and radicals, ex-Democrats and former Whigs, all agreed that slavery was the major issue of the 1850's. It was not surprising that Giddings should insist that "there is but one real issue between the Republican party and those factions that stand opposed to it. That is the question of slavery," or that Salmon P. Chase should declare that the election of 1860 had not turned on "subordinate questions of local and temporary character," but had vindicated the principle of "the restriction of slavery within State limits." But Orville H. Browning, as conservative as Giddings and Chase were radical, appraised the politics of 1860 in much the same way. "It is manifest to all," he declared, "that there is an unusual degree of political interest pervading the country—that the people, everywhere, are excited, . . . and yet, from one extremity of the Republic to the other, scarcely any other subject is mentioned, or any other question discussed . . . save the question of negro slavery. . . ." Ex-Democrats in the Republican party fully agreed. Both Francis Spinner and Preston King rejected suggestions that Democratic economic policies be engrafted onto the Republican platform, on the ground that these must await settlement until the slavery issue had been decided. As Spinner tersely put it, "Statesmen cannot make issues for the people. As live men we must take the issues as they present themselves." The potency of the slavery issue, and the way in which it subordinated or absorbed all other political questions, was noted by the anti-Lecompton Democrat from New York, Horace Clark, on the eve of the 1860 campaign:

> It is not to be controverted that the slavery agitation is not at rest. It has absorbed and destroyed our national politics. It has overrun State politics. It has even invaded our municipalities; and now, in some form or other, everywhere controls the elections of the people.

In a recent study of Civil War historiography, Roy F. Nichols observed that we still do not know whether either section had reached its own consensus on major issues by 1861. Some historians have interpreted the strong showing of Stephen A. Douglas in the free states as proof that a substantial portion of the electorate rejected the Republican brand of anti-slavery. Though there is some truth in this view, it is important to remember that by 1860 the Douglas Democrats shared a good many of the Republicans' attitudes toward the South. One of the most striking aspects of the Democratic debate over the Lecompton constitution was the way in which the Douglasites echoed so many of the anti-southern views which anti-Nebraska Democrats had expressed only a few years earlier. There is a supreme irony in the fact that the same methods which Douglas had used against dissident Democrats in 1854 were now turned against him and his supporters. Buchanan applied the patronage whip ruthlessly, and anti-Lecompton Democrats complained that a new, pro-slavery test had suddenly been imposed upon the party. And like the anti-Nebraska Democrats, who were now members of the Republican party, the Douglasites insisted that they commanded the support of most northern Democrats. Historians have tended to agree with them. Roy Nichols suggests that the enthusiasm Douglas's anti-southern stand aroused among rank and file Democrats was one reason why he refused to accept the compromise English bill to settle the Lecompton controversy, and recent students of Pennsylvania and Indiana politics agree that the vast majority of the Democracy in those states favored Douglas against the administration.

The bitterness of Douglas Democrats against the South did not abate between 1858 and 1860. They believed that the South had embarked upon a crusade to force slavery into all the territories, and protested that endorsement of such a goal would destroy the northern Democracy. "We have confided in their honor, their love of justice, their detestation of what is wrong," Henry Payne, a prominent Ohio Democrat, said of his southern colleagues in 1858, "*but we can do it no more.*" And many Republicans believed that, even if Douglas made his peace with the Democratic organization, many of his followers had acquired "a feeling against Slavery and its arrogant demands which *if cherished* will prevent their going back. . . ." A few Democrats did defect to the Republican party in 1858, 1859, and 1860, including a former chairman of the Iowa Democracy, several anti-Lecompton Congressmen, and F. P. Stanton, the former Democratic governor of Kansas. That there were not more defections largely reflected the continuation into 1860 of Douglas's contest with the administration, which increasingly took on what one historian calls "a semi-free-soil" tone. And when the 1860 Democratic national convention broke up over the South's insistence on a platform guaranteeing slavery in the territories, the bitterness of the Douglasites knew no bounds. The reporter Murat Halstead observed that he had "never heard Abolitionists talk more rancorously of the people of the South than the Douglas men here." For their part, southerners insisted they would not accept popular sovereignty since this would be as effective as the Wilmot Proviso in barring slavery from the territories.

There were, of course, many important differences between the Douglasites and Republicans. Douglas still insisted in 1860 that the slavery question was not important enough to risk the disruption of the Union, he was much more inclined to use racism as a political weapon, and, as one Republican newspaper put it, in words echoed by several recent scholars, Douglas "does not recognize the moral element in politics. . . ." Yet in their devotion to the Union and their bitter opposition to southern domination of the government, Republicans and Douglasites stood close together in 1860. There was much truth in the observation of one Republican that "the rupture between the northern and southern wing of the democracy, is permanent with the masses . . . ," and the experiences of the Douglas Democrats in the years preceding the Civil War go a long way toward explaining the unanimity of the North's response to the attack on Fort Sumter. The attitude of the Douglasites toward the South on the eve of the

Civil War partially reflected their assessment of northern opinion regarding slavery. Politicians of all parties agreed that northerners opposed slavery as an abstract principle, although they disagreed on the
intensity of this sentiment. John C. Calhoun had estimated in 1847
that while only 5 per cent of northerners supported the abolitionists,
more than 66 per cent viewed slavery as an evil, and were willing to
oppose its extension constitutionally. Similarly, a conservative Republican declared in 1858, "There is no man [in the North] who is an
advocate of slavery. There is no man from that section of the country
who will go before his constituents and advocate the extension of
slavery." Northern Democrats had the same perception of northern
sentiments. Even the Hunkers of New York, who consistently opposed
the Wilmot Proviso, refused to say "that they are not opposed to
slavery." For as William L. Marcy declared in 1849, "In truth we all
are."

Anti-slavery as an abstract feeling had long existed in the North. It
had not, however, prevented abolitionists from being mobbed, nor
anti-slavery parties from going down to defeat. Democrats and Whigs
had long been able to appeal to devotion to the Union, racism, and
economic issues, to neutralize anti-slavery as a political force. "The
anti-slavery sentiment," Hamilton Fish explained in 1854, "is inborn,
and almost universal at the North . . . but it is only as a *sentiment*
that it generally pervades; it has not and cannot be inspired with the
activity that even a very slight interest excites." But Fish failed to fore-
see the fundamental achievement of the Republican party before the
Civil War: the creation and articulation of an ideology which blended
personal and sectional interest with morality so perfectly that it became the most potent political force in the nation. The free labor
assault upon slavery and southern society, coupled with the idea that
an aggressive Slave Power was threatening the most fundamental values
and interests of the free states, hammered the slavery issue home to
the northern public more emphatically than an appeal to morality
alone could ever have done.

To agree with Rhodes that slavery was ultimately the cause of the
Civil War, therefore, is not to accept the corollary that the basis of
the Republican opposition to slavery was simple moral fervor. In a
speech to the Senate in 1848, John M. Niles listed a dozen different
reasons for his support of the Wilmot Proviso—but only once did he

mention his belief that slavery was morally repugnant. And thirteen years later, George William Curtis observed that "there is very little moral mixture in the 'Anti-Slavery' feeling of this country. A great deal is abstract philanthropy; part is hatred of slaveholders; a great part is jealousy for white labor, very little is consciousness of wrong done and the wish to right it." The Republican ideology included all these elements, and much more. Rhodes argued that northerners wished to preserve the Union as a first step toward abolition. A more accurate formulation would reverse the equation and say that many Republicans were anti-slavery from the conviction that slavery threatened the Union. Aside from some radicals, who occasionally flirted with disunion, most Republicans were united by the twin principles of free soil and Unionism. Cassius M. Clay even suggested that the Free-Soilers in 1851 adopt the name "Liberty and Union" party, in order to impress their essential goals upon the electorate. The New York *Times* emphasized this aspect of Republican thought in 1857: "The barbaric institution of slavery will become more and more odious to the northern people because it will become more and more plain . . . that the States which cling to Slavery thrust back the American idea, and reject the influences of the Union."

Still, Unionism, despite its importance to the mass of northerners, and obviously crucial to any explanation of the Republicans' decision to resist secession, was only one aspect of the Republican ideology. It would have been just as logical to compromise on the slavery question if the preservation of the Union were the paramount goal of Republican politics. Nor should Republicanism be seen merely as the expression of the northern drive toward political power. We have seen, to be sure, that resentment of southern power played its part, that many Democratic-Republicans had watched with growing jealousy the South's domination of the Democratic party and the national government, and that many former Whigs were convinced that the South was blocking economic programs essential for national economic development. But there is more to the coming of the Civil War than the rivalry of sections for political power. (New England, after all, could accept its own decline in political power without secession.)

In short, none of these elements can stand separately; they dissolve into one another, and the total product emergies as ideology. Resentment of southern political power, devotion to the Union, anti-slavery based upon the free labor argument, moral revulsion to the peculiar institution, racial prejudice, a commitment to the northern social order and its development and expansion—all these elements were intertwined in the Republican world-view. What they added up to was the conviction that North and South represented two social systems whose values, interests, and future prospects were in sharp, perhaps mortal, conflict with one another. The sense of difference, of estrangement, and of growing hostility with which Republicans viewed the South, cannot be overemphasized. Theodore Sedgwick of New York perhaps expressed it best when he declared during the secession crisis: "The policy and aims of slavery, its institutions and civilization, and the character of its people, are all at variance with the policy, aims, institutions, education, and character of the North. There is an irreconcilable difference in our interests, institutions, and pursuits; in our sentiments and feelings." Greeley's *Tribune* said the same thing more succinctly: "We are not one people. We are two peoples. We are a people for Freedom and a people for Slavery. Between the two, conflict is inevitable." An attack not simply on the institution of slavery, but upon southern society itself, was thus at the heart of the Republican mentality. Of all historians, I think Avery Craven caught this feature best: "By 1860, slavery had become the symbol and carrier of *all* sectional differences and conflicts." Here and elsewhere, Craven describes the symbolic nature of the slavery controversy, reflected as it was in the widespread acceptance among Republicans of the Slave Power idea—a metaphor for all the fears and resentments they harbored toward the South. But Craven did leave out something crucial. Slavery was not only the symbol, but also the real basis of sectional conflict, for it was the foundation of the South's economy, social structure, aspirations, and ideology.

"Why do we Meddle with Slavery?" the New York *Times* asked in an 1857 editorial. The answer gives us a penetrating insight into the Republican mind on the eve of Civil War:

> The great States of the North are not peopled exclusively by quidnuncs and agitators. . . . Nevertheless, we do give ourselves great and increasing concern about the existence of Slavery in States over whose internal economy we have no right and no wish to exercise any control whatever. Nevertheless, we do feel, and the feeling is growing deeper in the northern heart with

every passing year, that our character, our prosperity, and our destiny are most seriously involved in the question of the perpetuation or extinction of slavery in those States.

What is striking about this statement is a concern directed not only against the extension of slavery, but against its very existence. Lincoln put the same concern even more succinctly to a Chicago audience in 1859, "Never forget," he said, "that we have before us this whole matter of the right or wrong of slavery in this Union, though the immediate question is as to its spreading out into new Territories and States."

Lincoln and the editors of the *Times* thus made explicit that there was more to the contest over the extension of slavery than whether the institution should spread to the West. As Don E. Fehrenbacher puts it, the territorial question was the "skirmish line of a more extensive struggle." Only by a comprehension of this total conflict between North and South, between Republican and southern ideologies, can the meaning of the territorial issue by fully grasped. Its importance went even beyond the belief shared widely in both sections that slavery required expansion to survive, and that confinement to the states where it already existed would kill it. For in each ideology was the conviction that its own social system must expand, not only to insure its own survival but to prevent the expansion of all the evils the other represented. We have already seen how Republicans believed that free society, with its promise of social mobility for the laborer, required territorial expansion, and how this was combined with a messianic desire to spread the benefits of free society to other areas and peoples. Southerners had their own grandiose design. "They had a magnificent dream of empire," a Republican recalled after the war, and such recent writers as C. Stanley Urban and Eugene Genovese have emphasized how essential expansionism was in the southern ideology. The struggle for the West represented a contest between two expansive societies, only one of whose aspirations could prevail. The conflict was epitomized by two statements which appeared in the Philadelphia *North American* in 1856. Slavery, the *North American* argued, could not be allowed to expand, because it would bring upon the West "a blight whose fatal influence will be felt for centuries." Two weeks later the same paper quoted a southern journal, which, in urging slavery expansionism, used precisely this logic in reverse. Such expansion, the southern paper argued, would "forbid the extension of the evils of free society to new people and coming generations."

Here then was a basic reason why the South could not accept the verdict of 1860. In 1848, Martin Van Buren had said that the South opposed the principle of free soil because "the prohibition carries with it a reproach to the slaveholding states, and . . . submission to it would degrade them." Eight years later, the Richmond *Enquirer* explained that for the South to abandon the idea of extending slavery while accepting Republican assurances of non-interference in the states would be "pregnant with the admission that slavery is wrong, and but for the constitution should be abolished." To agree to the containment of slavery, the South would have had to abandon its whole ideology, which had come to view the institution as a positive good, the basis of an enlightened form of social organization.

Although it has not been the purpose of this study to examine in any detailed way the southern mind in 1860, what has been said about the Republican ideology does help to explain the rationale for secession. The political wars of the 1850's, centering on the issue of slavery extension, had done much to erode whatever good feeling existed between the sections. The abolitionist Elihu Burrit suggested in 1857 that a foreigner observing Amercian politics would probably conclude "that the North and South were wholly occupied in gloating upon each others' faults and failings." During the 1856 campaign, Burrit went on, sectional antagonisms had been brought "to a pitch of rancor, never reached before" in American politics. This was precisely the reason that Union-loving conservatives like Hamilton Fish dreaded the mounting agitation. "I cannot close my eyes to the fact which all history shows," Fish wrote Thurlow Weed in 1855, "that every physical revolution (of governments) is preceded by a moral revolution. [Slavery agitation] leads to estrangement first, and next to hostility and hatred which end inevitably in separation." By the time of the secession crisis another former Whig could observe that "the people of the North and of the South have come to hate each other worse than the hatred between any two nations in the world. In a word the moral basis on which the government is founded is all destroyed."

It is thus no mystery that southerners could not seriously entertain Republican assurances that they would not attack slavery in the states. For one thing, in opposing its extension, Republicans had been logically forced to attack the institution itself. This, indeed, was one of the reasons why radicals accepted the emphasis on non-extension. "We are disposed to select this single point," Sumner explained to Chase, "because it has a peculiar practical issue at the present moment, while its discussion would, of course, raise the whole question of slavery." Frederick Douglass agreed that agitation for the Wilmot Proviso served "to keep the subject before the people—to deepen their hatred of the system—and to break up the harmony between the Northern white people and the Southern slaveholders. . . ." As we have seen, many Republicans, both radicals and moderates, explicitly stated that non-extension was simply the first step, that there would come a day when slavery would cease to exist.

As southerners viewed the Republican party's rise to power in one northern state after another, and witnessed the increasingly anti-southern tone of the northern Democrats, they could hardly be blamed for feeling apprehensive about the future. Late in 1859, after a long talk with the moderate Unionist Senator from Virginia, R. M. T. Hunter, Senator James Dixon of Connecticut reported that the Virginian was deeply worried. "What seems to alarm Hunter is the *growth* of the Anti-slavery feeling at the North." Southerners did not believe that this anti-slavery sentiment would be satisfied with the prohibition of slavery in the territories, although even that would be bad enough. They also feared that a Republican administration would adopt the radicals' program of indirect action against slavery. This is why continued Democratic control of Congress was not very reassuring, for executive action could implement much of the radicals' program. Slavery was notoriously weak in the states of Missouri, Maryland, and Delaware. With federal patronage, a successful emancipation movement there might well be organized. And what was more dangerous, Lincoln might successfully arouse the poor whites in other states against the slaveholders. "Cohorts of Federal office-holders, Abolitionists, may be sent into [our] midst," a southern Senator warned in January 1861; ". . . Postmasters . . . controlling the mails, and loading them down with incendiary documents," would be appointed in every town. One southern newspaper declared that "the great lever by which the abolitionists hope to extirpate slavery in the states, is the aid of the non-slaveholding citizens of the South." The reply of Republicans to these warnings was hardly reassuring. Commenting on one southern editorial, the Cincinnati *Commercial* declared that the spread of anti-slavery sentiment among southern poor whites was "an eventuality against which no precautions can avail." And by December 1860, Republican Congressmen were already receiving applications for office from within the slave states.

For many reasons, therefore, southerners believed that slavery would not be permanently safe under a Republican administration. Had not William H. Seward announced in 1858, "I know, and you know, that a revolution has begun. I know, and all the world knows, that revolutions never go backward." Did not Republican Congressmen openly express their conviction that "slavery must die"? The Republican policy of preventing the spread of slavery, one southerner wrote to William T. Sherman, "was but the entering wedge to overthrow it in the States."

The delegates to South Carolina's secession convention, in their address to the people of the state, explained why they had dissolved the state's connection with the Union:

> If it is right to preclude or abolish slavery in a Territory, why should it be allowed to remain in the States? . . . In spite of all disclaimers and professions, there can be but one end by the submission of the South to the rule of a sectional anti-slavery government at Washington; and that end, directly or indirectly, must be—the emancipation of the slaves of the South.

Emancipation might come in a decade, it might take fifty years. But North and South alike knew that the election of 1860 had marked a turning point in the history of slavery in the United States. To remain in the Union, the South would have had to accept the verdict of "ultimate extinction" which Lincoln and the Republicans had passed on the peculiar institution.

The decision for civil war in 1860-61 can be resolved into two questions—why did the South secede, and why did the North refuse to let the South secede? As I have indicated, I believe secession should be viewed as a total and logical response by the South to the situation which confronted it in the election of Lincoln—logical in the sense that it was the only action consistent with its ideology. In the same way, the Republicans' decision to maintain the Union was inherent in their ideology. For the integrity of the Union, important as an end in itself, was also a prerequisite to the national greatness Republicans felt the United States was destined to achieve. With his faith in progress, material growth, and the spread of both democratic institutions and American influence throughout the world, William Seward brought the Republican ideology to a kind of culmination. Although few Republicans held as coherent and far-reaching a world view as he, most accepted Lincoln's more modest view that the American nation had a special place in the world, and a responsibility to prove that democratic institutions were self-sustaining. Much of the messianic zeal which characterized political anti-slavery derived from this faith in the superiority of the political, social, and economic institutions of the North, and a desire to spread these to their ultimate limits.

When a leading historian says, therefore, that the Republican party in 1860 was bound together "by a common enmity rather than a common loyalty," he is, I believe, only half right. For the Republicans' enmity toward the South was intimately bound up with their loyalty to the society of small-scale capitalism which they perceived in the North. It was its identification with the aspirations of the farmers, small entrepreneurs, and craftsmen of northern society which gave the Republican ideology much of its dynamic, progressive, and optimistic quality. Yet paradoxically, at the time of its greatest success, the seeds of the later failure of that ideology were already present. Fundamental changes were at work in the social and economic structure of the North, transforming and undermining many of its free-labor assumptions. And the flawed attitude of the Republicans toward race, and the limitations of the free labor outlook in regard to the Negro, foreshadowed the mistakes and failures of the post-emancipation years.

The Impeachment of President Andrew Johnson

C. VANN WOODWARD

• Many American presidents have had irascible tempers, or have had difficulty in getting on with members of Congress, or have been ineffectual in dealing with major problems besetting their administrations. Despite their flaws, however, few congressmen have ever seriously considered removing the president from office. In the case of two presidents, however, Andrew Johnson in 1868 and Richard M. Nixon in 1974, Congress viewed their transgressions as so gross that the constitutional remedy of impeachment seemed in order.

The cases of Andrew Johnson and Richard Nixon are strikingly different from one another. Congress considered removing the former primarily because he posed an obstacle toward implementing a reconstruction policy which a majority of the Republicans in the nation thought appropriate. In the case of Richard Nixon, on the other hand, opposition developed because many members of Congress believed that he had been part of a conspiracy to obstruct justice by covering up criminal activities surrounding the break-in of the Democratic National Headquarters in the Watergate complex in Washington in June 1972 and that he had also abused the powers of his office by politicizing agencies such as the FBI, CIA, and the Internal Revenue Service.

In the following essay C. Vann Woodward summarizes the arguments used in the impeachment trial of Andrew Johnson in 1868. The parallels between Johnson and Nixon were, of course, of major interest in 1973 and 1974, but President Nixon's resignation in August 1974 ended the impeachment process in Congress. Nevertheless it is instructive to compare the two cases. The Johnson incident occurred clearly because of political differences between the president and Congress.

Originally appeared as "That Other Impeachment," in *The New York Times*. Copyright © 1974 by The New York Times Company. Reprinted by permission.

> In Nixon's case there was sufficient basis to warrant impeach-
> ment on the grounds of possible criminal involvement or
> actual violation of existing laws.

One thing that gives history its edge of priority and peculiar sense of
immediacy in America is a national habit of mind. To find out where
they go from here, Americans characteristically look, not forward, but
backward to find what they did in the past. In moments of critical national decision such as the present, they search for precedents. History
is seen to be full of parallels, analogies—"lessons." It is one of the few
genuinely conservative traits of national character. But it is not without its perils.

Between two of the leading participants in the impeachment of
President Andrew Johnson in 1868 on the one hand and the two historians who later treated the event most fully on the other, there is
remarkable agreement about its "lesson" for the future. The "lesson,"
in brief, is—"never again."

Among the many enemies of President Johnson, none were more
passionate in their enmity nor more zealous in their efforts for his conviction and removal than Charles Sumner of Massachusetts and Thad-
deus Stevens of Pennsylvania. They went to great extremes and
stretched the law further than any of the other impeachers. Yet when
the ordeal was over and the failure evident, Sumner said that, "if his
acquittal is taken as a precedent, never can a political offender be found
guilty again." Stevens went even further. "I have come to the fixed
conclusion," said the old man a month after the trial and five weeks
before his death, "that neither in Europe nor America will the Chief
Executive of a nation be again removed by peaceful means." He added
darkly, "If tyranny becomes intolerable, the only resource will be found
in the dagger of Brutus."

The two historians, though separated by three generations in time
and at opposite poles in their attitude toward Johnson and their interpretation of his impeachment, are in basic agreement with each
other and with the two great impeachers over the "lesson." A huge
book by D. M. DeWitt, "The Impeachment and Trial of Andrew

Johnson," though published in 1903, is still the most comprehensive work on the subject. DeWitt was as friendly to Johnson and hostile to his impeachment as Sumner and Stevens were hostile to Johnson and eager for his conviction. Yet, he concludes: "Never will the practice of deposing Presidents by political impeachment become domiciliated in this Republic. Centuries will pass by before another President of the United States can be impeached, unless the offense of which he is accused is clearly nonpolitical and amounts unmistakably to a high crime or misdemeanor."

Seventy years after DeWitt there appeared a slighter work by M. L. Benedict that bears exactly the same title but could hardly be more different in its interpretation. Admittedly attuned to the current mood, which has "become more sympathetic to the radical Republicans in recent decades," the author, in 1973, is far closer to Sumner and Stevens than to Johnson and DeWitt. "But," he concludes, "the unquestionable fact remains that it is almost inconceivable that a future President will be impeached and removed. . . . Impeachment was Congress's defensive weapon; it proved a dull blade, and the end result is that the only effective recourse against a President who ignores the will of Congress or exceeds his powers is democratic removal at the polls."

Most Americans who remember anything they were taught about President Johnson and his impeachment probably shared the same impression—that impeachment was something that was tried and found wanting and should never be tried again. Their teachers shared that view and so have many historians. But is that lesson valid? Does the Johnson case say anything useful for the present, and future, or not?

It is important to remember first that it is the only precedent on which to generalize. Only one of the first 36 Presidents has been impeached by the House and tried by the Senate. He was acquitted. The effort was a failure. Some would call it a fiasco. It has been called much worse names: divisive, subversive, farcical, unjust, ludicrous, tragic, comic, futile. The whole thing left a bad taste in the mouths of participants on both sides and later in the mouths of historians as well. Their reaction has been to place "impeachment" firmly and forever in that abysmal dustbin of never-again national experiences—along with others labeled "secession," "appeasement" and "isolationism"—to be recalled only with a shudder and an admonition.

To do so, of course, is to beg a lot of questions. It is to assume, for one thing, an unproved analogy between the facts and peculiar conditions of Johnson's impeachment and the occasions and circumstances of all future impeachments. Among possible differences to explore before accepting the analogy are, for example, the nature of the "high crimes and misdemeanors" charged, the impeachability of the Presidential offenses, the evidence to support the allegations, the comparative character, scope and number of offenses, the extent of their depravity, the threat they pose to constitutional integrity, moral order and national interest.

The only Senator from a Confederate state to oppose secession, Andrew Johnson of Tennessee had fought his way up from the bottom as a fierce opponent of what he called the "slave aristocracy." He was an obvious asset to the Union cause. Lincoln appointed him military governor of war-torn Tennessee in 1862. He performed that difficult assignment so courageously and loyally that Lincoln picked this Southern Democrat as his running mate for the newly named National Union party in 1864. After Lincoln's assassination in April, 1865, therefore, the dominant Republicans faced a President elected by their votes who was a member of the opposing party, and the victorious North had a President presiding over reconstruction of the defeated South who was himself a Southerner.

President Johnson's instant promises to punish rebels and "make treason odious" quieted suspicions temporarily. Even the radical Senator Ben Wade of Ohio said, "Johnson, we have faith in you." Since Congress was in recess and would not reconvene until December, Johnson proceeded without its advice or consent to effect his own plan of reconstruction. The South did not know what to expect and feared the worst. The answer came in the Proclamation of Amnesty, May 29, 1865, to the immense relief of ex-Confederates. They were promised pardon upon taking a simple oath of allegiance to the United States. Their leaders were required to apply to the President for pardons, but they had little trouble obtaining them.

Their legal and political rights regained, their expropriated lands mostly restored, ex-Confederates proceeded under friendly provisional governors appointed by Johnson to set up new civil governments. Required only to accept the emancipation of slaves, repeal secession and repudiate Confederate debts, they wrote new constitutions, held elections without black voters and restored as much of the old racial order as was possible. "Home Rule," "White Supremacy" and "Restoration" seemed assured. Conservatives in the North were ready to regard the issue as settled.

But Southerners were not behaving like a defeated people is expected to behave. Having no more experience with defeat prior to this than other Americans, they had no one to teach them what was expected. Johnson was a poor instructor. The conquered showed little remorse or repentance or proper respect for their conquerors and few real signs of submissiveness. They probably regarded submissiveness as "un-American," as much so as other Americans. One appalling sign of their unregeneracy was their election of four Confederate generals, four colonels and numerous Confederate civil officers including the Vice President to Congress. They had yet to reckon with Northern opinion.

When Congress met in December it refused to seat the Southern Congressmen or admit their states to the Union. To have done so would have broken Republican control over the Administration. Instead, Republicans created a committee under Thad Stevens to investigate conditions in the South. Testimony before the committee told of forced labor of freedmen, black codes depriving them of civil rights, insults to Union soldiers, mistreatment of Southern unionists, injustice in the courts, disrespect for the flag and many stories of Southern arrogance, intransigence and cruelty. Ugly race riots occurred in New Orleans and Memphis. Congress passed a Civil Rights Bill and Johnson vetoed it. It passed a new Freedmen's Bureau Bill and he vetoed that. It offered the 14th Amendment as a condition for readmission of Southern states, and with Johnson's encouragement they rejected it.

Feeling grew in the North that the victors had been cheated of their victory, their great sacrifice dishonored, that the defeated were being pampered, encouraged in their recalcitrance and rewarded by the President. The fall elections of 1866 gave the Republicans a stunning victory and a majority in Congress large enough to override any veto. Turning down the more radical proposals of confiscation and redistribution of property, Republicans then passed their own Reconstruction Act. This act abolished the Johnson state governments and placed the Southern states under military rule pending their acceptance of conditions of readmission. These would include enfranchisement of Negroes and the disfranchisement of whites who could not take an

"Iron Clad Oath" that they had not given voluntary aid to the Confederate cause.

This act was passed over the President's veto and it now became Johnson's duty to administer it. This he proceeded to do grudgingly and in no more compliant or cooperative spirit than he had exhibited before. With power of appointment and command over the military, he removed officers who proved cooperative with Congress and appointed officers more compliant with his views. His Attorney General interpreted the law so as to frustrate enforcement. His Cabinet members disregarded the test-oath law and appointed many ex-Confederates in the large patronage under their control.

"Sir, I am right. I know I am right and I am damned if I do not adhere to it." That was the real Andy Johnson speaking. And anybody who differed with him was *wrong*. Flexibility, doubt, compromise were unthinkable. However deplorable his racial views and antiquated his political theories, Johnson undoubtedly believed he was right. The Republicans were the real disunionists, "traitors," he called them. Secession was unconstitutional. The Southern states had never been out of the Union. Now the Republicans were keeping them out. He would support his views with plenty of traditional states-rights rhetoric. But back of all that was the terrible experience seared in his memory—and he was the only politician among them who had endured it—the experience of actually governing one of the Southern states himself by military force. He knew what that meant. He was determined that some other way must be found—whatever the cost.

Republican Congressmen had grown increasingly desperate in their frustration. Daily they saw their laws flouted, their Southern allies persecuted, their friends among Army officers badgered, handicapped and humiliated, their Confederate enemies favored, flattered and encouraged and the freedmen robbed of their rights and driven back to forced labor. Many of the Republicans were deeply and sincerely concerned about the plight of the freedmen. But even those who were not had bitter grievances against Johnson to share with those who were. The President was busily filling the war-swollen list of Federal jobs with their political enemies and undermining their party strength in the North.

The state elections of 1867 in the North were disasters for the party. In 18 states its strength declined, and there was reason to believe that much of this was due to Northern racial bias and the unpopularity of Republican policy on Negro franchise in the South. While Negro voting was being forced on Southern states, every Northern state that voted on black enfranchisement for itself defeated it. A Presidential election was coming up. The Southern states might determine the outcome. "Reconstructed," they could go Republican. The President was clearly bent on keeping them in the Democratic column. The answer for an increasing majority of Republican Congressmen was: Johnson had to be impeached and removed.

The question was how. Of what impeachable "high crimes and misdemeanors" was he guilty? His offenses were intolerable, his speeches and veto messages outrageous, but vetoing bills, making political speeches, appointing his friends to office, removing his enemies, and dragging his feet in the enforcement of laws while denouncing them as unconstitutional—the intolerable offenses and the real issue between Congress and President—were hardly impeachable crimes. Had the broad view of impeachment held by the radical minority prevailed there would have been no difficulty in convicting and removing Johnson for failure to enforce the law faithfully. But the prevailing view was the narrow one that held him impeachable only for violating a criminal statute. That was the conservative Republican view and with it the impeachers were stuck.

Johnson had broken no law. He had exercised his constitutional powers. Had he violated any criminal statute, the impeachers would surely have discovered it. No previous President had ever been subjected to such ruthless investigation. No rumor was too absurd, no charge too fantastic, no witness or gossip too patently incredible to be neglected. His sex life, his financial affairs, his most obscure personal and political connections were thoroughly scrutinized. Spies were set on him and his friends. General U. S. Grant stooped to having a janitor secretly turn over the contents of the President's wastebasket. His bank account was examined—with his consent. He withheld nothing. He defied no court degree, no Congressional subpoena. He had nothing to hide, he said. It did not occur to him to add that he was no crook.

All the sleuthing was of no avail. Nothing was found. And here at last is something for the "lesson" seekers. President Johnson, whatever his numerous faults, had not enriched himself in the White House.

He had not evaded income taxes, or bought exotic houses and billed the Government for millions of dollars in improvements, or accepted large personal gifts from wealthy citizens or foreign governments, or huge campaign donations from corporations to whom he then granted favors. He could not be charged with subornation of perjury, or with conspiracy to cover up crimes of his close associates. He had not been surrounded by aides and secretaries and counsel who were to come under indictment or serve sentence in jail. He had not fired on a foreign country without Congressional authorization and lied about it. None of his Cabinet members had been indicted or convicted of crime. He had not ordered or condoned a private security service to spy on political opponents or burglarize private houses. He had not ordered or condoned payment of hush money. He had not subverted and secretly used Government agencies to discredit or defame opposing candidates and political critics. Had the impeachers of 1868 had just a few of these items to bring forward—and many others come readily to mind—they could have impeached, tried, convicted and removed Andrew Johnson, even on their narrow theory of impeachment, at the drop of a hat. No problem at all.

The impeachers were not stopped for want of a criminal record. They had started their efforts in 1866. The first attempt that reached the House Judiciary Committee came early in 1867 and was largely the work of Congressman James M. Ashley of Ohio, a nut with an *idée fixe*. His idea was that three Presidents had been done in by ambitious Vice Presidents: William Henry Harrison by John Tyler, Zachary Taylor by Millard Fillmore and Lincoln by John Wilkes Booth in conspiracy with Andy Johnson, who was guilty of murder most foul. After several months the committee tired of such nonsense and voted that no grounds for impeachment were found.

Infuriated by additional defiance and vetoes from the White House, impeachers returned with a second attempt in July. This time they advanced what could properly be called the "real" issues between them and the President. They charged that he had abused his pardoning power, his power of appointment and removal and failed to execute laws against ex-rebels—all "to defeat the will of the people," in other words, the programs of Congress. They succeeded in bringing these charges to a vote in the House, where they were defeated 2 to 1. They were rejected not because Johnson was believed innocent of them, but because they were not regarded as impeachable—no violation of a law. "Give us a specific offense!" was the cry—"a smoking gun," so to speak.

The President seemed ready to oblige. In August, while the Senate was not in session, he suspended Secretary of War Edwin M. Stanton and appointed General Grant as ad interim Secretary. Stanton had been secretly conniving with the impeachers, had refused to resign from the Cabinet, and Johnson was determined to remove him. Control of the Army was a "real" issue and Stanton's removal was a challenge to the purpose of the Tenure-of-Office Act passed over Johnson's veto in March to prevent the removal. It was characteristic of Stanton's duplicity that in the Cabinet he had pronounced the act unconstitutional as an infringement of Presidential powers and assisted in preparing the veto message.

The Tenure-of-Office Act was the unsatisfactory result of maneuver and compromise. It contained ambiguities that puzzled both its framers and its opponents. The original purpose was to stop Johnson's wholesale removal of rank-and-file Federal officeholders appointed with the consent and advice of the Senate and assure each of them tenure until a successor was similarly approved. The radicals, however, added a provision specifically protecting Cabinet members as well. Senate moderates objected, but accepted a House-Senate compromise that covered Cabinet members during the term of the President who appointed them. Since Secretary Stanton was appointed by Lincoln, several Senators assumed that the law did not apply to him. Senator John Sherman even said, to his later embarrassment, that it was inconceivable that a Cabinet member should cling to his office if he learned that the President desired his resignation. Violations of the act were to be deemed "high misdemeanors."

In January the Senate refused to approve the suspension of Stanton. Grant then broke what Johnson declared a solemn promise and abandoned the office to Stanton. The General's attempts to answer the President's accusation were embarrassing. Impeachers seized on the suspension as a conspiracy to violate the Tenure-of-Office Act and introduced a resolution of impeachment. To adopt it, however, since it takes two to make a conspiracy, would be to discredit Grant, who was being groomed for the Republican Presidential nomination in three months. This did not trouble the radicals, who did not want Grant but Senator Ben Wade, who as President pro tem of the Senate, would become President on Johnson's conviction. Conservative Republicans tabled the impeachment resolution in committee.

Then Johnson really threw down the gauntlet and in doing so united the divided Republicans. On Feb. 21, 1868, he ordered the removal of Stanton and nominated Gen. Lorenzo Thomas in his place. The next day, on this evidence alone, the Reconstruction Committee reported a resolution of impeachment and two days later the House adopted it— charges still unspecified, the articles undrafted—by a strict party vote of 120 to 47. There appeared to be no concern for the lack of bipartisan support. Johnson stood impeached on short order, and that was that. The articles of impeachment, 11 in number, were adopted on March 3 after cursory debate.

With short shrift and equal dispatch, the Senate convened as a court to try the case 10 days later on March 13. Presiding over the scene was Chief Justice Salmon P. Chase, an impressive figure in his robes, who tried with indifferent success to preserve order, assure some degree of fairness in procedure and make an intractable Senate behave like a court. He had his troubles from the start. Rules of evidence and procedure were repeatedly brushed aside.

Johnson himself never appeared in person but was represented by hurriedly assembled counsel. They included the most towering figures of their profession: Benjamin R. Curtis, former Justice of the Supreme Court, William M. Evarts, future Secretary of State, and Henry Stanbery, former Attorney General. They petitioned for 40 days to prepare their defense. "Forty days!" exclaimed Ben Butler. "As long as it took God to destroy the world by flood!" They were grudgingly allowed 10.

Their opposite numbers, the House Managers, cut poor figures by comparison. The three leaders were Ashley, the *idée fixe* man (still at it), George S. Boutwell of Massachusetts, who had advanced the charge that "Johnson was accessory to the murder of Lincoln," and loudest, most vituperative and bombastic of all, the incredible Ben Butler. He enlivened the occasion in many ways, once by literally waving a bloody shirt and thereby launching a tradition. *The Nation*, which favored impeachment, characterized Butler's legal style as "pettifogger's balderdash." Defense counsel, on the other hand, impressed all, even the opposition, by the learning, logic, cool reserve and the authority and dignity of their bearing.

Public interest in the trial was intense, at times hysterical; it had certainly been given no time to cool. Senate galleries were packed and sometimes uncontrollable in their partisan cheering and applauding. The press outdid itself with sensational rumors and "leaks." The 54 Senators occupied the front rows and members of the House crowded in behind them. The taste in oratory and the style of histrionics belong to a remote era, and it is hard to recapture the appeal the orators undoubtedly had. "Orations" there were, two three-day performances included, ending in elaborate "perorations." Drama was heightened by one challenge to a duel. Ailing and expiring statesmen and orators, determined to give all, were lifted on and off the floor. The voice of the feeble Stevens failed him and Butler had to finish reading his speech—recalling to all Calhoun's last address, 20 years before. The elegant Stanbery was stricken but returned to the floor dramatically, defying his "watchful physician," yielding to "irresistible impulse," and responding to "voices inaudible to all others." All agreed that as public drama, it was the high point of the century.

The radicals still clung hesitantly to the broad view of impeachment, that Johnson could be found guilty, "without violating a positive law," as Butler put it, merely for "the abuse of discretionary powers from improper motives." Sumner agreed and held that "the proofs are mountainous" of both abuse and motive. Stevens declared, "The question is wholly political." Boutwell would convict Johnson as "a tyrant, a usurper, an apostate and a traitor." Butler told the Senators, "You are bound by no law," and, "You are a law unto yourselves." But the fact was that they were stuck with the narrow view, impeachment for violation of the law in removing Stanton: "a trip-hammer to crack a walnut," Judge Curtis quipped.

Nine of the eleven articles of impeachment were confined to some aspect of that charge. The articles were, in fact, a can of worms, convoluted in syntax, tortuously complicated and repetitive. Only three were ever voted on. The 10th article, on Butler's insistence, charged Johnson with defaming Congress in speeches, but few took that one seriously. The 11th or "omnibus article" threw in everything in the hope of collecting a few votes for the rejected broad view of impeachment. But the case for conviction boiled down to proof that the President had violated the Tenure-of-Office Act, and even on that the impeachers had a flimsy case.

The provision of the law that the Managers tortured into covering Stanton said that Cabinet members "shall hold their offices respectively for and during the term of the President by whom they may have been appointed and for one month thereafter, subject to removal by and with consent of the Senate." Since Stanton was appointed by Lincoln in 1862 and Lincoln died in 1865, the law, as the defense counsel pointed out, did not cover Stanton and Johnson had not violated it in removing him. The Managers tried to maintain that Johnson had no term and was still serving Lincoln's term, but the defense had little trouble with the quibbling.

Thornier problems confronted the impeachers. Was the Tenure-of-Office Act constitutional at all? Did it not violate the Constitution in invading exclusive executive prerogative and curtailing the President's power to remove a member of his Cabinet? Power of removal had prevailed since 1789. Even Sumner admitted the act reversed the practice of some 80 years. Legal opinion went heavily against the Managers here. So did it also on the question of whether a President could be punished for disobedience of an unconstitutional statute. His oath to "protect and defend the Constitution," defense contended, obliged him to protect the President's constitutional powers from Congressional invasion. In a dispute between Congress and President, Congress was not the constitutional judge of its own powers, nor could it settle the dispute unilaterally by impeachment. The evidence was that Johnson made bona fide efforts to bring the dispute before the courts, and that Congress repeatedly held that the courts could not determine Congressional powers either—only Congress itself. And finally, even if the law was constitutional and did cover the Secretary of War, Johnson had not actually removed him: he only attempted to do so and was frustrated by the clownish marplot General Thomas, whose behavior permitted Stanton to hang on, barricaded and living in his office.

The arguments were closed by a tempest of rhetoric on May 4 after less than six weeks of regular sessions. The Senate then prepared to vote, still not sure of the outcome.

Government by Congress was largely suspended during the trial, but not politics. National attention was focused on the Senate, and the Senators were eager to complete the trial in time to attend the Republican National Convention, which was being held in Chicago and was expected to nominate Grant. Meanwhile, Congress became a sort of preliminary session of the convention. Senator Ben Wade and his friends had other plans for the next President—namely Wade himself, who would automatically succeed to the office on Johnson's removal and was expected to appoint Ben Butler Secretary of State. He intended to vote on the matter himself and left no doubt how. Defeated for re-election to the Senate, Wade seemed capable of any scheme to put him in the White House. One plot that came near success was his midnight bill to admit Colorado as a state and thereby add two Senate votes for conviction. The prospect of a *President* Wade gave some Republicans pause. During impeachment procedures in Washington, most of the reconstructed Southern states completed their organization and now awaited admission; the newly elected carpetbag Senators were already in the capital. Stevens got a bill through the House admitting five of the states—and their Senators—but the Senate refused to take up the bill.

Every newspaperman and scribbler in the country knew that 36 votes were required to convict and 19 to acquit. A majority of the 54 Senators had made no secret of their intentions during the trial. Twelve were regarded as sure votes for acquittal and 29 as sure for conviction. That left 13, all Republicans, in the doubtful or undecided column, and seven of those would determine the outcome. They were so reticent that, as one of them said, he "could not ascertain their position, and they were liable to change their minds at any moment before the final vote was taken."

As the day approached every sort of pressure bore down upon the doubtful Senators. The chairman of the Republican National Committee wired party leaders in their states, and back came telegrams, delegations, resolutions and editorials demanding conviction. Some doubters were burned in effigy and all were watched in every movement—where they dined, whom they visited, with whom they talked or corresponded. For five days preceding the vote impeachment Managers seized all telegrams dispatched from Washington or Baltimore and forced banks to disclose accounts of Senators. Washington was described as "swarming, simmering, half-delirious" and "crowded with all sorts of people from all parts of the country—everyone intent on the impending result."

The anguish of the undecided, their whole future and peace of mind at stake, was often painful. The final holdout was Senator Edmund G. Ross from "Bleeding Kansas," with impeccable abolitionist credentials. Yet no threat, intimidation, bribe or blackmail could extract a commitment from him. He entered the Senate chamber on voting day, May 16, still uncommitted, watched in every move. All members of the Senate were present save one.

The Senate voted first on the 11th, or "omnibus," article in the hope that it had the best chance. As the roll was being called, hopes for impeachment were lowered when James W. Grimes of Iowa, known to favor acquittal and believed possibly too ill to attend was carried in at the last minute and voted not guilty. The roll call continued, and the result was still unsettled when Chief Justice Chase called: "Mr. Senator Ross, how say you? Is the respondent, Andrew Johnson, guilty or not guilty of a high misdemeanor as charged in this article?"

The answer came without hesitation, "Not guilty." That settled it. Johnson would be acquitted. The Senate tried votes on two more articles 10 days later, all with the same result, 35 to 19, one vote short of conviction.

Johnson had remained aloof in the White House throughout the proceedings at the other end of Pennsylvania Avenue. For lack of the still uninvented telephone, he had followed the trial by means of a telegraph wire between the Capitol and Willard's Hotel, a block from the White House. He received the news of his acquittal as he had prior developments in his impeachment and trial—"without visible emotion." His supporters were less restrained. Congratulations poured in from conservatives all over the country and the celebrators crowded the White House. Reactions of the frustrated Republicans were bitter, and some of them planned new impeachment efforts. It was remarkable, however, how quickly the impeachment struggle was forgotten by the public. The two Presidential nominating conventions followed quickly after the trial, and national attention turned to the campaign.

President Johnson had nine months left to serve in the White House, and there was much apprehension over what he would do. Grant feared he would "trample the laws under foot," and others feared the worst. On the surface, however, an air of tranquillity returned to Washington as government settled back into routine. A mutually acceptable replacement for Stanton was found in Gen. John

Schofield for Secretary of War, and the Senate confirmed William Evarts, the President's counsel at trial, as Attorney General after petulantly rejecting Stanbery, who had resigned the office to defend the President. Congress kept a tight rein on appropriations, removals and appointments in such a fashion as to curb White House initiative. Johnson was also disappointed at being passed over for the Democratic Presidential nomination, which went to Horatio Seymour, a colorless candidate. After the November elections President-elect Grant was the center of attention.

Two historians believe that the President was "frightened" by his close call and became more compliant. But the incorrigible Andy did not act very frightened. He proceeded to veto bills readmitting eight states, issued two more amnesty proclamations, and appointed a conservative Democrat to the command post in Louisiana. He also proposed the repeal of the offensive Tenure-of-Office Act. The House, preparing for a President of its own, meekly voted down the act that it had recently impeached Johnson for violating. Grant refused to ride to his inauguration with Johnson, and the ex-President cheerfully returned to Tennessee. Six years later he returned to Washington as Senator from his state, the only American ex-President so honored, and found many changes at the scene of his late trial.

It had been downhill most of the way for the radical cause since impeachment failed. Ashley and Wade were both defeated for re-election. Stevens died shortly after the trial, and Chase and Sumner soon followed. Reconstruction went to pieces in the South as white America moved closer to the deplorable racial views of Senator Andrew Johnson—if indeed white America had ever departed very far from them. President Grant was better known for other things than a zeal for racial justice.

The seven Republicans who saved Johnson by voting not guilty have earned a reputation for heroism that may be partly deserved. It is true that none of them won re-election, though neither did the majority of Republicans who voted the other way. As their party moved away from radicalism, the seven "recusants," as they were called, gained more influence in its councils. The unflappable Senator Ross, whom Horace Greeley's *Tribune* doomed to "everlasting infamy" and pronounced "the greatest criminal of the age," did show rather unseemly haste in asking favors from Johnson after the trial.

Of those who voted the other way few had much to say by way of justification in later, more conservative days. James G. Blaine wrote that "sober reflection" had "persuaded many who favored impeachment that it was not justifiable on the charges made, and that its success would have resulted in greater injury to free institutions than Andrew Johnson in his utmost endeavor was able to inflict." John Sherman took much the same line.

The "lesson" of all this? It seems improbable that any historian would hold up this particular impeachment as a model for any future one. If nothing else, the reckless haste of the impeachers precludes that. The House committee took just one day of deliberations to recommend impeachment in 1868—as compared with 11 weeks in 1974. The deliberations of the latter committee have taken almost as long as the whole procedure, from the violation charged through House debate and Senate trial, took in the earlier instance. The same reckless haste is reflected in the flouting of rules of evidence and procedure, the shoddiness of counsel and its lack of preparation, the blatant partisanship on every hand. With the earlier example of confinement to the narrow view of impeachable offense—violation of a criminal statute—at hand, it seems inconceivable that it should be followed again.

These are all negative lessons, to be sure. But to extend this negativism to preclude any further resort to impeachment is absurd. The abuse of a constitutionally granted power is no argument for its abandonment—especially on the basis of one precedent. Such a rule would put an end to all government and the institutions that support it. That other impeachment constitutes no historical roadblock to a second. But should the never-again "lesson" nevertheless be applied in the present instance, then the great sword the Framers forged for the defense of constitutional liberty may indeed rust unused and never again be drawn.

Reconstruction: Ultraconservative Revolution

ERIC MC KITRICK

• The phrase "radical reconstruction" appears in almost every textbook in American history. It is difficult, however, to point to any permanent changes of a radical nature that resulted from Reconstruction policies. The Civil War led to the Thirteenth Amendment which abolished slavery and the Fourteenth which granted citizenship to anyone born or naturalized in the United States and which required states to proceed with "due process of law" (however ambiguous that may be) before depriving any citizen of life, liberty, or property. These constitutional amendments passed through Congress before Reconstruction in the South began. Beginning in 1867 military forces occupied the southern states and influenced the region's politics for almost a decade. But in crucial areas such as social mobility, education, and occupational opportunities, little was done to help the former slave. No major political or military figures of the Confederacy suffered anything more than temporary imprisonment and suspension of political rights for a few years. The structure of southern society remained relatively intact and the descendants of the pre-Civil War leaders emerged as the key personages in the post-Reconstruction South. For all of these reasons, as well as others discussed below, Eric McKitrick argues that Reconstruction was not radical but "ultraconservative." His analysis also provides insights into some of the more troubling questions of our own era.

From *The Comparative Approach to American History*, edited by C. Vann Woodward. Copyright © 1968 by C. Vann Woodward. Reprinted by permission of Basic Books, Inc., Publishers, New York.

It had been understood for some time that the American Civil War was a revolution. But more than a hundred years have had to pass before Americans can finally begin to understand what sort of revolution it actually was. Not so many years ago our historians were still arguing that the Civil War—"the Second American Revolution," as the late Charles Beard called it—represented the final victory of Northern capitalism in its relentless aggressions against the agrarian economy of the South, and that slavery was in no true sense the central issue. Such a point of view was first encouraged by Marx and Engels, who observed the war and followed its course with great interest, and arguments based on some version of that same viewpoint have not entirely disappeared from the discussions of historians even today. Other writers in turn have argued that the Civil War should not be considered as a Marxian revolution of North against South, but rather as a revolution of the South against the United States—that slavery *was* indeed the central issue, and that in order to preserve slavery the Southern states were willing to undertake a war of liberation. The true revolutionary act, then, was the South's effort to achieve separation from the Federal Union. And yet by viewing the Reconstruction that followed the Civil War, and by considering it and the war together as parts of the same process, we begin to see that perhaps the North was, in a larger sense, the revolutionary aggressor after all. Moreover, by connecting these events with the events of today as part of an even larger pattern, we may see at last what sort of revolution it really was. We may see that its deepest, most pressing, most fundamental issue was, and still is, the proper place of the American Negro in American life. And we may even wonder, as we consider the experience of Reconstruction, whether the American political and constitutional structure itself provides a truly adequate framework within which the revolution may be brought to a satisfactory as well as peaceful close.

It has been very difficult for historians or anyone else to view all this as a single revolutionary cycle. One reason is that the cycle has been so long: it began at least a generation before the Civil War and has not yet ended. But the more important reason is that its central problem—the Negro's place in American life—was one which Americans were never willing to confront directly, even at the most critical phases of the revolution, those of the Civil War and Reconstruction.

This confusion, this ambiguity, this reluctance to face the implications of a problem of such magnitude, have had curious effects on Americans' very habits of historical thought. Despite the enormous and persistent interest in the Civil War, and despite the lesser but still considerable interest in Reconstruction, the latter period has become intellectually encapsulated. It has been isolated within the national consciousness and the national memory in a very unusual way, considering the things that a revolution does to a nation's life. With regard to the objectives of the Reconstruction, even of the Civil War, the quality of our writing, our thought, and our public discourse has been very diffuse and has shown a remarkable lack of precision. Nevertheless, the demands of the 1960's have made it clear that the revolution is not yet finished, that it has not gone nearly far enough, and that the original character of the revolution must be considered all over again.

The problem, indeed, was systematically quarantined from the very first, even while society was beginning to concede its urgency. In a way this is understandable. In almost every ordinary sense the United States on the eve of the Civil War was politically, socially, and economically one of the most stable countries in the world. A political and constitutional system had been established which was acceptable to virtually the entire population. It was characterized by universal white manhood suffrage and a level of citizen participation not seen since the days of the Greek republics. Its electoral practices may have included strong elements of demagoguery and vulgar carnival appeal, but the result was a system of party government which was in many respects the most sophisticated in the world. And whereas most European countries at mid-century were permeated with the ferment of social revolution, the United States was perhaps the one nation in the Western world where the overwhelming bulk of the population was profoundly committed to laissez-faire capitalism. It had no tory class, no tory socialism, no aristocracy with traditions of noblesse oblige or a sense of responsibility for checking the excesses of laissez faire. American society, as Tocqueville had discovered a generation earlier, had become intensely egalitarian and intensely committed to the ideal of equal opportunity and careers open to talent. It would be difficult for most Europeans to understand that those values normally regarded elsewhere as "bourgeois" were in 1860 the values of the American farmer, the American workingman, and the American enterpreneur.

All of these values were embodied in the career and person of Abraham Lincoln, who was to be the leader of the "revolutionary" party of 1860. Lincoln, rising from the poorest possible origins, largely self-educated, a leader in politics while still a young man, becoming a successful railroad lawyer, and emerging from state politics in Ilinois to become the Republican nominee for the Presidency, insisted again and again that there was no real gulf between capital and labor. "There is no permanent class of hired laborers amongst us," he announced in one of several speeches he made on this subject in 1859. "Twenty-five years ago, I was a hired laborer. The hired laborer of yesterday, labors on his own account today; and will hire others to labor for him to-morrow. Advancement—improvement in condition—is the order of things in a society of equals." Probably few men of any class who heard these words would have thought of doubting their essential truth. For most Americans living in the North, this highly satisfactory state of affairs had come to be directly connected with the continued stability of the Federal Union. The one great flaw in it, as Lincoln reminded his audiences in each of these speeches, was the continued existence of a very rigid system of chattel slavery.

Americans had inevitably been brought to confront this problem. But they did so reluctantly, despite the steady growth of antislavery feeling which had already begun to force itself into national politics by the 1840's. This feeling could only be admitted into the realm of political discourse and contention by placing all stress upon the Union and virtually none upon the Negro, in order to maintain some sort of unity even in the North. It was done not by a direct assault upon slavery, but through the formula of "Free Soil": not by challenging slavery where it was, but by declaring that it should not be carried into new places where it did not yet exist. In short, men did face the issue, but they deliberately avoided facing it directly as long as they possibly could.

Even after the war broke out, they continued to avoid it. In order to prevent the alienation of a sizable portion of the Northern people, to say nothing of the border states which had not seceded, the administration felt it necessary to declare that its sole purpose in waging war was to restore the Federal Union. Lincoln announced this on many occasions in the most solemn tones. "I would save the Union," he insisted; "I would save it the shortest way under the Constitution. The sooner the national authority can be restored, the nearer the Union will be 'the Union as it was.' . . . My paramount object in this struggle is to save the Union, and is *not* either to save or to destroy slavery." And yet the man to whom this was written—Horace Greeley, editor of the influential New York *Tribune*—himself represented a growing sector of public opinion which was insisting that emancipation should be made one of the objects of the war. It had already become obvious to Lincoln by the summer of 1862 that without the support of this sector the continued vigor of the war effort might itself be undermined; and although he had told Greeley, "If I could save the Union without freeing any slave, I would do it," he also conceded that if he "could do it by freeing all the slaves," he would do that. But if he conceded this much, he was hardly prepared to go the whole way, because he too understood public opinion, probably better than Greeley. The Emancipation Proclamation (which, according to one of our historians, "had all the moral grandeur of a bill of lading") was presented not as a statement of high purpose but as a measure of military necessity.

It was the same with regard to the use of Negro troops in the Union Army. Two objectives might be served by accepting Negro enlistments. One of them directly concerned the Negro himself: "Once let the black man get upon his person the brass letters, U.S.," as the Negro abolitionist Frederick Douglass expressed it, ". . . and there is no power on earth which can deny that he has earned the right to citizenship in the United States." The other was that Negro soldiers might augment the declining strength of the army and thus assist in suppressing the rebellion. Of the two objectives, the Northern public would accept only the second. Even this could occur only after the war was well under way, and after many discouraging military reverses. Few concessions were made to the Negro's representing any more than a matter of military policy. Negro regiments could have no Negro officers, and the United States Congress refused to grant them equal pay with white troops until the war was nearly over. The Negro's proper role, even in the society of wartime, could not be considered on its own terms but only in the interest of some other objective. Even the President, despite his "oft-expressed personal wish that all men everywhere could be free," could still think of no more satisfactory way of dealing with slaves who had been freed than to encourage them to leave the country. His "first impulse," he had stated in 1854, "would be to free all the slaves and send them to Liberia"; eight years later, on the very eve of emancipation, he was earnestly urging a committee of Negro leaders to colonize themselves and their families in Central America, as the best example that could be offered to American Negroes everywhere.

II

Once the war was over, the problem of dealing both with the Negro and with the readmission of Southern states to the Federal Union dominated all else. But all emphasis was placed upon the latter. And again, the first instinct was to change as little as possible. By constitutional amendment the Negro had been given his freedom, but few steps were taken to adjust him to his new status. At the same time elaborate efforts were made by the administration of Lincoln's successor, Andrew Johnson, to re-establish state governments in the South which would be more or less identical with those in existence before the war. Certain things were rejected almost out of hand. There was to be no redistribution of land, either with or without compensation. There was no insistence that Negroes be accorded rights of citizenship. Federal responsibility for education and welfare was regarded as being only of the most temporary and limited kind. Legislation to expand even the minimal services of this sort that did exist— those performed by the wartime Freedmen's Bureau—was opposed by the President, and there were not enough votes in the national Congress to enact it over his veto. It is certainly true that the President's position on these questions lagged behind that of the Republican majority in Congress, and perhaps even somewhat behind the center position in public opinion. But the differences, in 1865 and 1866, were hardly more than differences in degree.

The revolution was destined to go considerably further than anything Andrew Johnson had in mind. But its conservative nature would still be such, even at its height, as to make it hardly comparable to any other revolutionary or counterrevolutionary movement known to modern Western history. Not one political prisoner, for example, was ever put to death. The political head of the rebellion was kept in prison for two years and then set free, while the rebellion's military chief was never molested at all. The President of the United States spent much of his time during the first year of peace over matters of amnesty and pardon; and a few years later, while Congressional Reconstruction was still in full force, an act of general amnesty in effect removed that problem from further contention altogether. The government of Soviet Russia was executing enemies of the Revolution years after the Revolution itself was over. Even in England, whose revolution was one of the earliest and mildest, the revolutionary party felt it expedient to execute the head of the state, after having done away with his two chief advisors, and to massacre priests, women, and children in Ireland. With the Restoration, only the genial disposition of the king himself prevented a blood bath of vengeance and limited the number of executions to a dozen regicides.

The political, constitutional, legal, and administrative changes effected in the United States through the Civil War and Reconstruction were almost invisible compared with those that remained in France from the French Revolution, even after the restoration of the Bourbon monarchy. There, the provincial boundaries of the Old Regime were eliminated forever (in the America of 1865 and 1866, the very thought of such a thing made men turn pale with consternation); while the new geographical boundaries were designed in such a way that the resulting "departments" could be uniformly administered through the central government in Paris. (In the American South, even today, mere "interference" by the central government is the issue most likely to unite the entire population.) The most sweeping changes in property, class, fiscal, and jurisdictional relationships throughout French society, effected by the Revolution and codified by Bonaparte, were never reversed despite all efforts by the Bourbons to turn back the clock. The American "Bourbons," as the South's post-Reconstruction leaders were called, hardly needed to turn back the clock at all. No changes on this scale had been effected in the first place. As for the emancipated slaves, far less was done for them by the United States government in the way of land distribution and social planning than was done during that very same period for the emancipated serfs of autocratic imperial Russia.

By 1867 the extraordinary refusal of President Andrew Johnson to

cooperate with Northern leadership on any of the problems of read-
justment, plus the determination of the South to resist even the
minimal implications of change, had brought the North—still
reluctantly—to see the need for stronger measures. The result was
called "Radical Reconstruction." These measures, designed to protect
Negroes and those Southern whites who had supported the Union,
represented the high point of revolutionary action. The military occupation, followed by the enfranchisement of the entire Negro male
population, the temporary disqualification of former Confederate
leaders from suffrage and officeholding, and the establishment and
support of state governments heavily dependent upon Negro votes
and operated by pro-Union whites and Negroes constituted the
closest thing to a revolutionary situation that was reached.

This situation, which began deteriorating almost at once, lasted
no more than a few years. By 1877 all of the so-called "Radical" state
governments had been expelled, mostly through the force of local
pressure. Two general criticisms of this experiment may be made, not
counting the traditional one that the Southern white people had been
forced for a time to accept regimes which they did not want. One
is that this relatively radical political program was not accompanied
by anything systematic in the way of social and economic welfare.
Much of what was accomplished in matters of education, for example,
had to be undertaken through private efforts by Northern philan-
thropic groups, and in the face of enormous local resistance. There
was no confiscation of estates, and no systematic effort to aid the
freedmen in acquiring holdings of their own. Thus it might be said
that the true priorities were reversed: that the Negro was given the
vote before he had either the education or the economic power that
would enable him to make effective use of it. The other criticism
is that, even if it were granted that political rights ought to have
come first after all, the federal government was still unprepared to
undertake the massive commitment of long-term supervision, combined with continuing force, that would have been needed to preserve
those rights.

Thus in the face of corruption, inefficiency, and chronic local aggression and unrest, the federal government gradually withdrew its
support and allowed the white community in each state to re-establish

full control. By 1877 the political, social, and economic systems of the South had become remarkably similar to what they had been in 1860, except that now the Negro was a landless laborer rather than a legally bound slave. A final stage of reaction remained. In the general effort to reconstitute the structure which had been disrupted by the Civil War and Reconstruction, even the Negro's small political gains—to say nothing of the minimal social rights he had acquired, in no way commensurate with the total effort and sacrifices implied in that war—were systematically removed. One by one, and with no interference whatever, the Southern states now began by law to impose systems of social segregation and disfranchisement which set the Negro entirely outside the mainstream of Southern civic life. By 1900 the process was virtually complete.

III

Without a clear center of gravity, historical discussion of this entire problem has had a somewhat erratic character. For the most part, it has been considered well within the context of the American constitutional system, and with very cautious assumptions, quite orthodox and traditional, as to where the boundaries of that system are located. One line of thought, probably more persistent than any other, regards the whole episode of Reconstruction with the most profound distaste, because it prolonged into peacetime the internal conflicts and alienations which had driven the American people into fratricidal war. The Civil War and Reconstruction thus represented a breach that must above all be healed, smoothed over, reknit. Perhaps the definitive statement of this position was made by Paul Buck in his *Road to Reunion, 1865–1900.* Yet it may also be significant that the terminal date of Professor Buck's study coincides with that very point in time at which the Negro's own exclusion from American society had been made all but complete.

My own study of Andrew Johnson's role in Reconstruction, published seven years ago, also assumes reunion to be a primary value, without questioning the limits of the system as it then existed. I argued, perhaps somewhat conservatively, that within those limits, and without violating the basic assumptions and values of the most enlightened men of the time, far more might have been done toward solving the problems of Reconstruction, as well as of reunion, than was in fact done. And yet these assumptions might themselves be questioned. An English historian of great perception and intelligence, William R. Brock, has recently looked at the subject of Reconstruction through the eyes of an outsider. He concludes that the very system of federalism, as established by the Constitution and construed by two generations of pre-Civil War Americans, was simply not adequate for the containment of a problem of such dimensions and magnitude.

As the problem confronts us all over again in the 1960's, we might well consider the bare possibility, at least, of Brock's being right. It could be argued that the decision to commit federal power to Reconstruction would not have been taken at all but for the abnormal stimulus of a crisis between the executive and legislative branches of the federal government. Then, as the will to maintain that commitment began to wane, there remained to the states—thanks to the federal "balance"—all the power they needed to expel with relative ease those features of Reconstruction they found not to their liking. By the turn of the century the states, using the authority of their state governments to render federal law inoperative, could place restrictions on the political and social rights of Negroes which the judicial branch of the federal government could overlook only by allowing the law to be construed in a highly strained and dubious way. These restrictions—virtual disfranchisement and complete social segregation—remained until World War II almost wholly unchallenged. As late as 1964 the Assistant Attorney General in charge of civil rights, Burke Marshall, was not optimistic about the future of federal law enforcement. At that time Mr. Marshall devoted two public lectures at a major university to the inherent restrictions imposed by the very structure of the federal system. Even the guarantee of voting rights, despite a series of federal laws beginning in 1957 which simply attempted to enforce the Fifteenth Amendment, had been for practical purposes frustrated in innumerable Southern communities.

Thus in view of what is minimally indispensable to complete the revolution begun with emancipation and Reconstruction, the restrictions of the federal structure do indeed seem formidable. The minimum obligations go well beyond political rights. They include